# BRITAIN'S CHANGING PARTY SYSTEM

*Edited by*
Lynton Robins,
Hilary Blackmore
and Robert Pyper

**Leicester University Press**
**London and New York**

*Distributed in the United States and Canada by St. Martin's Press*

Leicester University Press
(a division of **Pinter Publishers Ltd.**)
25 Floral Street, London WC2E 9DS, United Kingdom

First published in 1994

Distributed exclusively in the USA and Canada by St. Martin's Press, Inc., Room 400, 175 Fifth Avenue, New York, NY10010, USA


**British Library Cataloguing in Publication Data**

A CIP catalogue record for this book is available from the British Library

ISBN 0 7185 1494 7 (hb)
      0 7185 1505 6 (pb)


**Library of Congress Cataloging-in-Publication Data**

A CIP catalog record for this book is available from the Library of Congress

Typeset by Mayhew Typesetting, Rhayader, Powys
Printed and bound in Great Britain by Biddles Ltd., Guildford and King's Lynn

# BRITAIN'S CHANGING
# PARTY SYSTEM

**Frontispiece** Cartoon in *The Guardian*, 4 January 1993, by David Simonds. Used with kind permission of the cartoonist.

# Contents

# Contents

# List of contributors

**Arthur Aughey** is Senior Lecturer in Politics at the University of Ulster at Jordanstown. He has published widely in the field of Northern Ireland politics and is the author of *Under Siege: Ulster Unionism and the Anglo-Irish Agreement* (1989). He is currently working on a study of developments in Irish politics in the 1990s.

**Hilary Blackmore** is a Senior Lecturer at Charles Keene College, Leicester. She teaches politics and education. Her research interest is citizenship and education.

**John Gyford** is Reader in Urban Politics and Planning at University College London. His books include *Local Politics in Britain*, *The Politics of Local Socialism* and *Citizens, Consumers and Councils*; he has eighteen years experience as a local councillor.

**Andrew Heywood** is Course Director for Politics and History at Orpington College, and a GCE 'A' Level Chief Examiner. He is the author of *Political Ideologies: An Introduction* (1992) and *Political Ideas and Concepts: An Introduction* (1994). He is currently writing a book on British politics and is carrying out research on the role of nature in political theory.

**Stephen Hunt** is a lecturer in the Sociology Department at the University of Reading. He specialises in political sociology and the sociology of health and medicine. He has published work in social movements and on issues related to race. Currently he is conducting research into contemporary Christian movements.

**Stephen Ingle** is Professor and Head of Department of Politics at the University of Stirling. He has written extensively in the field of British political parties and has a special interest in adversarial politics in Westminster-type systems. His other main interest is in politics and literature and he has recently published a political life of George Orwell.

**Alistair Jones** is a lecturer in politics and public administration at De Montfort University, Leicester. He graduated from the University of

Canterbury, New Zealand, and his research interests include electoral reform, voting behaviour and the European Union.

**Richard Kelly** is tutor in politics at Manchester Grammar School and Manchester University's Department of Extra-Mural Studies. He is the author of *Conservative Party Conferences* (1989), co-author of *British Political Parties Today* (1993) and a contributor to *Conservative Century* (1994).

**Roger Levy** is Professor and Head of School of the School of Public Administration and Law at The Robert Gordon University, Aberdeen. After undergraduate and graduate study at Leicester and Glasgow Universities, he completed his doctorate in Political Science at McGill University in 1984. His thesis on the Scottish National Party was published in 1990 and he has published regularly on Scottish government and politics over the last 10 years. His current research interests also include the control and management of the EU budget.

**Joni Lovenduski** is Professor of Comparative Politics at Loughborough University. She is author of several books on gender and politics and on European politics, and is co-director of the British Candidate Study (funded by the ESRC). Her current research is on equality policy in Europe, state feminism and gender and urban government.

**Allan McConnell** is a Lecturer in Public Administration at Glasgow Caledonian University. He obtained his PhD in 1992 and has published in the fields of policy formation, the poll tax, and select committees. He is currently working on a book entitled *State Policy Formation and the Origins of the Poll Tax*.

**Pippa Norris** is Associate Director of the Joan Shorenstein Barone Center on Press, Politics and Public Policy and Lecturer at the Kennedy School of Government, Harvard University. She works on legislative recruitment, comparative electoral behaviour, the politics of the media, and women and politics. She is co-director of the British Candidate Study, (funded by the ESRC) and the American Candidate Study (funded by the National Science Foundation).

**Philip Norton** is Professor of Government, and Director of the Centre for Legislative Studies, at the University of Hull. His most recent publications are *The British Polity* (3rd edn, 1994), *Does Parliament Matter?* (1993), *Back from Westminster* (with D. Wood, 1993), *Parliamentary Questions* (jt ed., 1993), *New Directions in British Politics?* (ed., 1991), *Legislatures* (1990), and *Parliaments in Western Europe* (ed., 1990). He is President of the Politics Association.

**Robert Pyper** is Senior Lecturer in public administration at Glasgow Caledonian University. He is author of *The Evolving Civil Service* (1991) and *The British Civil Service* (forthcoming). He is assistant editor of *Talking Politics*, the journal of the Politics Association.

**Lynton Robins** teaches politics at De Montfort University, Leicester. He is co-author of *Contemporary British Politics* (1989) and co-editor of *Public Policy Under Thatcher* (1990) and *Two Decades in British Politics* (1992). He is editor of *Talking Politics*.

# List of abbreviations and acronyms

AWL     Alliance for Workers' Liberty
BNP     British National Party
CCO     Conservative Central Office
CLP     Constituency Labour Party
CLPD    Campaign for Labour Party Democracy
CMP     Campaign Management Team (Lab)
CPGB    Communist Party of Great Britain
DUP     Democratic Unionist Party (Northern Ireland)
GLC     Greater London Council
GMC     General Management Committee (Lab)
IMG     International Marxist Group
LLB     London Labour Briefing
NCC     National Constitutional Committee (Lab)
NCP     New Communist Party
NEC     National Executive Committee (Lab)
NF      National Front
NSR     new suburban right
NU      National Union of Conservative Associations
NUL     new urban left
OMOV    one member one vote
PLP     Parliamentary Labour Party
PPC     Prospective Parliamentary Candidate
PR      proportional representation
SACC    Standing Advisory Committee on Candidates (Con)
SCA     Shadow Communications Agency
SCLV    Socialist Campaign for a Labour Victory
SDP     Social Democratic Party
SL      Socialist League
SNP     Scottish National Party
SDLP    Social Democratic and Labour Party (Northern Ireland)
SLD     Social and Liberal Democrats
TGWU    Transport and General Workers Union
UUP     Ulster Unionist Party
WRP     Workers' Revolutionary Party

# Introduction: The British party system in transition

*Lynton Robins, Hilary Blackmore and Robert Pyper*

Political parties are deeply flawed, politicians are more unpopular than ever, and the party system is failing in its operation – these criticisms have a timeless quality about them. For over a hundred years political science literature has included periodic warnings that Britain's political parties were in serious danger from one development or another, were in decline (Finer, 1984), or were becoming increasingly irrelevant (Rose, 1984; Ingle, 1989). Yet parties have survived and, although substantially weaker and less popular than in the recent past, no one seriously doubts their future survival. This is not to argue that current anxiety about the poor state of health of Britain's parties is misplaced, but simply that it should be kept firmly in perspective.

Few would contest the view that parties have slipped from the position they occupied in the immediate post-war years. However, the causes of party decline have been the subject of considerable debate, with the development of the mass media; alternative forms of participation provided by increasing numbers of specialised pressure groups and social movements; the recurrent failure of government to deliver what party members wanted; social changes which have fractured links between party and class; and increased leisure opportunities, identified as crucial factors. More recently attention has focused not only on the decline of party but on the failure of the party system to provide alternative government. The seeming permanent grip on power by one party has in turn led to suspicions of corruption in political patronage and party finances, as well as to a more general concern over the effect of one-party dominance on the quality of political leadership in Britain. This book examines recent changes which have taken place within parties and the party system, and considers the likely impact of the most commonly discussed reforms.

It was assumed for much of the post-war period that Britain's two-party system facilitated Labour and Conservative alternating in power (Drucker, 1979). Indeed, there has been a commonplace belief that after

1

two successive periods in office governments become tired, lack fresh ideas, and need a period on the opposition benches in order to recover. Fourteen years of uninterrupted Conservative government, its continuance into the next century barely challenged, have led to the view, examined by Andrew Heywood in Chapter 1, that the party system has broken down. A multi-party electorate, a two-party Parliament, and a dominant-party government must surely add up to a system failure? Heywood argues that the answer to the question depends on which perspective is taken on recent events. On the one hand, for example, there was no certainty about a Conservative victory in the run-ups to recent elections. Other possibilities seemed likely. Poll data indicated that Labour might win or that, at the very least, there would be a hung parliament. Four consecutive Conservative victories do not guarantee a fifth and 'one more heave' might well bring Labour to power in 1996–97. On the other hand, it is possible to identify factors working in ways which consolidate the dominant-party system. These include the fragmentation of working-class communities which provided Labour's traditional bedrock support and the regional split of the anti-Conservative vote between Labour and the Liberals. And in addition to this it must not be forgotten that when in full working order the two-party system delivered only two clear-cut victories to Labour and denied every Labour prime minister a second full term in Number Ten.

A consequence of the pendulum becoming stuck in favour of Conservative rule is that the dominant-party system increasingly comes to resemble a one-party system, exhibiting many of the unwelcome characteristics of a government immune from removal. The politicisation of the bureaucracy blurring the distinction between party and state, ministerial indiscretions both in the public and private realm, as well as government of the type which brought in the poll tax, are symptoms of one-party dominance. Yet this dominance is based on little over 40 per cent of the popular vote which goes to the Conservatives in general elections. The electoral system, once recognised as the bulwark of the two-party system, now supports perpetual one-party dominance of government.

As Heywood mentions, some blame for the continued existence of the dominant-party system might be laid at Labour and Liberal Democrat doors for their refusal to collaborate against the Conservative Party. Electoral typography changed during the 1980s and 1990s, yet Labour and the Liberals planned their respective strategies as if there had been no such change. Despite electoral reform remaining unobtainable, some argued that the means to oust the Conservatives already lay in the hands of the opposition parties if only they would come to some form of electoral arrangement, pact or deal. In other words, according to this argument, the pendulum is stuck only for as long as Labour and the Liberal Democrats allow.

Labour's reflex action to each successive election defeat has not been a consideration of electoral pacts for the future. Rather, as Richard Kelly recounts in Chapter 2, Labour has looked inward for changes it hoped would bring future victory; an ideological shift towards socialism, followed by programmatic moderation, topped off with structural and constitutional change. But the new model Labour Party, capable of leading in opinion polls, armed with moderate policies, and less influenced by trade union links, still faces serious problems. Despite modernisation, Labour still lacks credibility with voters in the South and perhaps because of modernisation, it has declined at the grassroots (Seyd and Whiteley, 1992). Traditionally activists joined Labour in a campaign to usher in a New Dawn; today the crusade is for mere electoral victory.

As Kelly observes, Labour's reforms have resulted in a more centralised power structure, allowing the leadership to act in ways consistent with Robert McKenzie's account of their party. Conservative leaders, on the other hand, could only wish that it applied to their party. For permanence in office has made a considerable impact on the Tory grass roots. Whilst efforts to democratise the Conference have so far failed, grass-roots influence is exerted informally throughout the conference system. And fourteen years of championing individualism and citizen empowerment have not passed the Conservative Party organisation by. Tory grass-roots members are no longer willing to be led this way or that way at the discretion of the leadership. Rather, they expect to influence their leaders. More party democracy, particularly the more formalised forms proposed by the Charter movement, may come to be seen as a crucial measure to stop the rot which is eating away at many constituency associations.

There is no evidence of the decay which has eaten into the mass parties being present in parliamentary parties. Philip Norton identifies 1979 as a watershed after which the major parliamentary parties became less closed, less structured and less predictable. The parliamentary environment, seen in the past as having a deradicalising effect on parties, changed in ways which removed constraints on the political behaviour of the back-benchers. Already willing to rebel against the Heath government, Conservative MPs were even more ready to vote against the Thatcher government. At the same time, the new departmental select committee system ended any notion that MPs were mere lobby fodder. Parliamentary reform was complemented by party reform, with Conservative back-benchers playing an increasingly influential role through the election of their leader and, within the 1922 Committee, helping shape ministerial careers.

Labour, too, has experienced the benefits bestowed by parliamentary reform measures as well as by an improving political situation. The bad old days of back-bench defections to the Social Democratic Party, deselection rows in the constituencies, and policy paralysis over the European Community, are over. Party morale has risen accordingly. The government's slender majority, with the possibility of by-election defeats narrowing it still further, gives Labour prospects of some important parliamentary victories. In short, parliamentary parties are in better health now in terms of greater activity and more energy than at any other time in the post-war years.

Critics of the parliamentary parties have drawn attention to the similarity of Conservative and Labour policies on the European Community at the time of the 1992 general election, thus denying the electorate the possibility of registering an alternative preference. It is the case that the European issue is one which has presented the major parties with a variety of problems over the course of time. The question of British membership of the then Common Market possessed many of the characteristics of a minority-interest foreign policy issue during the 1960s, when it was discussed principally in terms of possible consequences for the Commonwealth and likely risks of a close association with Germany. During the 1970s and particularly since entry was successfully negotiated, the issue has become firmly embedded in Britain's domestic politics. By the 1980s political manoeuvres resulted in the Conservatives in government remaining the party of Europe, with Labour distinctly anti-EC in tone if not in form. However, the propagation of Thatcherism at home and Euro-federalism in Brussels was to fracture this simple alignment.

In Chapter 4 Alistair Jones explores the potential for partisan realignment around the European issue and tests the substance behind parliamentary commentators' claims to have discovered that two new parties, the Anti-Maastricht Party and the Pro-Maastricht Party, had replaced the old and familiar ones. Although the 'new' parties had some of the trappings of formal parties, such as whips, and despite much cross-bench liaison, they lacked the substance of 'real' parties. It is anticipated that members of a political party will not necessarily share one set of values, but there has to be some attitudinal commonality as a basis for joint membership. What united Labour and Conservative MPs who passed through the same lobby on Maastricht was superficial agreement only, there being no positive consensus on why they were doing what they were doing. In this sense the new Maastricht parties of the Commons bore much similarity to their cousins at one remove in the European Parliament, being more in the way of coalitions for voting purposes than of authentic parties.

In their studies of British political parties, Robert McKenzie (1955) and Samuel Beer (1965) discussed the Liberals in the space of a few pages. Justified then, perhaps, but today such scant attention would be inappropriate. There was speculation in the early 1980s that the party system might be transformed by the intervention of a third party (Ball,

1981; Berrington, 1983). The beneficial changes, it was argued, would include greater continuity between one regime forged in coalition and the next, thereby moderating the excesses of left and right, and the eventual replacement of an adversarial political culture by one based on cooperation and partnership. In Chapter 5 Stephen Ingle examines the impact of the emergence of the Social Democratic Party and its alliance with the Liberals on party politics. The birth of a new party, massive media attention, and some spectacular by-election victories are remarkable political phenomena by any standards. There were heady days, when the two-party system seemed as if it really was being recast around a new alignment. The Falklands War interrupted the Alliance's take-off but nevertheless a dramatic 1983 general election result put it only 2.3 per cent behind Labour in the popular vote. But only a handful of Alliance MPs were returned and, in this sense, Ingle argues that the Alliance ultimately failed since it did not dislodge Labour as the main opposition party. It was, however, far from total failure since SDP members could comfort themselves that their defection from Labour had accelerated the pace of that party's internal reforms, so that Labour was to become the radical non-socialist opposition the SDP set out to be. In other words, without the electoral threat by the SDP/Liberal Alliance, Labour would have remained an ideological party attracting fewer and fewer voters.

To some Liberals the sole purpose of their alliance with the SDP was to strengthen the campaign for electoral reform. This drew attention to the riddle which is posed to any national third party in terms of electoral arithmetic. In order to secure proportional representation the Alliance needed to get into government, but the chances of the Alliance being in government were minimal without proportional representation. Also, as Ingle argues, no matter how seriously the Liberal Democrats viewed electoral reform as a constitutional issue, its emergence in the 1992 campaign smacked of an opportunist electoral gimmick to put a Labour prime minister into Number Ten. At national level the most that the now merged Liberal Democrats can hope for is a fair crop of by-election successes and a hung, or 'balanced', general election outcome. Opportunism, therefore, remains their best strategy; yet it is one which masks the true strength of the Liberal Democrat contribution.

Liberal Democrats have made large gains in local government representation since 1979. A fourfold increase in the number of Liberal Democrat councillors has resulted in the aspiration of power-sharing becoming a reality at local level. Liberal Democrat-controlled councils along with a variety of hung-council arrangements in which Liberal Democrats play a significant role are commonplace in the world of local government. It is argued that the local government electorate is influenced by national party politics, yet the national party system is not faithfully replicated at the local level. For in local government elections, the Labour/Conservative two-party dominance has been eroded by third-party intervention. In Chapter 6 John Gyford reviews the variety of new strategies negotiated in hung councils which enabled them to discharge their day-to-day duties. The pivotal rule which has eluded the Liberals at national level, including the Lib-Lab pact, has been available within many hung and minority-ruled councils, given a willingness on their part to innovate, constantly if necessary and sometimes across a wide front, in order to move forwards with policy and administration. It is also worth noting that the growing influence of Liberals has taken place during a time of increased polarisation in local government, with the new urban left and the new suburban right frequently being more ideologically intense than their parliamentary counterparts. Negotiating government in a world of zealots means that many of the old ground rules no longer apply and new ones have to be created in order to facilitate the coalition process.

An important function of political parties has been the recruitment of political leaders (Lees and Kimber, 1972) although harsh words have been said about the raw material which makes up the talent pool from which candidates for office are drawn. Ostrogorski (1902) saw local organisations bringing forward 'local mediocrity, and then installing it in the counsels of the party'. Beatrice Webb, as recounted by McKenzie (1955), had even less respect for party members, seeing them as 'groups of nonentities dominated by fanatics and cranks, and extremists . . .'. The contemporary situation is examined by Joni Lovenduski and Pippa Norris in Chapter 7 and they are able to draw a more flattering picture of those selected from the rank and file, although it is not one without flaws. The typical MP is white, male, middle-class, and better educated than his average constituent, and the candidate list from which he was selected will have been of a similar social composition. Whilst there are no constitutional reasons why MPs' backgrounds need be other than they are, since MPs are elected to represent constituencies and not sectional or social groupings, common sense dictates that patterns of recruitment should relate more closely to Britain's social structure. A stagnating unresponsive pattern of political recruitment would serve only to make Parliament appear more remote, more elitist, and less trusted than its members would want. But how is change accomplished?

Lovenduski and Norris examine the parties' differing selection procedures, then proceed to explore reasons for social bias within the process. It is far from easy to establish the point of balance which explains recruitment patterns between discrimination in selection procedures and the reluctance of female and ethnic minority community members to put themselves forward. Nevertheless, there have been some encouraging changes in recent years in terms of greater female and ethnic minority presence on both short-lists and in members returned to the Commons. Any immediate improvement in social representation could only be gained through reforming the candidate selection procedures, such as Labour's politically sensitive quota proposal.

The nationalist parties of Scotland and Wales are examined by Roger Levy. In Scotland the years since 1979 have been ones of generally increasing constitutional strain, resulting from permanent Conservative rule from Westminster accompanied by a decline in the number of Tory MPs representing Scottish constituencies. These political circumstances have provided fertile ground for developing Scottish National Party politics, but they have led also to Scotland's Labour and Conservative parties adopting a more distinctly nationalist tone. Some commentators have always been quick to dismiss the importance of the nationalist issue and argued, for example, that what exercises voters' thinking in Scotland – unemployment, the NHS and education – are foremost in the minds of English voters as well. Assessments which habitually played down the significance of nationalism in Scottish party politics have, however, failed to appreciate how far the SNP has developed from being the home of the protest vote to winning broad support for its nationalist platform. Levy notes that the SNP and Plaid Cymru share some similarities in terms of developing from a political movement base into organisations having within them centralised, efficient electoral machines. Also both parties became more socialist during the 1980s, principally as a response to Thatcherite English nationalism. However there are differences between the two nationalist parties; where the SNP developed across a broad front, Plaid remained a culturally based party. The consequence is that the goal of independence has differing political meanings. For Plaid Cymru independence is seen as a means to defend the Welsh language and associated culture, whilst for the SNP independence is an end relating to autonomous public policy making.

Nationalist and Unionist party politics of Northern Ireland revolves around the constitutional question which, unlike its presence in Scotland and Wales, is organised around contested visions held by distinct communities. Whilst the nationalist parties of Scotland and Wales are riven by factions, the party system of Northern Ireland is based on rival Unionist parties competing for the overwhelmingly Protestant vote and rival Irish Nationalist parties competing for the Catholic vote. In Chapter 9 Arthur Aughey examines the impact of recent events – the Hunger Strikes, the Anglo-Irish Agreement and the 'Talks' process – on the behaviour of the Ulster Unionist and Democratic Unionist parties, the Social Democratic and Labour Party, and Sinn Fein. Added ingredients, such as paramilitary politics and proportional representation, confirm the mainland view of Northern Ireland being 'a place apart'. There has been an attempt to make Northern Ireland's party politics less distinctive and less polarised through the importation of mainland parties, but this has made little impact to date.

Other parties compete within Britain's party system which from time to time have made an impact upon electoral politics. Fringe parties, because of their minimal levels of popular support, have also adopted a strategy of entryism into other political organisations in pursuit of their goals. Stephen Hunt examines the parties of the extreme right and left, and he notes that 1979 was a watershed year for the then vanguard of the far right, the National Front. In the general election of that year the Front attempted to present itself as a major player and fielded over three hundred candidates. It was rewarded with less than 200,000 votes; Thatcherite populism had drawn support away from the Front and the following years were to be ones of political decline. Support for the far right did not receive much publicity until, after the departure of Mrs Thatcher from Number Ten, its new voice in the shape of the British National Party won a local government by-election in Millwall. The far left also experienced a general decline during the 1980s; its parties experienced electoral humiliation, expulsion from Labour, and decline into political obscurity.

The party system suppresses the electoral breakthrough of authoritarian and anti-democratic parties, but the same system also suppresses the emergence of new parties devoted to grass-roots democracy. The Green Party, which began the period under review as the Ecology Party, offered an alternative vision not based on the conventional ideological framework which underpins the party system. In this sense the Green Party is located on the radical but not extremist political fringe. A Green surge in the 1989 elections to the European Parliament resulted in much speculation about the imminent arrival of a 'new' politics, but even at the height of its success the party was dogged by factionalism. The Party's most substantial success came in the form of imitation by the major parties donning green clothes in order to persuade the electorate that they too cared about the environment.

The years since 1979 have thus witnessed considerable changes and developments in Britain's parties. In the concluding chapter Allan McConnell considers the accounts provided by the other contributors and assesses whether the weaknesses could have been avoided and, indeed the strengths reinforced, by greater involvement of the state in funding parties. At most state funding would make life more comfortable for the main parties, loosening their dependence on sectional support and thereby removing some of the distortion from current representative democracy. At the very least, it would make little or no difference since improved funding arrangements are not relevant to the range of problems discussed. But McConnell does not close the book on the issue of state funding since he foresees the possibility of circumstances akin to 1974: the need to fight two general elections in quick succession, leaving the parties strapped for cash. He would not be surprised if Lord Houghton's report was taken off the shelf, the dust blown off its covers and the arguments for state funding rediscovered.

## References

Ball, A.R. (1981), *British Political Parties: The Emergence of a Modern Party System*, London, Macmillan.

Beer, S.H. (1965), *Modern British Politics: Parties and Pressure Groups in the Collectivist Age*, London, Faber and Faber.

Berrington, H. (1983), 'Change in British Politics: an introduction', *West European Politics*, 6 (4): 1–25.

Drucker, H.M. (Ed) (1979), *Multi-party Britain*, London, Macmillan.

Finer, S.E. (1984), 'The Decline of Party' in V. Bogdanor, *Parties and Democracy in Britain and America*, New York, Praeger.

Ingle, S. (1989), *The British Party System*, Oxford, Blackwell.

Lees, J.D. and Kimber, R. (1972), *Political Parties in Modern Britain*, London, Routledge and Kegan Paul.

McKenzie, R.T. (1955), *British Political Parties: The Distribution of Power within the Conservative and Labour Parties*, London, Heinemann.

Ostrogorski, M. (1902), *Democracy and the Organization of Political Parties*, London, Macmillan and Co.

Rose, R. (1984), *Do Parties Make a Difference?* London, Macmillan.

Seyd, P. and Whiteley (1992), *Labour's Grass Roots: The Politics of Party Membership*, Oxford, Clarendon Press.

# 1
# Britain's dominant-party system

*Andrew Heywood*

Almost two decades of academic debate about the nature of Britain's party system was brought firmly – and at the time surprisingly – to an end in the early hours of Friday, 10 April 1992. The conventional view that Britain possesses a two-party system had been under attack since February 1974. The central feature of such a system is an alternation in power between two major parties, commanding sufficient support between them to exclude other parties from government. However, the revival of the Liberals in 1974 – securing more than six million votes – reduced combined Conservative and Labour support to a post-war low of 75 per cent, compared with over 95 per cent in the 1950s. Moreover, for the first time since 1929, neither major party gained an overall majority in the House of Commons. No longer was it possible to dismiss the Liberals as a 'third party'. But what was going to take the place of the two-party system? What kind of party system was emerging in Britain?

The split in the Labour Party which led to the formation of the SDP in 1981 and to the speedy conclusion of the Alliance with the Liberals later that year appeared to herald the emergence in Britain of three-party politics. At the time, Alliance supporters proclaimed that their objective was to 'break the mould of British politics', by which they meant to destroy its duopolistic tendencies and, in particular, to overthrow the Conservative–Labour stranglehold (Bradley, 1981). By gaining over a quarter of the votes in the 1983 general election, they seemed to be well on the way to achieving this goal. Many, believing the Labour Party to be in terminal decline, looked to a more radical breakthrough: a reshuffling of the two-party system with the Alliance replacing Labour as the principal alternative to the Conservatives. After all, in 1983 Labour recorded its worst election result since 1918, and stood only a bare 2 per cent ahead of the Alliance.

If anything, speculation about the party system mounted during the 1992 election campaign, with a number of possible developments appearing viable (Butler and Kavanagh, 1992). For instance, the prospect of a 'hung' parliament, persistently if inaccurately predicted by the opinion polls, pointed to a likely Labour–Liberal Democrat coalition government. Such a government was very likely to introduce some kind of electoral reform, thereby entrenching in Britain a continental-style, multi-party system. At the same time, the possibility of a single-party Labour government could not be discounted, a development that would have brought history full circle with the re-establishment of the traditional Conservative–Labour two-party system. However, as the election results came in, confirming a fourth successive Conservative victory, it became patently clear that each of these scenarios was flawed: Britain has a dominant-party system.

Is the matter that simple? Has the two-party 'mould' of British politics, celebrated even by Gilbert and Sullivan, finally collapsed and been replaced, not as the Alliance had hoped by three-partyism, but by a dominant-party system? To examine this question it is helpful to look at the British party system in light of the experience of countries like Japan, Sweden and India, which have had a long history of dominant-party rule. Perhaps the more important question, however, is: does it really matter? Is the party system merely an issue of academic debate, or is it crucial to the political process and vital to the health of democratic government? This issue has caused particular alarm because of the fear that dominant-party rule means that Britain has effectively become a one-party state. If this is the case, it is likely that Britain will start to exhibit characteristics more commonly associated with the Soviet Union of old than with more typical Western liberal democracies.

## Defining the dominant-party system

How does a dominant-party system differ from other party systems? In the first place, it is essential to distinguish a dominant-party system from the one-party systems typically found in now-collapsed communist states like the Soviet Union, and in surviving ones such as China, Cuba and North Korea. The principal feature of a one-party system is that government power is invested in the hands of a single, 'ruling' party, whose monopoly of power is usually constitutionally guaranteed. Thus all forms of opposition or political competition are legally prohibited. By contrast, a dominant-party system is open and pluralistic, at least in the sense that a number of parties compete for power in regular and popular elections. In other words, the general public possesses the constitutional ability to remove the government from office, but chooses not to use it. A dominant-party system is, therefore, a competitive party system dominated by a single major party that consequently enjoys a prolonged period of government power.

This apparently neat definition, however, runs into the problem of determining what a 'major' party is, and of deciding how long a 'prolonged' period in power might be. A 'major' party, as opposed to a 'minor' one, is government-orientated in the sense that it enjoys sufficient electoral support to have a realistic prospect of winning power; in short, it is 'electable'. However, does this include parties that have a realistic prospect of power but only as junior partners in a coalition government? Moreover, in federal political systems or in ones in which a strict separation of powers operates, it is often unclear which level of government and which institutions a party has to control to be considered to be 'in power'. Still greater difficulties arise from the fact that 'major' party status has as much to do with the future prospects of a party as it does with past performance. The British Labour Party, for instance, may have lost four successive elections, but is it now 'electable'? Deciding what a 'prolonged' period in power might be is no more straightforward. In practice, a 'prolonged' period surely encompasses several electoral terms, whose duration will, of course, vary from country to country. But how many is 'several' – three, four, five? A further problem is that prolonged one-party dominance may be punctuated by brief periods during which a rival party or parties form governments. But how frequent and long-lived do these governments have to be before the notion of a dominant-party system has to be discarded?

Japan is usually cited as the classic example of a dominant-party system. Until its fall in 1993 the Liberal-Democratic Party (LDP) had been in power continuously for thirty-eight years, having failed to gain an overall majority in the House of Representatives, the lower chamber of the Japanese Diet, only in 1976, 1979 and 1983. LDP dominance has been underpinned by the Japanese 'economic miracle'. It also reflects the powerful appeal of the party's neo-Confucian principles of duty and obligation in the still-traditional Japanese countryside, and the strong links the party has forged with business elites. The best European example of a dominant-party system is Sweden, where the Social Democratic Labour Party (SAP) remained in power, either alone or as the senior partner in a coalition, from 1951 until 1992, with the sole exception of the 1976–78 period. The SAP was able to appeal to a broad welfare consensus in Sweden while pursuing moderate policies that did not alienate business interests. It was also bolstered, at least until the late 1980s, by sustained economic growth.

The dominant-party system in India, however, had very different roots. The Congress Party enjoyed an unbroken spell of thirty years in power commencing with the achievement of independence in 1947, and until 1989 Congress had only endured three years in opposition, following Indira Gandhi's 1975–77 'State of Emergency'. Congress had the advantage of developing out of the victorious independence movement and, unique in Indian politics, a cross-caste and cross-religious appeal. Quite clearly its success was also related to the unifying leadership of the Nehru-Gandhi dynasty, and has faltered since the assassination, first, of Indira Gandhi in 1984 and then in 1991 of her son Rajiv. In some respects Australian politics exhibits similar dominant-party tendencies. Under the leadership of Robert Menzies, the Liberal Party held power for seventeen consecutive years in the immediate post-war period. However, since 1983, the Labour Party has won five consecutive general elections, even surviving the party coup in which Bob Hawke was replaced by Paul Keating to win the 1993 election. The Liberals, nevertheless, remain strong in state politics.

More debatable examples of dominant-party systems would include Italy and the United States. In Italy, the Christian Democratic Party (DC) dominated every one of the country's fifty-two post-war governments until the party's effective collapse in 1993 amidst mounting allegations of corruption. However, given Italy's highly proportional electoral system, the Christian Democrats were always constrained by the need to form coalitions, sometimes serving under prime ministers drawn from other parties. In addition, these coalitions were held together by a common desire to keep the other major party, the Italian Communist Party (now Democratic Left), out of power. This meant that apart from the 'historic compromise', 1977–78, the Communist Party, consistently the second largest party in the country, was a permanent party of opposition. In recent years, US politics has also displayed some dominant-party features. Until Clinton's victory in November 1992, the Republicans had won five out of the previous six Presidential elections and so had held the White House since 1969, except for the Carter interlude, 1977–81. This dominance, however, was achieved almost exclusively in relation to Presidential politics. Even while Republicans like Nixon, Reagan and Bush were in the White House, the Democrats dominated Congressional politics, a dominance that has much older roots. Since 1955, the Democrats have had unbroken control of the House of Representatives and only lost their Senate majority in the 1981–87 period. In the same way, the Democrats have retained entrenched power in many, especially Southern, states.

## A dominant-party system in Britain?

For much of the 1980s debate about the party system in Britain focused not upon Conservative dominance but on the prospect that a centre party breakthrough would establish a three-party or multi-party system. This prospect has now receded. Alliance support dropped by 3 per cent between 1983 and 1987, and the 18 per cent the Liberal Democrats gained in 1992 marked a further 5 per cent fall. Despite by-election victories and continued progress in local government, especially in the South West, the Liberal Democrats are no closer to 'breaking the mould' of British politics. In such circumstances, the case against the dominant-party system would seem to rest upon the assertion that elements of two-partyism survive: Labour is still a major party. Britain, so the argument goes, remains a two-party system, but one that has since 1979 temporarily ceased to function. Those who argue that Labour is once again 'electable' point out that since its nadir in 1983, when the party gained less than 28 per cent of the vote, electoral support has risen in the two subsequent elections and so is on a steadily upward path. The 35 per cent eventually achieved in 1992 may have been disappointing in view of opinion poll predictions at the time, but at least confirms the wisdom of the policy review conducted after the 1987 defeat and provides a sound basis for regaining power at the next election. This interpretation has come to be known in Labour circles as the 'one last heave' thesis. Indeed, some have gone as far as to argue that Labour was electable in 1992; its defeat is put down to 'political' circumstances, errors made during the election itself. These include the 'Kinnock factor', the clouding of the health issue by controversy over the 'Jennifer's ear' election broadcast, the misconceived Sheffield rally, and, of course, the mishandling of the party's tax proposals. In short, a Conservative victory was by no means inevitable.

Unfortunately for the Labour Party, such arguments present its position in the most favourable possible light and ignore compelling evidence of long-term decline. The simple fact is that the Conservative Party has held power alone since 1979 and can now, after its fourth successive general election victory, expect to remain in government until at least 1996 or 1997. Surely seventeen years in power, though modest by Japanese or Indian standards, is sufficiently 'prolonged' for the Conservatives to be considered 'dominant'; the alternation in power which is crucial to any two-party system has simply ceased to occur. Moreover, it is difficult for Labour to find alibis for its 1992 defeat in view of the fact that it was fought in the depths of a recession, circumstances in which no other twentieth-century government has clung on to power. However, there are also reasons to believe that Conservative dominance may be yet more protracted.

There is little doubt that the Labour Party has a mountain to climb if it is to return to office. The party's electoral support remains below the level achieved in 1979, and even if the approximately 3.5 per cent improvement registered in 1987 and 1992 were to be repeated in 1996, Labour would still be short of the 40 per cent usually needed to form a government. The 1992 result was, after 1983 and 1987, Labour's worst since 1918; and the seven-point lead over Labour which the Conservatives now enjoy would require the largest swing in any election since 1945 to be overturned. Labour's task in 1996 or 1997 is, in addition, certain to be made more difficult by parliamentary boundary changes which will cost the party, on current estimates, between three and thirteen seats. However, the gloomiest possible picture for Labour emerges from an analysis of long-term social and demographic trends, all of which point towards continued Conservative success. Labour, for example, has been damaged by the shrinkage of the manual working class, the decline of public-sector employment and consumption patterns, and the shift of population from urban to rural areas; more worryingly for Labour, all evidence suggests that these trends will continue into the foreseeable future (Crewe, 1991).

Taking a longer perspective, it could be argued that Britain has had a dominant-party system through much of the twentieth century and certainly since the old Liberal–Conservative two-party system collapsed after the First World War (Ball, 1987). In the seventy years leading up to 1992, the Conservatives had been in government, either alone or as the dominant member of a coalition, for fifty of them. Two-party politics undoubtedly took place during this time but was largely confined to the 1964–79 period, when Labour won four out of five general elections. The important point is that Labour has only twice, in 1945 and 1966, recorded decisive election victories, and at no time has the party managed to serve two consecutive full terms in office. With hindsight, the Labour governments of 1924, 1929–31, 1945–51, 1964–70 and 1974–79 merely punctuated Conservative dominance but did not succeed in breaking the mould of twentieth-century British politics. The 1992 general election may therefore only have highlighted an older and firmly-established trend.

It would be a great mistake, nevertheless, to assume that Conservative dominance of the party system reflects the dominance of its values and beliefs in society at large, as Hugo Young of the *Guardian* (11.4.92) implied when he interpreted the 1992 result as evidence that Britain is 'a deeply conservative country'. Party systems are fashioned as much by technical factors like the electoral system as they are by social, historical and cultural ones. For example, had the 1992 election been fought under any one of the proportional representation (PR) electoral systems it would have produced a Labour–Liberal Democrat coalition government. For all its 'dominance', the Conservative Party has only gained 50 per cent or more electoral support twice in the twentieth century, in 1931 and 1935, and then when the Labour Party was deeply split. Since 1979, in fact, the Conservatives have not gained more than 43 per cent of the vote, a smaller percentage than the winning party gained in every election between 1945 and 1970 and, more surprisingly, a smaller percentage than the 'losing' party managed in 1951 and 1955. When almost 58 per cent of the electorate votes for parties other than the Conservatives, as it did in 1992, is it really possible to describe Britain as a 'conservative nation'?

Moreover, as Ivor Crewe (1988) has argued, consistently backed up by opinion polls and Social Trends surveys, there is very little evidence of the growth in British society of 'Thatcherite values', such as self-reliance, enterprise and rugged individualism. Instead, social democratic values appear to be more deeply rooted than they were in the 1970s – even if self-interest rather than moral principle seems to influence voting behaviour. Such evidence suggests that the dominant-party system has less to do with the ascendancy of the Conservative Party, or of the values for which it currently stands, than it does with a crisis of opposition in British politics: the failure of any party since the pre-First World War Liberals to mount a sustained challenge to the Conservatives. Given the broad coalition of interests and ideas which it represents, Labour has been far less effective than the Conservative Party as a vehicle for winning and retaining power. The party has traditionally been more prone to factional in-fighting than the Conservatives, and has undoubtedly been less adept at changing its policies and its image in response to electoral pressure. It is instructive, for instance, to contrast Labour's 1987–89 policy review, which came after a party split in 1981 and three successive election defeats, with the speed with which the Conservatives adopted a social democratic platform after their 1945 defeat. The willingness of the party to dispense with a three-time election victor like Margaret Thatcher in November 1990 further illustrates its ruthless determination to hold on to power.

## Consequences of the dominant-party system

Once immediate, and predictably partisan, reactions to the 1992 result began to fade, a deeper debate about its long-term implications started to take place. From the Conservative point of view, of course, the result was a triumph, a victory for both the party *and* the British people, whose re-endorsement of continuity surely reflected satisfaction with thirteen years of Conservative government. The people had examined the alternatives and decided to stick with John Major; this was democracy at work. However, others have expressed darker concerns about the affect that continued Conservative government was having upon the political system itself. Paddy Ashdown, for example, warned about what he called 'the slow death of pluralism in our democracy'. Evidence from other countries, as well as from recent British experience, suggests that a dominant-party system, whichever party is in power, poses a serious threat to the political process and may even be corrosive of the democratic spirit. The central concern is that, in effect, a dominant-party system allows a country to be governed like a one-party state.

### The relationship between the party and the state

The distinctive feature of a one-party state is that, in the absence of institutionalised opposition and political competition, the party in power effectively becomes the government and so dominates the entire state apparatus. It becomes a 'ruling' party. In the Soviet Union, for example, the Politburo and Central Committee, organs of the Communist Party, functioned as the highest executive institutions, and the state bureaucracy was subject to pervasive party control (McAuley, 1977). Liberal democratic systems, on the other hand, establish a clear distinction between the party in power, the 'government of the day', and the institutions of the state. The state is meant to be neutral, it exists to promote the permanent interests of society – the maintenance of public order, stability and prosperity, and defence against external aggression – while the party in government is motivated by narrower and partisan objectives, such as the desire to remain in power, to keep major backers happy and to translate its ideological convictions into action. If the governing party succeeds in subordinating the power and authority of the state to its partisan goals, it begins to assume the mantle of a 'ruling' party, and the level playing field of political competition, the heart of electoral democracy, is seriously compromised.

One simple but effective guarantee of a distinction between the state and the government of the day is that in a liberal democracy governments are temporary while the state is permanent. When governments come and go, state officials and institutions are encouraged to remain neutral for fear of becoming over-dependent upon any single party and in order to have the flexibility to adjust to an incoming government with new political and ideological priorities. When, however, power ceases to alternate, an insidious process of politicisation takes place and the distinction between party and state becomes blurred. This has been particularly evident in Japan, where the LDP's status as a 'permanent' government led to an unhealthily close relationship with the state bureaucracy. For instance, about one-quarter of the party's Diet members are former civil servants, creating a 'revolving door' that made political neutrality in the bureaucracy virtually impossible.

In Britain, it could be argued that an alternation in power is all the more crucial given the absence of the usual liberal democratic constraints upon government – a written constitution, a Bill of Rights and an effective separation of powers. Britain's highly centralised system of government means that, once elected, governments inherit enormous power, including the ability to re-shape the state system itself. This has been evident since 1979 in a series of profound changes that have taken place within Whitehall (Hennessy, 1990). In the early 1980s, for instance, a new senior appointments mechanism was introduced into the civil service, prompting allegations of politicisation and even 'Thatcherisation'. This was followed by an efficiency drive, which has witnessed the transfer of responsibilities to executive agencies outside the Whitehall system, and to the introduction of competitive tendering. More subtly, however, a free-market and more commercial ethos has taken root amongst senior Whitehall officials, whose participation in conferences organised by right-wing 'think-tanks' like the Adam Smith Institute or the Institute of Economic Affairs stimulates little comment in the 1990s. While in the early 1980s the Thatcher government encountered senior civil servants who had served previous Labour administrations, the Major government is advised by officials who have over the years adjusted, possibly unconsciously, to the ethos and philosophy of the Conservative Party.

Furthermore, crucial areas of public life in Britain have been reformed and re-modelled as a result of prolonged Conservative rule. This has particularly affected health, education and training, where, by stark contrast with the government's alleged desire to 'roll back the state', policy making has been placed in the hands of a growing number of powerful quangos. One thousand, four hundred and twelve quangos were in existence by 1992, responsible for spending between £10bn and £14bn of public money, and leaving about forty thousand jobs at the disposal of ministers, from the Prime Minister downwards. These include many newly-created organisations, such as the London Residuary Body, the Docklands Development Corporation and the funding councils which now control universities and colleges. Not only does this development raise questions about the decline of public accountability, but it also creates the spectre of widespread politicisation. The neutrality of public bodies ranging from the BBC to health authorities and hospital trusts has been compromised by a policy of 'packing' them with appointees who openly sympathise with the government's political and economic objectives (Baxter, 1993). In the same way, the ethic of public service which is supposed to reign in state education and public health has been progressively displaced by an emphasis upon efficiency, cost-cutting and 'consumer' responsiveness, concerns which reflect the ideological priorities of the modern Conservative Party.

### The dominant party

An extended period in government can also have a disturbing effect upon the dominant party itself. When a party starts to regard itself as a 'permanent' government, the result can either be complacency and intellectual flabbiness or, on the other hand, an uncritical and unlistening arrogance. In extreme cases, complacency can undoubtedly lead to financial corruption. The course of Japanese and Italian politics has, for example, regularly been interrupted by scandals, usually involving allegations of corruption. Indeed, the most serious threats to LDP dominance in Japan have resulted from events such as the Lockheed bribery scandal in 1979, which provoked the resignation and later imprisonment of Prime Minister Tanaka. Although it is clearly misleading to put corruption down to a single cause, the fact that politicians can remain in power for long periods of time without fearing loss of office is surely a contributory factor. This was dramatically illustrated by the Italian Christian Democrats in their 'fortress city' of Naples, where very close links were formed between DC leaders and the Camorra, the city's infamous Mafia organisation.

Although its image was tarnished by allegations of gerrymandering made against its 'flagship' council, the London Borough of Westminster, as well as questions concerning the propriety of party financing, the British Conservative Party has not been afflicted by Japanese- or Italian-style corruption scandals. Nevertheless, prolonged success has arguable had an effect upon the party's ideological orientation. The Thatcher period commenced with an attempt to 'think the unthinkable'; the party leadership set out to challenge social democratic values that were deeply rooted in the British state and the Conservative Party itself. Early battles between the 'wets' and the 'drys' were meaningful confrontations, provoking debate about both policy and ideological direction. After fifteen years in power, however, free-market principles stand virtually unchallenged within the party, with the result that major policy rifts and ideological disagreements have, with the all too painful exception of Europe, largely disappeared. What was once 'unthinkable' has now become unquestioned dogma, meaning that, for all his attempts to establish a distinct political and ideological identity, John Major cannot break loose from his Thatcherite heritage. The decision to privatise coal and the railways, and the persistence with health and education reforms against the advice of the professionals involved, perhaps demonstrates an inability to think beyond what are now firmly-entrenched ideological parameters.

The existence of seldom-questioned ideological goals also means that policy mistakes are more likely to occur, simply because the other side of the argument is no longer being put. The most spectacular example of this was, obviously, the ease with which Thatcher was able to gain cabinet and parliamentary approval for the poll tax, whose unpopularity quickly threatened the party with the possibility of electoral defeat. Internal debate within the government party is particularly crucial in a dominant-party system because of the ineffectiveness of other parties. The focal point of politics shifts from competition between parties to factional rivalry within the dominant party. However, when the range of ideological disagreement is as narrow as that between, say, John Major and Michael Portillo, there is little reason to believe that the main thrust of government policy will be seriously questioned or scrutinised from within. This is a particularly disturbing prospect when the radicalism of the government's programme is taken into account. John Major may certainly be less ideological and more pragmatic than his predecessor, but he is nevertheless presiding over changes in public and political life which will have a permanent affect upon British society.

Finally, when a party ceases to fear the judgement of the electorate, it becomes less sensitive to external pressures. Once again, this is particularly important in a country with an unwritten constitution like Britain where constitutional rules are upheld very largely by a sense of propriety on the part of the governing party. Some have suggested that the last decade has witnessed a gradual decline in the standards of public life, perhaps not unconnected with the fact that a single party has been in power throughout the period (Graham and Prosser, 1988). This can be seen in increasingly partisan appointments to supposedly neutral state bodies, but is also evident in the declining significance of the doctrine of ministerial responsibility. There is no doubt that individual ministerial responsibility has not functioned in its classic form for many years – possibly not since Sir Thomas Dugdale's resignation over Critchel Down in 1954, taking responsibility for a blunder made by his officials – but the cases of David Mellor and Norman Lamont suggest that the convention may be on the verge of becoming entirely irrelevant.

Major's reluctance to sack Mellor in the summer of 1992 for fear of succumbing to pressure from the tabloid press may be understandable in political terms. However, it also meant that Mellor remained in office while it was clear to a growing number of Conservative back-benchers that by accepting gifts and a holiday he had acted in a manner unacceptable for a Secretary of State. Lamont's case is even more telling. Once again, Major's desire to keep him makes political sense – Major may have recognised that Lamont had become the 'lightning conductor' of the government, drawing criticism away from the Prime Minister himself. Furthermore, he may have refrained from acting out of a genuine sense of personal loyalty. Nevertheless, as Chancellor, Lamont had presided in September 1992 over the ERM fiasco which saw the collapse of what was acknowledged to be the centrepiece of the government's economic strategy. Moreover, an estimated £5bn was squandered in an attempt to support an unsustainable pound. In other words, a policy blunder of the first magnitude had occurred, but no minister had taken responsibility for it, or even acknowledged that mistakes had been made. That Lamont was sacked the following year in an attempt to bolster the government's flagging popularity merely supports the view that resignations are now dictated more by political convenience rather than by constitutional principle.

*The quality of opposition*

Effective opposition is an essential ingredient of democratic politics. It is only through scrutiny and criticism that the electorate can gain a balanced understanding of government policies and therefore be in a position to make meaningful choices at election time. In any competitive party system the burden of this responsibility falls on opposition parties and, in Britain's case, upon Her Majesty's Opposition. However, as already mentioned, a dominant-party system creates 'permanent' opposition parties, whose capacity to question, scrutinise and check the governing party is severely restricted.

Criticism itself is no obstacle to government; what forces government to heed criticism and enter into meaningful policy debate is that it is made by a party perceived to be a genuine rival for power, a 'government in the wings'. When the Opposition ceases to be regarded as an alternative government, its views and opinions, however well expressed, no longer carry weight and can be dismissed with impunity. Moreover, the longer the period in opposition, the more insuperable these problems are likely to become. 'Permanent' parties of opposition may also exhibit a tendency towards internal disputes and divisions, resulting from mounting frustration and the fact that the prospect of power is perhaps the best guarantee of party unity. They may lack drive and direction, losing confidence in traditional ideological positions and coming to shadow those of the governing party, and find increasing difficulty in attracting talented and ambitious recruits.

Opposition, for instance, to the LDP in Japan has traditionally been weak and fragmented. The principal opposition party is the Japan Socialist Party, which split in 1960 with the formation of a breakaway, more right-wing Democratic Socialist Party, and again in 1977 with the formation of the smaller Social Democratic Federation. There are also the Japanese Communist Party and Komeito, the political wing of an eight-million strong Buddhist sect. Opposition to the SAP in Sweden has been similarly fragmented and includes the conservative Moderate Party, the Liberal Party, the Centre Party representing agrarian interests, the Christian Democratic Party, the former-communist Left Party and a rising Green Party. The usual alternative to SAP domination, a broad centre–right coalition, has therefore typically lacked cohesion and been, in most cases, short-lived.

Similar tendencies have been evident in Britain since 1979. Conservative dominance of the House of Commons during the 1980s was not simply a consequence of its large majorities but also a reflection of the weakness of opposition parties – in particular, the poor performance of Labour and the division in opposition ranks between Labour and the Alliance, later the Liberal Democrats. In Labour's case, the period of factional in-fighting dated from the early 1980s and can be put down not to prolonged opposition so much as to the division within the party between socialists and social democrats which had been exacerbated by the party's long-term decline and was brought to a head by the 1979 defeat. However, the experience of its third successive defeat in 1987 had a dramatic affect upon the Labour Party. Kinnock succeeded in persuading a defeat-shattered party to undertake a comprehensive policy review, effectively re-casting Labour as a continental-style social democratic party (Heywood, 1992). The 'new model' Labour Party is also more telegenic, offering a more moderate and, above all, a more unified image to the electorate. As a result of this, Labour was able, in the run-up to the 1992 election, to present itself as both more disciplined and better organised than the Conservatives.

This process may, nevertheless, not so much reflect a determination to get back into power as the fact that Labour, battered by successive defeats, no longer has a sense of its own ideological identity. What is clear is that, under both Kinnock and Smith, Labour has increasingly aligned itself with an individualist platform that more closely resembles Liberal Democratic policies, and even Thatcherism, than it does the party's collectivist heritage. There is a sense, furthermore, in which Labour's new, unified image may be fragile. Factionalism has been contained by the fact that the 1983 defeat in particular, fought as the election was on a radical manifesto, has demoralised the Left, leaving it, some would argue, intellectually bankrupt. However, unity has also been maintained because the gap between Labour and the Conservatives closed in 1987 and 1992, albeit modestly, keeping alive the expectation of an early return to office. In other words, the party still has something to be unified for. How Labour will react if opinion polls and by-election results do not sustain its election hopes is, however, another matter. Unity will be particularly difficult to maintain given the controversial nature of the issues now confronting Labour: electoral reform, the party's relationship with the unions, a further overhaul of policies, electoral pacts with the Liberal Democrats and even the possibility of a wholesale realignment of the centre-left in British politics.

*The political culture*

Ultimately, the quality of democracy is dependent upon the values and political attitudes of the general public. 'Government by the people' has long since ceased to mean popular self-government but at least still means that government is regularly accountable to the people through the mechanism of competitive elections. This accountability, of course, requires that the public is both well-informed and capable of making independent judgements, but it also depends upon the public's willingness to question, challenge and, finally, remove the government. A dominant-party system tends to have a profound but insidious influence upon the political culture. Long periods of one party rule engender the belief that that party is the 'natural' party of government; in the popular mind the dominant party is linked with security and stability, the 'natural' order of things. Hugo Young, for instance, commented upon the 1992 result under the headline 'Sticking with the Nurse' (*The Guardian*, 11.4.92). In effect, longevity appears to invest the dominant party with a 'right' to govern, a fact that tends to encourage deference, conformity and a fear of change.

The prospect of a change in government is disturbing precisely because it is a journey into the unknown. Parties like Labour, whose last period in power is not even a memory to a growing number of voters, clearly have a credibility problem to overcome. This is compounded, quite obviously, by a growing problem of inexperience. John Smith, for example, is now the only member of Labour's shadow cabinet ever to have held a ministerial post of cabinet rank. In a sense, therefore, a dominant-party system is psychologically self-perpetuating. In contrast to the democratic spirit, it generates an increasingly cautious and deferential political culture which works to the benefit of those already in power and clearly against those who aspire to replace them. Many explanations, for instance, have been suggested for the last-minute surge in Conservative support which confounded the pollsters in April 1992, but surely a desire for security and familiarity was not irrelevant to the outcome. It is also interesting to note the parallels between the British 1992 election and the 1993 election in Australia. In both, a party that had enjoyed a prolonged period in power succeeded in gaining re-election, despite consistent opinion-poll evidence to the contrary and the fact that the economy was in deep recession.

## Breaking the mould?

If a dominant-party system does exist in Britain, how can it be challenged or overthrown? This question has stimulated considerable debate within the Labour Party, at least among those who no longer believe in an automatic return to two-party normality, and also within the Liberal Democrats. Without doubt, frustration with prolonged Conservative rule has pushed Labour towards a programme of constitutional reform that, in many respects, resembles the policies of the Liberal Democrats. Labour's conversion to the cause of devolution, a Bill of Rights and a reformed second chamber was completed before the 1992 election; the more difficult issue of electoral reform for the House of Commons has consumed much of its energy since. From one point of view, embracing constitutional reform is designed to broaden the party's electoral base, probably attracting support away from the Liberal Democrats and strengthening Labour in the South of England. However, it also reflects an attempt to place obstacles in the way of a 'permanent' Conservative government.

If the Conservatives cannot be removed from power, or if Labour is only capable of punctuating Conservative dominance for brief periods, at least the government's freedom of manoeuvre can be limited, and rival centres of power can be established. This is why electoral reform is so crucial: it creates the possibility of excluding the Conservatives from power by the construction of an anti-Conservative coalition. The obvious weakness of such an approach, however, is that, given the Conservatives' unbending and understandable commitment to a constitutional structure that currently benefits them, they have to be removed from office before any such reforms can be introduced. As explained earlier, that prospect may still be remote. This is why so much attention has been paid to the politics of realignment.

The prospect of realignment on the centre-left of British politics has a powerful and obvious appeal. If the Conservatives are kept in power with the support of approximately two-fifths of the electorate, surely it must be possible to harness the votes of the remaining three-fifths to remove them. By dividing the non-Conservative vote, Labour and the Liberal Democrats conspire to keep the Conservative Party in government. This is, however, very superficial logic. Realignment can, broadly speaking, take one of three forms. In the first place, it can involve nothing more than a willingness by Labour and the Liberal Democrats to work more closely together in the process of policy formation. This has already occurred in drawing up proposals for a future Scottish Parliament and in relation to Labour's Commission on Social Justice, on which Liberal Democrats sit. A more concrete form of realignment would take the form of a willingness to enter into a post-election deal, requiring that the two parties fight the next election either on a joint manifesto or on separate but clearly compatible ones. Both these forms of realignment are nevertheless doomed to fail in the absence of an electoral pact that ensures that Labour and Liberal Democrat candidates do not fight one another, thereby splitting the non-Conservative vote. In other words, there is little reason to believe that the non-Conservative vote would grow simply because the opposition parties proposed to work together. And there is some danger that it might shrink if the Conservatives can exploit fears of coalition government as they did in the final week of the 1992 campaign.

The third and perhaps only realistic form of realignment would therefore involve a pre-election pact, through which Labour and the Liberal Democrats could agree upon joint candidates. This need not mean an arrangement as ambitious and comprehensive as the deal which the SDP and the Liberals negotiated before the 1983 and 1987 elections. Rather, it could involve targeting those Conservative marginals in which one or other of the opposition parties is particularly weak. This may apply, for instance, in the South of England, where Labour has little realistic chance of winning. In total, there are eighty-three seats in England and four in Scotland, where Labour gained 15 per cent or less in April 1992. Indeed, such deals were evident in the local government elections of May 1993, and succeeded in depriving the Conservatives of a number of seats. Moreover, surprisingly few ideological obstacles now stand in the way of some kind of Labour–Liberal Democrat Alliance – Labour's 1992 manifesto was, after all, remarkably similar to the policies the breakaway SDP adopted in 1981.

Significant problems do nevertheless exist. In the first place, any move by Labour in the direction of an electoral pact would be tantamount to an admission that it can no longer win power on its own, that it is no longer a major party. This explains the Labour front-bench's determination to field a candidate in the Eastleigh by-election, despite the fact that the party had no realistic chance of victory. More seriously perhaps, there are doubts about whether an electoral pact would work, even if one could be constructed. In particular, a significant, if unquantifiable, proportion of Liberal Democrat supporters would defect to the Conservatives if confronted by a choice between a Labour–Liberal Democrat coalition government and a single-party Conservative one. In short, the non-Conservative electoral majority in Britain is not necessarily an anti-Conservative majority. As a result, and particularly while the 'one last heave' thesis retains credibility in the minds of the Labour leadership, it is unlikely that the party will countenance any but the most modest form of realignment.

## References

Ball, A. (1987), *British Political Parties: The Emergence of the Modern Party System*, London, Macmillan, second edn.

Baxter, S. (1993), 'The Sleaze at the Heart of Tory Britain', in *New Statesman and Society*, 1 October 1993.

Bradley, I. (1981), *Breaking the Mould: The Birth and Prospects of the Social Democratic Party*, Oxford, Martin Robertson.

Butler, D. and Kavanagh, D. (eds) (1992), *The British General Election of 1992*, London, Macmillan.

Crewe, I. (1988), 'Has the Electorate become Thatcherite?' in Skidelsky, R. (ed.), *Thatcherism*, London, Chatto and Windus.

Crewe, I. (1991), 'Labour Force Changes, Working Class Decline, and the Labour Vote: Social and Electoral Trends in Postwar Britain', in Piven, F.F. (ed.), *Labour Parties in Post-industrial Societies*, Oxford, Polity Press.

Graham, G. and Prosser, T. (eds) (1988), *Waiving the Rules*, Milton Keynes, Open University Press.

Hennessy, P. (1990), *Whitehall*, London, Fontana, revised edn.

Heywood, A. (1992), *Political Ideology: An Introduction*, London, Macmillan.

McAuley, M. (1977), *Politics and the Soviet Union*, Harmondsworth, Penguin.

# 2

# Power and leadership in the major parties

*Richard Kelly*

It remains one of the most remarkable features of political science that, until Robert McKenzie's seminal thesis was published in 1955, little academic attention was devoted to the question of power and leadership inside Britain's major parties. Since then, there has been a series of additional and usually more specific studies designed to update, refute or modify McKenzie's conclusions (Minkin, 1978; Seyd, 1987; Shaw, 1988; Kelly, 1989). Events since 1979 have indeed provided a further stimulus to discussion, as both major parties have undergone vital changes concerning their structures and procedures, as well as the behaviour and attitude of leaders and members alike. Furthermore, many of these changes have profound implications for the sort of policies and image each party projects to an ever more volatile electorate.

The aim of this chapter is to chronicle most of the key developments that have occurred within the parties since the Conservatives came to power, and to offer some thoughts upon the relevance of party activism as the century draws to a close. Any imbalance in the amount of attention given to each of the parties is easily explained: the Labour Party, having been out of office for over thirteen years, has inevitably been drawn to a greater degree of introspection and, therefore, a greater degree of internal reform. The Conservatives, by contrast, have an organisation which, for all its warts, has at least seen the party win four successive elections.

## The Labour Party

Since 1979 scarcely a year has passed by without some important alteration to Labour's internal structure, a factor which has made life both challenging and frustrating for students of intra-party democracy. It is, however, possible to discern four distinctive phases in the changes that have taken place, phases which correspond roughly to the four phases of Conservative government since 1979.

*Phase 1: the Bennite ascendancy (1979–83)*

In the two years following Labour's loss of power, Tony Benn became the pivotal figure in an extraordinary debate about the location of authority inside the Party. Benn's analysis was at once a vindication and refutation of McKenzie's aforementioned thesis. McKenzie had argued that, despite the democratic tone of Labour's 1918 constitution, real power in the party rested with the parliamentary leadership. For McKenzie, this covert oligarchy was defensible on practical grounds (given the unpredictability of parliamentary life and the related need for swift, dynamic responses from principal parliamentary spokesmen), on ethical grounds (given the ethos of parliamentary democracy and the 'representative' as opposed to 'delegate' character of MPs) and on the grounds of the parties' electoral self-interest. Regarding the latter grounds, in light of the militant views attributed to most activists by McKenzie, party leaders who wished to be electorally attractive had to be able to appeal over the heads of party activists and assemble policies that would interest instead the more centrist electorate.

Benn (1980) agreed that the 1974–79 governments largely substantiated McKenzie's theory of power inside the Labour Party; as serving cabinet member throughout, he could also claim to speak with some authority. Yet far from the conduct of those governments (*vis-à-vis* party activists) producing electoral success, as McKenzie had indicated, Benn claimed it had contributed to electoral ignominy: by ignoring the wishes of Labour's activists, Labour's parliamentary leaders had lost touch with the wishes of its 'natural' working class electorate, paving the way for Mrs Thatcher's victory in 1979. Benn thus contested that organisational reform had become necessary not just to satisfy abstract theories of party democracy, but to ensure that future Labour governments did not 'betray' the socialist ideas developed in opposition and did not therefore suffer any further loss of confidence among voters.

This analysis had been anticipated at least five years earlier by the Campaign for Labour Party Democracy (CLPD), a leftist pressure group which believed that the struggle to guarantee the implementation of its ideas in government could not be divorced from organisational reform inside the party – reform which enhanced the influence of constituency party (CLP) activists at the expense of Labour MPs (the PLP). The CLPD's prospects were naturally raised after 1979, with Benn as its principal champion. Yet despite Benn's eloquence, the success CLPD was to enjoy could not have been achieved without the support of key trade unions, notably the Transport and General Workers Union

(TGWU), whose block votes ensured the CLPD powerful backing at Labour's annual conference, the arena in which all constitutional change must eventually be ratified (Seyd, 1987).

At the 1980 conference, Benn and his allies scored two historic victories. The first of these was mandatory reselection. Labour MPs were now obliged, as a matter of procedure, to again go through the process of being selected as Labour candidates by their CLPs before each general election. This was not so much an opportunity for deselecting MPs, which had always existed anyhow (*vide* Reg Prentice, who was deselected in 1976 by his Newham NE CLP), but a deterrent to those moderate MPs who might otherwise defy their CLPs' wishes.

The second reform involved taking away from the PLP its exclusive right to elect Labour's leader and deputy leader. It was alleged that this served to provide leaders who were unrepresentative of the party as a whole (although Foot's subsequent victory over Healey rather undermined this argument). After the decision had been taken to widen the franchise, a special conference was convened in January 1981 to determine the exact mechanics. At that conference 94 per cent of delegates voted in favour of an electoral college, whereas only 6 per cent supported David Owen's idea of a postal ballot involving all party members (Punnett, 1992). These figures reflected the fact that this special conference, like all Labour conferences, was dominated by the unions' block votes. Indeed, it was these same block votes which determined the composition of the new electoral college, giving 40 per cent of its votes to the trade unions and only 30 per cent each to the PLP and CLPs. It was also confirmed that this new device could be used to challenge Labour leaders in or out of government; Labour PMs had hitherto been protected from such an indignity, even though the Tories had themselves removed such protection after 1974 (see Figures 2.1 and 2.3).

The impact of these changes in the years that immediately followed seemed to justify the CLPD's prognosis; that is, they seemed to push the party in a leftward direction. The electoral college hastened the formation of the SDP and the subsequent defection of almost thirty right-wing Labour MPs. It was also demonstrated that it could saddle Labour MPs with a leader they might not otherwise have chosen, while depriving them of one they admired. In the 1981 deputy leadership contest, Benn came within 1 per cent of ousting Denis Healey, even though Benn never achieved more than a third of PLP support. Similarly, Neil Kinnock (who then still had leftist credentials) won an overwhelming victory to become Labour leader despite failing to get even half of the PLP's vote (see Table 2.1).

The effects of mandatory reselection were, on the surface, less severe than might have been imagined; only 8 MPs were deselected in the run-up to the 1983 general election. However, many of those who defected to the SDP faced deselection, as did a number who chose retirement

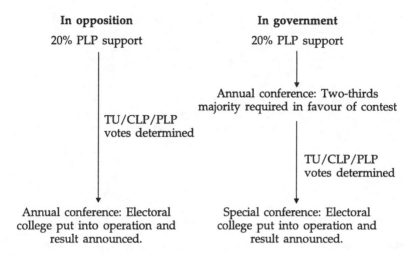

| In opposition | In government |
|---|---|
| 20% PLP support | 20% PLP support |

Annual conference: Two-thirds
majority required in favour of contest

TU/CLP/PLP
votes determined

TU/CLP/PLP
votes determined

| Annual conference: Electoral college put into operation and result announced. | Special conference: Electoral college put into operation and result announced. |

*Notes:*
a) PLP = Labour MPs and MEPs (30 per cent of electoral college); TU = Trade Unions (40 per cent of electoral college); CLP = Constituency Labour parties (30 per cent of electoral college).
b) When there is a vacancy (as in 1992), the NEC may decide to bring forward the ballot and pre-empt the conference. John Smith was thus elected almost three months before the conference assembled.
c) Originally 5 per cent, the 20 per cent figure was brought in after Benn's abortive challenge in 1988 (see Table 2.1). The effect was to limit quite severely the number of candidates.
d) The rules do not specify a closing date for nominations, but precedent seems to indicate a period of at least three months before the electoral college is convened.
e) Each MP and MEP is entitled to one vote; each CLP has one vote regardless of size; each TU's vote is determined by the size of its affiliated membership – in 1992, two-thirds of the TU vote were cast by four unions.
f) The votes of each MP, MEP, CLP and TU are recorded and subsequently disclosed.
g) The victor needs an overall majority of votes cast. If not achieved, the bottom candidate's second preferences are distributed among remaining candidates (see 1981 deputy leadership contest, Table 2.1).
h) At the 1993 conference, the composition of the electoral college was changed, giving the TUs, PLP and CLPs a third of the votes each. Though not a realisation of OMOV, as Smith had initially sought, it did nudge the system in that direction. In addition, TUs must no longer cast their votes as a block but split them in accordance with the voting patterns of their individual levy-paying members, with only those registering their support for Labour being allowed to vote.

**Figure 2.1** Procedures for contesting Labour leadership (1981–92)

*Source*: Garner and Kelly (1993: 176–9).

rather than the reselection procedure. In addition, many Labour MPs did seem to take more notice of their CLPs' opinions and modified their behaviour accordingly (Seyd 1987).

One final change during this period was scarcely noticed at the time and has been barely discussed since, partly because it was taken away

**Table 2.1**  Labour leader/deputy leader election contests since 1981

| | PLP section (30%) | Constituency section (30%) | TU section (40%) | Total |
|---|---|---|---|---|
| **1981 Deputy Leader** | | | | |
| Benn | 6.7 (10.2) | 23.5 (24.3) | 6.4 (15.0) | 36.6 (49.6) |
| Healey | 15.3 (19.8) | 5.4 (5.7) | 24.7 (25.0) | 45.5 (50.4) |
| Silkin | 8.0 | 1.1 | 8.9 | 18.0 |
| **1983 Leader** | | | | |
| Kinnock | 14.8 | 27.5 | 29.0 | 71.3 |
| Hattersley | 7.8 | 0.6 | 10.9 | 19.3 |
| Heffer | 4.3 | 2.0 | 0.1 | 6.3 |
| Shore | 3.1 | 0.0 | 0.1 | 3.1 |
| **1983 Deputy Leader** | | | | |
| Hattersley | 16.7 | 15.3 | 35.2 | 67.3 |
| Meacher | 8.8 | 14.4 | 4.7 | 27.9 |
| Davies | 3.3 | 0.2 | 0.0 | 3.5 |
| Dunwoody | 1.2 | 0.1 | 0.1 | 1.3 |
| **1988 Leader** | | | | |
| Kinnock | 24.8 | 24.1 | 39.7 | 88.6 |
| Benn | 5.2 | 5.9 | 0.3 | 11.4 |
| **1988 Deputy Leader** | | | | |
| Hattersley | 17.4 | 18.1 | 31.3 | 66.8 |
| Prescott | 7.2 | 7.8 | 8.7 | 23.7 |
| Heffer | 5.4 | 4.1 | 0.1 | 9.5 |
| **1992 Leader** | | | | |
| Smith | 23.2 | 29.3 | 38.5 | 91.0 |
| Gould | 6.8 | 0.7 | 1.5 | 9.0 |
| **1992 Deputy Leader** | | | | |
| Beckett | 12.9 | 19.0 | 25.4 | 57.3 |
| Prescott | 9.4 | 7.1 | 11.6 | 28.1 |
| Gould | 7.7 | 3.9 | 3.0 | 14.6 |

*Note*: Where a second ballot took place, the results of the second ballot are shown in parentheses.

*Source*: Punnett (1992: 110).

from the glare of Labour's conference. The PLP, as a response to the party's iconoclastic mood, decided in conjunction with the Party's National Executive Committee (NEC) that future Labour governments must, in their first year, include all those elected in the last PLP elections to the shadow cabinet. Of course, few PMs of either party have had the absolute right to appoint whomsoever they want to cabinet office (King,

1985). Still, this does represent a new formal constraint upon Labour leaders which students of government in general may care to consider.

The culmination of these changes within the party was Labour's manifesto of 1983, arguably the most radical the party has ever produced. Yet if the 1983 manifesto was the Left's *apogee*, the 1983 general election result was to prove its nemesis – as organisational changes during the next nine years were to demonstrate.

*Phase 2: the revival of social democratic centralism (1983–87)*

The *débâcle* of the 1983 election was to prompt a revival of what Shaw (1988) termed 'social democratic centralism'. This involved the parliamentary leadership using its dominance of the NEC to extend its influence inside the party in order to secure support for the type of social democratic policies preferred by the electorate – a strategy deployed with some electoral success between 1945 and 1970. The major figure in the renewal of this strategy was obviously the new leader himself, for whom the 1983 election was a chastening realisation that Bennite policies were incompatible with a Labour victory (Leapman, 1987).

Kinnock was fortunate in acquiring quickly the *sine qua non* of any centralising strategy; namely, the support of the large trade unions upon whom the 1983 result had a similarly cathartic effect. This was to give Kinnock (via the NEC) the authority and confidence to start attacking the citadels of left-wing power within the party, the most controversial being Militant Tendency, which had in the early 1980s established a strong base in many urban CLPs (Crick, 1984). Between 1984 and 1985, the NEC carried out a much publicised purge at CLP level, climaxing with Kinnock's splenetic attack upon Labour councillors in Liverpool and Lambeth at the 1985 conference (see Chapter 10). Between 1985 and 1987, the NEC continued to show its determination to reshape the party at grass-roots level by shutting down the Knowsley North CLP (after allegations of Militant involvement) and imposing its own favoured candidate for the 1986 by-election. Likewise, the Lewisham and Nottingham East CLPs were ordered to re-run their candidate selection process following rumours that they had employed illicit 'black sections' by reserving places on their GMC for black constituency party members.

Meanwhile, Kinnock and his NEC allies moved to reorganise Labour's headquarters in Walworth Road – thought mainly responsible for Labour's shabby 1983 campaign – and to improve the party's overall media profile. To this end, Kinnock secured the services of Larry Whitty, who became General Secretary, and Peter Mandelson, who became the party's first Director of Communications and the guiding light for the new shadow communications agency, a body Mandelson set up to co-opt the assistance of pollsters, marketing specialists and media experts. By 1987, Whitty and (especially) Mandelson had, with the leader's unqualified support, rejuvenated Labour's national bureaucracy and crafted a new public image often dubbed as 'designer socialism'. The contrast between Labour's 1983 and 1987 campaigns was quite stunning, with the party winning much praise for its slick, professional approach. Less noticed was the way in which the 1987 manifesto was 'bounced' upon the rest of the party by the leader and a handful of fairly anonymous advisers. A number of left-wingers complained that, although the commitment to unilateral nuclear disarmament had been retained, conference's demand for large cuts in conventional military expenditure was brazenly ignored by both the manifesto and the official campaign (Hughes and Wintour, 1990).

*Phase 3: the apotheosis of social democratic centralism (1987–92)*

Labour's defeat in 1987 was only marginally less shameful than that of 1983. Yet far from weakening the leader's faith in the sort of changes he had already instigated, it merely strengthened his wish to see them intensified. As a result, four interlocking ideas were restated and undertaken between 1987 and 1992.

*Purging Militant*: During this period, a remarkable portion of the party's energy was devoted to the cause of self-cleansing. In the vanguard of this assault upon the 'enemy within' was the National Constitutional Committee (NCC), set up in 1986 after expelled Militants in Liverpool threatened legal action against the NEC on the grounds that it had, by acting as prosecutor, judge and jury, infringed 'natural justice'. The NEC responded by creating a body which was to be independent of the main executive and elected by the annual conference. Between 1986 and 1990, the NCC dealt with 251 disciplinary cases, 150 of which ended in expulsion; 112 of these related to Militant involvement. Other grounds for expulsion allegedly ranged from 'a sustained course of conduct prejudicial to the party' to 'insulting the party leader'. According to those who made these allegations, the NCC seldom conducted its inquiries in an even-handed manner and did much to undermine the morale of local party activity (Heffernan and Marqusee 1992).

It was astonishing, perhaps, that even in the year leading up to the 1992 election, when it might have been thought that party officials' attention would have been focused entirely on the wider political debate, the NEC and NCC carried out lengthy investigations into about a dozen of its own constituency parties; two of these actually led to the expulsion of MPs Dave Nellist (Coventry SE) and Terry Fields

(Liverpool Broadgreen). The justification for this was a belief that the party would benefit from being seen as tough with its extremists; this was plainly the view of Peter Kilfoyle, the Labour Party's chief organiser in the North-West, who was central to the attack on the hard left in Merseyside. On the other hand, the high profile of the purge may have worsened the situation by spotlighting the bitter divisions which happened to exist in a handful of CLPs. The assault upon Liverpool Walton, for example, provoked one ex-member to stand as the 'Real Labour' candidate in opposition to Kilfoyle's own official campaign in the 1991 by-election. Somewhat predictably, Labour's vote in the by-election fell by 11.4 per cent.

*'OMOV'* The second objective to receive much greater emphasis after 1987 was that of enhancing the influence of 'ordinary' (*qua* 'moderate') Labour supporters in the affairs of the CLPs. This was to be done, first, by converting more Labour voters into members, and second, in order to make the prospect of membership more alluring, by offering ordinary Labour members a more direct input in such matters as party elections. The idea behind this strategy was symbolised by the acronym OMOV (one member one vote).

Neither OMOV nor the recruitment drive (see below) were devoid of ulterior, political motives. OMOV was intended to herald a frontal attack on the union block votes which had long been recognised as an electoral handicap to the party. It could, in consequence, be depicted as a clear sign that Labour had moved away from its old 'workerist' base to a new political territory embracing all classes and sections of the community. But it was also hoped that a bigger membership, more closely reflecting Labour's voters, would offset any lingering Bennite influence among CLP officials and also in the trade unions, whose local affiliations were suspected of harbouring those no longer allowed to hold individual membership (a charge made in connection with the attempted deselection of Frank Field in Birkenhead). The end results, it was hoped, would ensure widespread party support for the social democratic policies insisted upon by the leadership. Once again, it must be emphasised that such a strategy was only viable because of the support given it by key union leaders, a new generation of which were prepared to accepted a curtailment of formal influence in order to boost the chances of a Labour government they so urgently wanted.

The OMOV campaign, supposedly concluded in 1993, had five tangible effects between 1987 and 1991. First, the 1987 conference voted for a change in the method of choosing parliamentary candidates, one that gave CLP members an enhanced role through the introduction of a new CLP electoral college in which union block votes would count for no more than 40 per cent (see Figure 2.2). Though not a precise

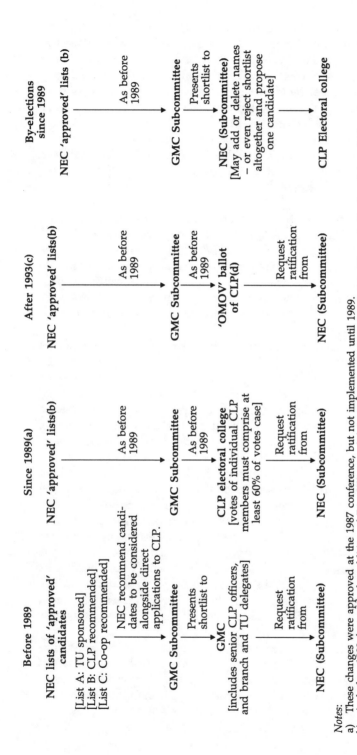

**Figure 2.2** The selection of Labour parliamentary candidates

*Source:* Garner and Kelly (1993: 162–7).

*Notes:*

a) These changes were approved at the 1987 conference, but not implemented until 1989.
b) As before 1989, but with the addition of 'List W' – candidates recommended by the Party's Women's Section, from which at least one candidate had to be drawn.
c) The decision to introduce OMOV was agreed at the 1990 and 1991 conferences, although the whole issue was reopened after the 1992 election.
d) The 1991 conference agreed that, before a selection contest, a ballot of CLP members be held on whether to allow affiliated trade unionists in the constituency to vote. If permitted, their votes would be one third the value of those cast by individual CLP members. At the 1993 conference, it was agreed to enfranchise only those affiliated TU members who 'top up' their political levy with a £3 payment to their CLP (levy plus'). Conference also resolved that Labour's regional organisers should ensure all-women shortlists in half of Labour's winnable seats.

realisation of the OMOV ideal, which had been rejected at the 1984 and 1987 conferences, it did represent a step in that direction (the 1990 conference confirmed that the OMOV principle should indeed be established by the end of the decade).

Secondly, the 1990 conference decided that the formal reselection of Labour MPs should only occur if a majority of the CLP members supported it in a ballot, a move which neatly combined the OMOV principle with the NEC's wish to avoid publicised disputes between MPs and activists. It also effectively killed off the mandatory principle for which Bennites fought so hard ten years earlier; it is in fact now harder for reselection to occur than in the 1970s, when a decision on whether to institute proceedings lay only with the CLP's General Management Committee.

Thirdly, it was decided in 1989 that, before casting their own block votes in Labour leadership contests, the CLPs should conduct ballots of individual members. The effects of this change were not of course visible until after the 1992 election, but the political reasoning behind the change seemed to be vindicated: the CLPs, which in the 1981 deputy leadership race gave all but 6 per cent of their votes to Benn, gave, in 1992, all but 0.7 per cent of their votes to John Smith (see Table 2.1).

Fourthly, the 1990 conference agreed to increase CLP voting strength at conference from about 10 per cent to 30 per cent, with a matching decrease in union representation from about 90 per cent to 70 per cent. Again, this was only a partial realisation of OMOV, but it was stressed that this was only an initial reform, with more ambitious changes envisaged later. In a bid to tie in this reform with the drive for more members, it was also agreed that CLP votes at conference would rise by 1 per cent for every increase of 30,000 in membership.[1]

Finally, the NEC ruled in 1991 that CLP votes for NEC elections also be preceded by OMOV ballots in each constituency. Once more, the political intention bore fruit: the CLP vote, traditionally a bastion of the Left, gave at the 1991 conference a place on the NEC to Gerald Kaufman, the first right-winger to be elected to the constituency section for sixteen years. Heffernan and Marqusee (1992), however, took a rather dim view of this reform, claiming that no more than 15 per cent of the membership bothered to cast a vote.

Lest it be assumed that the party's modernisers wished to sever the union link altogether, it is worth recalling that discussion did take place on how the OMOV scheme could be harnessed to an 'updated' relationship with the affiliated unions. For example, the 1988 conference resolved to recruit more affiliated union members by offering them a reduced subscription rate of £5 (see also note 'd', Figure 2.2). Heffernan and Marqusee are again scathing about this initiative, claiming that by 1991 fewer than 15,000 of the 4.5 million eligible took advantage of the offer.

*Positive discrimination* Here there has been some philosophical (though not political) inconsistency, with women being viewed much more favourably than Labour's ethnic minorities. It was hoped that the greater emphasis on sexual equality inside the party would offer further proof that Labour had moved towards a more cosmopolitan orientation, complementing Labour's stress upon such 'female-friendly' policies as a proposed Ministry for Women.

Organisational change between 1987 and 1992 took three specific forms. First in 1988, a stipulation that all CLPs must include one mandatory woman on their short-lists for PLP candidates – something which may help to account for the rise in the number of female Labour candidates from 93 in 1987 to 138 in 1992 (see Lovenduski and Norris below). Secondly, in 1989, that the PLP must vote for at least three women in its shadow cabinet elections. Thirdly, in 1990, that the NEC take steps to guarantee in the near future at least 40 per cent female representation.

The NEC responded with nothing like the same zeal to the demand, spearheaded by black MPs Bernie Grant and Diane Abbott, for separate black sections akin to women's sections. It seemed that the NEC feared that such a reform would evoke memories of Labour's 'loony left' during the early to mid-1980s, thought to have cost the party vast support in London, the one city not to swing Labour's way, in 1987.

*An imperious hierarchy* It may have appeared strange that a sub-section referring to the apotheosis of social democratic centralism should have gone on to allocate such a substantial section to a strategy (OMOV) ostensibly designed to elevate the rank-and-file. Yet the two are closely related. To begin with, the OMOV campaign, like positive discrimination for women, was wholly orchestrated by the parliamentary leadership in tandem with the NEC. As Hughes and Wintour (1990) affirm, all the changes discussed above were part of a top-down exercise, quite unlike the 'peasants' revolt' of the early 1980s. Furthermore, the new, and newly enfranchised, members Kinnock and the NEC wished to bring about were only expected to perform a basically negative role, *viz*, negating the influence of hard-left forces in the trade unions and among CLP officials. As Seyd and Whiteley (1992) point out, there was never any recognition by the NEC that ordinary CLP members could play a vital part in winning the party votes in their locality – apart, that is, from silencing the extremist voices which might otherwise damage the party's image.

When assessing how much positive faith was placed in the membership by the NEC, it is instructive that even the membership drive after 1989 took the form of a national campaign coordinated by the NEC's own John Evans. Under this scheme, interested individuals could apply for membership direct to Walworth Road and, if no objections were received from the applicant's CLP within eight weeks, a membership card would be issued by party headquarters. In a sense, the scheme was a mild success; Labour's official membership by 1991 was 311,152 as opposed to 265,927 in 1988. However, given that the aim was to double membership within four years, the scheme was plainly off target (membership has since fallen to pre-1988 levels). There have also been reports that the scheme was carried out in a grossly inefficient way, as already overburdened staff at Walworth Road struggled with a mounting backlog of applications; by 1991 they were supposedly taking over nine months to process the paperwork (Heffernan and Marqusee, 1992). Despite these difficulties, no effort was made to give the CLPs a more proactive role in recruiting members, the assumption being that a national approach must always be more effective than a local one.

The National Membership Scheme was a prime symptom of how, after 1987, Kinnock (through the NEC) resolved to expand his (and its) power. Moreover, one of the great ironies of Kinnock's domineering leadership was that it was facilitated largely by one of the reforms of the early 1980s designed to reduce the leader's autonomy.

This first became clear in early 1988, when a sizeable section of the PLP was rumoured to be unhappy with Kinnock's leadership, blaming him in no small way for Labour's failure to undermine Tory support (then higher than it had been at the 1987 election). It was suggested that, had the old system of leader selection survived, he could well have been the victim of a swift *coup*, similar to that which ousted Heath after 1974 (Kellner, 1988). Yet the cumbersome mechanics of the electoral college served to deter 'respectable' would-be challengers in the shadow cabinet, who were alarmed by the political damage likely to accrue from a drawn-out contest (Punnett, 1992). It was noted that whereas the PLP's election of Michael Foot in 1980 took just three weeks, the election of Kinnock in 1983 took over three months. In the event, a challenge did come (to both leader and deputy) from Benn, Eric Heffer and John Prescott. This somewhat maverick group of challengers simply allowed Kinnock to rally support from across the party, gain a crushing victory and claim a renewed mandate for his crusading style of leadership. Here again, the 1981 reform exemplified the law of unintended effects: it was now possible for an 'autocratic' leader to invoke a 'licence' from the whole party, a facility not available to any of Kinnock's predecessors. Benn's futile challenge also enabled the leadership to tighten the preconditions of any future leadership challenge, preconditions which remain much stricter than those obtaining in the Tory Party (see Figures 2.1 and 2.3).

Their confidence and authority strengthened by Benn's defeat, Kinnock and the NEC advanced their centralisation strategy in early 1989, not only through the National Membership Scheme, but in respect

37

of its by-election policy. Following the loss of a 19,509 majority at the Glasgow Govan by-election in late 1988, the NEC arrogated ultimate responsibility for the selection of by-election candidates (see Figure 2.2). In June 1989, it duly overruled the Vauxhall CLP's choice of a radical black feminist and ordained the candidature of the 'soft-left' Kate Hoey. The impeccably moderate candidate for Mid-Staffs nine months later was also a product of the NEC's self-styled 'school of excellence'. That both candidates proved extraordinarily successful was naturally used to exonerate the NEC's imperious approach.

Centralisation was also a feature of policy making *per se* during this period. The Policy Review, undertaken between 1987 and 1989, was not conspicuous for its grass-roots involvement (Garner, 1990). It revolved around seven policy groups overseen by conveners from the NEC and shadow cabinet. Mindful of the expeditious way in which the Review had ditched the policies disliked by the leadership, the NEC unveiled in 1990 plans for a new Policy Forum which would downgrade the policy-making role of the annual conference and echo the *modus operandi* of the Review.

The proposal was that the Forum would split up into small policy commissions, working on a two-year cycle and producing reports for the NEC's inspection and, ultimately, conference's approval. It looks as if this system will enhance the leader's control over detailed policy making: all the commissions will be coordinated by the appropriate shadow cabinet member, affiliated bodies will not be able to submit policy resolutions whilst the commissions are deliberating, while the conference will only be able to vote on the commission's reports *en bloc*, rather than specific items. The proposal is strikingly similar, in fact, to the system of policy making used by the 'Council' of the defunct SDP, a party which consistently emphasised the supremacy of its Parliamentary wing (Garner and Kelly, 1993).

Evidence of increased centralisation was most obvious, however, in the field of campaigning. The Shadow Communications Agency (SCA) continued to work closely with the leader's office, its ethos being that there should be a shift 'from grass-roots opinion forming to influencing electoral opinion through the mass media' (Hughes and Wintour, 1990: 52). Even before the 1992 election, there were widespread complaints that the SCA and leader's office worked in a clandestine, inaccessible fashion, with excessive power invested in unelected officials like Patricia Hewitt (Kinnock's political aide) and Charles Clarke (Kinnock's chief-of-staff). In the run-up to the 1992 election, the SCA spawned another rather arcane committee, the Campaign Management Team (CMT), of whose sixteen members only two were elected politicians. As Heffernan and Marqusee (1992) observed, never had the CLPs felt so divorced from a campaign to which they were prepared to devote so much effort.

*Phase 4: 1992 and after*

Labour's fourth consecutive defeat in 1992 has raised searching questions about the organisational principles underpinning Kinnock's leadership, also prompting bitter criticism from those who, like Prescott, always harboured doubts about its utility. In both 1987 and 1992, Labour fought polished, American-style campaigns meticulously planned by officials from Walworth Road. The fact that Labour was still unable to win much more than a third of the popular vote obviously casts doubt upon this approach. It has since been argued by renegades like Prescott that there was nothing inevitable about Labour's 1992 defeat, citing campaign errors by apparatchiks like Hewitt, poor coordination within the national campaign's bureaucracy (nobody on the CMT, for example, knew much about Hewitt's 'Last Week Unit'); and the marginalisation of constituency activists; a body called 'Network', set up to transmit voters' opinions (as gleaned by the CLPs) to the national campaign managers, later complained that its soundings were persistently ignored. For Prescott, this was a classic illustration of everything that had been wrong with Labour's organisation since 1987, *viz*, that it was top-heavy and unresponsive to the party's volunteers at local level. This view has since been endorsed in the studies of both Seyd and Whiteley (1992) and Heffernan and Marqusee (1992).

Does this mean, therefore, that Labour should increase the profile of its members? If it is sincere in its wish to boost membership figures, it may have no option: research indicates that those with centre-left opinions are not inclined to join a political party unless there is clear evidence that they may participate effectively (Shaw, 1988). This in itself is a problem, as on certain key issues Labour's current membership seems out of line with the leadership and average Labour voters (Seyd and Whiteley, 1992). Any further curbs on the union block vote also threaten to remove from the leadership its traditional weapon in crushing leftist dissent at CLP level, especially during periods of government (Minkin, 1978). Also, the fact that Labour members are now predominantly white-collar, with over a quarter holding university degrees, does not suggest a placid rank-and-file devoid of any independent ideas (Seyd and Whiteley). Yet it should be stressed that, on most policy matters, differences between members and leaders and members and voters are only marginal, with most members recognising the centrality of electoral success and the need to tailor policies accordingly (Seyd and Whiteley).

At the start of 1993, it appeared that Labour's conference later that year would back an emphatic shift towards OMOV, won narrowly in the event, in its debates on internal reform. An NEC report in the February lent support to a drastic reduction of union influence in respect of conference representation, candidate selection and leadership election, the latter made particularly urgent by the tortuous, yet tediously predictable, contest of 1992 (Jones, 1993). It remains to be seen whether such changes will represent a cosmetic exercise designed merely to impress voters, or a new and genuine desire on the part of the leadership to at last trust its constituency members.

## The Conservatives

The 1992 general election served to confirm that the Conservatives are indisputably Britain's most effective political party, having been in office for almost three-quarters of this century. It might have been assumed, therefore, that the distribution of power inside the Conservative Party would be of paramount concern to scholars of British politics and the object of intense academic debate. Instead, there has been no detailed, comprehensive study since that of McKenzie nearly forty years ago, with the party's internal workings remaining, even to insiders, 'governed by secrecy' (*Charter News*, 1986).

The arcane nature of Tory organisation owes much to the lack of any grand constitution outlining the powers and functions of its various organs. Indeed, a legal inquiry of 1982, involving Conservative Central Office and the Inland Revenue, found that 'the Conservative Party' did not even exist as 'a compact, legally recognized organization', consisting instead of 'three separate components' operating mainly on the basis of convention (*Charter News*, 1991). The purpose of this section is to examine developments in each of these three 'components', highlighting *inter alia* that the party is much less autocratic than many textbooks seem to allow.

### A top-down party?

Most accounts of the Tory structure begin with the party at Westminster, simply because it is normally considered pre-eminent (see Norton below). This pre-eminence is rooted in party history, with the organisation beyond Westminster instigated only by its parliamentary leaders in response to the extension of the franchise in 1867. Its role from the outset was to be that of an 'electoral handmaid', serving the interests of Tory MPs but never seeking to direct them (McKenzie, 1963: 146).

It is normally assumed that the power and autonomy enjoyed within the party by Tory MPs is duly invested in their leaders, thus giving rise to the party's 'oligarchic' reputation: he (or she) is acknowledged to have the last word on policy and to be free of any formal constraints from other party bodies; he is under no official constraints when choosing front-bench colleagues; he shapes the party bureaucracy through his appointment of the Party Chairman; he is elected by and accountable to only a tiny fraction of the party (its MPs) and is unencumbered by any elected deputy leader; finally, his supremacy is thought to be underpinned by what Gamble (1979: 40) termed a 'sleeping membership' indifferent to the fine print of party policy.

The period after 1979 offered considerable support for this traditional thesis. Mrs Thatcher 'exploited the leader's residual powers' for the sake of her eponymous 'revolution', and one of the most remarkable aspects of her premiership was the way in which the most significant Cabinet resignations were somehow linked to her 'hegemonic' style (Critchley, 1985). Gilmour (1992) has argued that Thatcherism itself was imposed upon the government by a cabal of ideologues, contemptuous of collective decision-making and acting largely from non-party think-tanks (such as the Centre for Policy Studies and Adam Smith Institute).

Although John Major was thought to signify a more consensual style of leadership, the manner in which the 1992 election manifesto was forged differed little from that of 1987 (Butler and Kavanagh, 1992). Major and his Downing Street Policy Unit were determined to make their own mark on the drafting process, with the only input from Central Office coming through a special liaison committee overseen by the leader's personal appointee, John Wakeham. In the first week of the campaign, Major seemed to make a special point of stressing his own personal imprint upon the manifesto: 'It's me, it's all me', a remark neatly complementing the orthodox view of power in the party.

Yet it remains the case that it was a Tory prime minister, and one of the most domineering this century, who was the first to be challenged (in 1989) and then ousted (in 1990) through a formal party ballot. In fact, it had long been true that the mechanisms for deposing a Tory leader were much more accessible than those used in the Labour Party (see Figures 2.1 and 2.3). Furthermore, the 1990 *coup* was only the latest example of how the Tories have shown little mercy to those leaders who appear as electoral liabilities (Shepherd, 1991). As McKenzie stated (1963: 145): 'The leader leads and the party follows, except when the party decides not to follow; then the leader ceases to be leader.' In the case of Thatcher, however, this oft-quoted explanation may not be wholly sufficient, as on numerous occasions during the 1980s a sizeable group of Tory MPs refused to 'follow' a particular policy but without indicating a wish to change the leader (see Norton below). Mrs Thatcher's fall may thus have been only the most explosive illustration of a much more far-reaching trend within the party at Westminster.

Any idea that this growth of dissent was a by-product of Mrs Thatcher's huge majorities was quickly scotched following Major's election victory. Within six weeks, twenty-one Tory MPs had voted against the first reading of the Maastricht Treaty, with over sixty later signing an early day motion asking for a 'fresh start' in the

Challenge to be announced within 14
days of a new Commons session or three
months of a new Parliament. Challenger
requires backing from (unnamed) 10% of
Tory MPs[a]

↓

MPs consult constituency associations

↓

1st BALLOT OF TORY MPs
Victory involves one candidate
achieving overall majority plus 15%
lead over nearest rival.[b] Otherwise . . .

↓

2nd BALLOT OF TORY MPs
Those not initially candidates may now
enter contest. Victory involves one
candidate achieving overall majority of
votes cast. Otherwise . . .

↓

3rd BALLOT OF TORY MPs
Involves the two leading candidates
from 2nd ballot[c]

↓

Winner (after whichever ballot)[d] confirmed
at party meeting comprising MPs, peers,
MEPs, parliamentary candidates and
members of National Union Executive

*Notes:*
a) The names of backers only had to be given prior to the contest of 1990, having
   been introduced after Meyer's 'frivolous' challenge in 1989. This provision was
   withdrawn in 1991 and the *status quo ante* resumed.
b) Since 1974, this has been based upon those entitled to vote.
c) Until 1991, there was no formal provision for the contest to end as a result of the
   leading candidate's rivals withdrawing after he had achieved only a plurality of
   support in the second ballot. Neither did the rules envisage a third ballot
   involving fewer than three candidates.
d) Since 1991, the rules allow for a fourth ballot should the third end in a dead heat.
*NB:* Although provision for Tory leadership contests had existed since 1965, it was
   not until the rules change of 1974 that a leader could be challenged in an annual
   ballot. Neither, until 1974, were MPs obliged to consult their associations before
   voting.

**Figure 2.3** Procedures for electing Tory leaders (Revised rules, 1991)

*Source:* Punnett (1992: 53–9).

government's dealings with the EC (see Jones below). In October 1992, the government's paving bill for the Treaty's final reading passed with the barest of majorities, while its proposal to close thirty-one coal mines was remoulded largely on account of the hostility it provoked on the Tory back-benches. The behaviour of newly elected MPs, normally thought the most reliable of government supporters, must also have given concern to the leadership. Over a third of the new intake of MPs were among those signing the aforementioned early day motion, prompting speculation that the new generation of Tory MPs represented 'Thatcher's children' rather than loyal backers of those who succeeded her.

There must be some doubt about Major's capacity to handle such tensions. His stumbling response to the divisions over Maastricht, coal and the ERM crises has indicated to some an unease with internal dissent. A number of Tories have already drawn gloomy comparisons with Balfour and Heath; two 'grey' men whose consensual rhetoric masked an inability to compromise and whose clumsiness eventually led the party to electoral disaster. At the beginning of 1993, another token leadership contest (similar to that of 1989) was not being ruled out inside the party.

### The National Union

The extra-parliamentary party's voluntary wing is enfolded by the National Union of Conservative Associations (NU). It was set up in 1867 by those who insisted that its deliberations be purely advisory and in no way a challenge to the judgement of its parliamentary representatives.

The NU's subservient position is widely thought to have survived, finding expression in the make-up of its key body, the NU General Purposes Committee, of whose sixty-five members only a fifth are elected by party members (the rest owing their *ex officio* positions to appointments made by either the leader or the Party Chairman). Unsurprisingly, it has been argued that this makes it difficult for ordinary grass-roots members to have much influence over party activity even outside Parliament, let alone in government. The NU's limitations were said to be further exposed by the conduct of its yearly autumn conference; the fact that it lacked any formal policy-making role was thought to be compounded by the obsequious atmosphere in which many of its debates were held – the post-Falklands conference of 1982 was declared by one journalist to be 'nothing more than a festival of worship for the leader' (*The Economist*, 15.10.88).

*Party Democracy: Tory-style* In recent years, however, Tory activists have also been prepared to use their conferences to transmit strongly felt

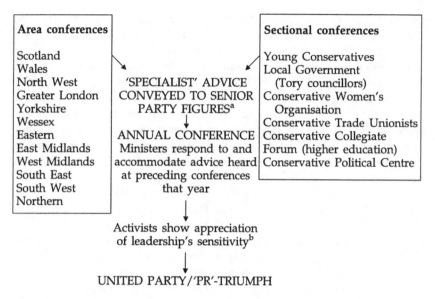

| Area conferences | | Sectional conferences |
|---|---|---|
| Scotland<br>Wales<br>North West<br>Greater London<br>Yorkshire<br>Wessex<br>Eastern<br>East Midlands<br>West Midlands<br>South East<br>South West<br>Northern | 'SPECIALIST' ADVICE<br>CONVEYED TO SENIOR<br>PARTY FIGURES[a]<br>↓<br>ANNUAL CONFERENCE<br>Ministers respond to and<br>accommodate advice heard<br>at preceding conferences<br>that year | Young Conservatives<br>Local Government<br>(Tory councillors)<br>Conservative Women's<br>Organisation<br>Conservative Trade Unionists<br>Conservative Collegiate<br>Forum (higher education)<br>Conservative Political Centre |

Activists show appreciation
of leadership's sensitivity[b]

↓

UNITED PARTY/'PR'-TRIUMPH

*Notes*:
All conferences supervised and organised by various officers of the National Union
Executive Committee
(a) This advice tends to be communicated through 'mood' rather than formal
balloted resolutions.
(b) Dissent at the Annual Conference is rare and often caused by ministers having
failed to absorb and react to grass-roots criticism at previous conferences, e.g.
Ridley 1987 concerning his plan to 'phase in' the Poll Tax (revoked after
persistent complaints from the floor).

**Figure 2.4** The Conservative conference system

*Source*: Kelly (1989).

opinions to the leadership (Kelly, 1989). As society becomes more
propertied, suburban and white-collar, there has been a parallel
tendency for conference-goers to see their vested interests and 'gut'
instincts as synonymous with those of the new typical voter.

This was underwritten after 1983 by an apparent connection between
the advice these conferences offered and the evolution of several
government policies; trade union reform, married women's taxation and
disability pensions being just three examples. Yet the conferences
concerned were not those which receive massive media coverage each
autumn, but the less publicised conferences held by the NU's various
areas and sections (see Figure 2.4). In this context, the autumn
conference becomes only the climax of an oblique 'conference system',
where ministers earn ovations only by showing sensitivity to advice
offered from the floor at earlier conferences held that year. The party's

desire for 'good PR' at the autumn conference was beyond dispute; what the 1980s brought into question was the way by which it was normally secured.

While in office, Mrs Thatcher was usually ready to acknowledge Tory conferences as reliable guides to common opinion and is said to have invoked their beliefs in her battles with more cautious cabinet members (Kelly, 1988). After 1990, there were also signs that, along with such allies as Lord Tebbit, she still valued conference's role – but this time as a means of deflecting the government from its original course by mobilising discontent at rank-and-file level. The 1992 conference proved one of the stormiest of any party this century, with the platform visibly chastened by Tebbit's fervently received diatribe against European integration. It seemed rather ironic that, after a period in which Labour's 'spin doctors' sought to emulate the supposedly stage-managed tone of Conservative conferences, Tory conferences themselves seemed now to be acting in a manner historically associated with the conferences of the Labour Party.

In spite of these developments, the influence of the membership still tended to be exercised, even at conference, in an informal or coded manner. Ballots, formalised resolutions and Labour-style number-crunching were still deemed vulgar and impolitic – assuming the leadership was receptive to advice. As a former NU Secretary explained: 'The trouble with voting is that it highlights the size of minorities and implies a lack of trust in our leaders . . . far better to pass on our views in a polite and informal way and trust our leaders to sense the prevailing mood.'[2]

*Sub-national organisation*  The NU is subdivided into provincial areas, including Scotland which has its own Central Office. The number was increased from twelve to thirteen after the 1989 conference resolved, against the leadership's wishes, to affiliate Tory activists in Northern Ireland (although none of the eleven candidates there in 1992 received much help or encouragement from the mainland party machine). Each area is governed by an area council, whose duties include coordinating the work of its individual constituency parties – the associations.

A number of studies have already contested that Tory associations have more autonomy than constituency Labour parties, one obvious reason being that they are much more financially independent (Pinto-Duschinsky, 1990). This has given them the self-confidence to resist the sort of centralisation that until recently proved unstoppable in the Labour Party. It was telling that Sir Basil Feldman's internal inquiry into the NU (1992–93) rejected any erosion of the associations' right to choose parliamentary candidates, particularly for by-elections, even though the Party Chairman (Sir Norman Fowler) had earlier indicated that this could be desirable. Even more telling was that Feldman's actual

**National level**

NATIONAL UNION STANDING
ADVISORY COMMITTEE

↓ Recommends most
applicants to

NATIONAL UNION PARLIAMENTARY
SELECTION BOARD

↓ Recommends c. 60%
of applicants to

NATIONAL UNION APPROVED LIST
(c. 800 candidates)

- - - - - - - - - - - - - - - - - - - - - - - -

**Association
(constituency)
level**

Interested
candidates
apply to

'Unapproved'
candidates[a]

EXECUTIVE SUB-COMMITTEE (c. 20)
Interviews c. 20 and reduces shortlist to
between 3 and 6

↓

EXECUTIVE COUNCIL (c. 60)
Interviews remaining candidates and
recommends one or more to whole association[b]

↓

GENERAL MEETING
*Either* makes final selection (if more than
one remaining candidate) *or* formally adopts
candidate recommended by Executive[c]

*Notes*:
a)  Dudley Fishburn, successful candidate at the Kensington by-election of 1988, is a
    rare example of a would-be MP sidestepping the Approved List. Such applicants
    must be endorsed by the Standing Advisory Committee, whose endorsement
    relates only to the association concerned.
b)  If only one candidate is recommended to the whole association, he or she must
    have gained an overall majority of votes cast at Executive Council. It is
    recommended, however, that three candidates should normally be submitted to
    the General Meeting. Much of the bitterness created in Cheltenham, following the
    adoption of John Taylor, sprang from his opponents' belief that these criteria had
    not been respected.
c)  The Standing Advisory Committee has the capacity to veto adopted candidates
    by refusing them official Party backing (even though the constitutional case for
    this being 'official' seems doubtful). In 1992, the candidate initially chosen for
    Western Isles was thus replaced, the *casus belli* being his assertion that 'Catholics
    cannot be considered Christian'. The exercise of the veto therefore occurs only in
    highly unusual circumstances.

**Figure 2.5**  The selection of Conservative parliamentary candidates

*Source*: Rules and Standing Orders of the National Union (1990).

proposals, which involved enhancing the NU Executive and General Purposes Committee at the expense of local autonomy, were emphatically rejected at the 1993 Central Council (the annual assembly of senior activists and the NU's 'sovereign' body).

The association's governing body is the executive council, whose principal duties naturally include overseeing the choice of parliamentary candidates (Figure 2.5). Apart from the creation of the NU's Parliamentary Selection Board in 1979, designed to assess a candidate's 'intellectual ability, practical skills and personal character', there have been few procedural changes in this sphere (Lovenduski *et al.*, 1991). There have, however, been subtle changes in the attitude of selectors themselves; emboldened by social change and electoral success, they have tended towards selecting candidates to whom they can 'relate' rather than those displaying the *gravitas* traditionally expected of Tory MPs (Heffer, 1991). Further evidence of this change came through in 1992. Among newly elected Tory MPs and unsuccessful candidates, only a minority were public school educated, with a clear shift in occupational background from 'professional' to 'commercial' (Butler and Kavanagh, 1992: 223–6).

The change in selectors' attitudes is also echoed in the associations' changing view of readoption. No longer, after 1987, did activists seem quite so prepared to tolerate whatever interpretation of Conservatism their MPs chose to project in Parliament. The most conspicuous example of this came in Clwyd NW, where Sir Anthony Meyer was deselected shortly after his leadership challenge in 1989. Similarly, nine of the MPs who publicly supported Heseltine's bid in 1990 were forced to repel votes of no confidence held in their associations – Sir Peter Emery (Honiton) and Cyril Townsend (Bexleyheath) coming closest to defeat. Indeed, the fact that Tory MPs ousted Mrs Thatcher in clear defiance of opinion at association level might only undermine further the goodwill and respect formerly accorded them by local activists. In an open letter to the *Daily Telegraph* (26.11.90), the Vice-Chairman of the NU actually warned Tory MPs that 'there can no longer be any whining about loyalty and solidarity if constituency parties take steps to deselect them'. Although such a possibility at first alarmed senior party figures, including the Vice-Chairman of the NU, by 1992 there were signs that they were being harnessed. During the Maastricht debates, a number of rebel MPs (such as Nicholas Winterton) alleged that Central Office had put pressure upon their constituency chairmen in the hope that they, in turn, would issue dark warnings to their maverick back-benchers. At least one such chairman, Walter Sweeney in the Vale of Glamorgan, both confirmed and endorsed this manoeuvre. As indicated below, however, such rapport between Central Office and local parties is not *de rigueur*.

*Central Office*

Conservative Central Office (CCO) was created in 1870 and is the professional or bureaucratic wing of the extra-parliamentary party. Although theoretically separate from the party's two other components, many CCO officials are *ex officio* members of the NU's key committees, while CCO's own command structure shows a clear link with the parliamentary leadership (see Figure 2.6).

The basic function of the CCO is said to be that of serving the associations by meeting their demands for literature, political ammunition and organisational advice. Few activists believe it performs this function well, arguing that it behaves 'as if it were master rather than servant' (*Charter News*, 1988). These complaints usually point to the fact that responsibility for CCO rests not with someone elected by activists themselves, but with the Party Chairman appointed by the leader. Since 1979, certainly, the occupant of the post has been a close ally of the leader when appointed (Thorneycroft 1975; Parkinson 1981; Gummer 1983; Tebbit 1985; Brooke 1987; Baker 1989; Patten 1990; Fowler 1992) and, in Thorneycroft's case, replaced if there were serious differences over CCO's management. Pinto-Duschinsky has argued (1972) that the Chairman's task is to make CCO not the tool of the membership, but the leader's 'personal machine'. Recent changes seemed to corroborate this view. The streamlining of CCO into directorates by Brooke in 1988 was a response to Thatcher's disgust at its performance during the 1987 election, reflecting her wish for a more manageable headquarters (Tyler, 1987).

CCO's most persistent critics are still to be found in the Charter Movement, set up by activists in Kent in 1981 to campaign for greater grass-roots control over the party's bureaucracy; Charter claims that its principal demand – the election of the Party Chairman by NU members – is irrefutable given the government's policy since 1979 of making trade union officials electable and accountable to ordinary trade unionists (*Charter News*, 1988). Yet it is also claimed that it would eliminate CCO's 'gross inefficiency', evidence for which is the colossal debt it has accumulated since 1982 – £19 million in March 1993 (Fowler, 1993: 21). The rumour that much of this debt stems from an expensive refurbishment of CCO in 1991 adds weight to Charter's claim that, in politics, efficiency and democracy go together.

*Fowler's reorganisation* The 1992 election did little to rescue CCO's reputation inside the party, with most activists claiming they won despite, rather than because of, its national campaign. Particular criticism was reserved for CCO's 'brat pack', a group of inexperienced, young apparatchiks guided by CCO's Director of Communications, Shaun Woodward (himself under 40). As after 1987, it was said that

*Central Office:*

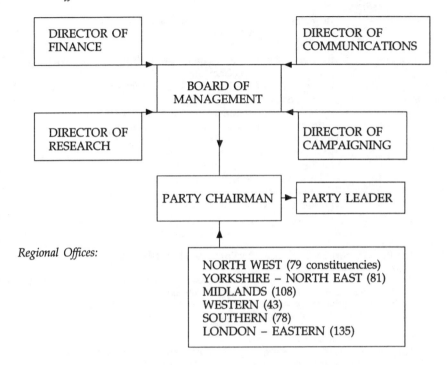

*Regional Offices:*

Notes:
i) The six Regional offices in England and Wales replace the eleven Area offices created in 1930. Scotland retains its separate Central Office.
ii) The structure within each Regional office will broadly replicate that of Central Office, headed by a new Regional Director.
iii) Given the composition of the Board of Management (Figure 2.6), it is clear that the influence of the National Union (*ergo* Tory activists) upon the Party's bureaucracy remains slight.
——▶ Denotes direction of responsibility.

**Figure 2.6** The professional extra-parliamentary Conservative Party (since 1993)

*Source*: Fowler (1993: 19–25).

CCO exuded 'uncertainty, confusion, slowness and conceit' (*Charter News*, 1992).

In response to this grievance, Sir Norman Fowler headed a working party to overhaul the professional extra-parliamentary wing, stating its aim to be an increase in managerial efficiency and the reduction of CCO's huge debt. His report, published in February 1993, announced a 'rationalisation' of both CCO and its provincial satellites, with the old area offices being replaced by a smaller number of regional headquarters (Figure 2.6); that the professional extra-parliamentary wing is now

*Composition:*

> The Party Chairman (Chairman of the Board)
> A Deputy Party Chairman
> The Director-General
> The Chairman of the National Union (formerly known as NU Executive Chairman)
> The President of the National Union (formerly known as NU Chairman)
> The Senior Vice-President of the National Union (formerly known as NU Vice-Chairman)
> The Chairman of the 1922 Committee
> The Leader of Conservative MEPs
> The Senior Party Treasurer
> A senior figure from local government
> Two non-executives
> The Secretary of the Board

*Notes*:
i) The Board's purpose is to 'bring together the elected, voluntary and professional parts of the Party'.
ii) Its six broad aims are to: review and approve plans for the extra-parliamentary wings of the party; to review and approve annual budgets; to coordinate fund raising strategies; advise on efforts to increase party membership; to approve plans for all major party events and activities; to undertake or commission special studies on key issues.
iii) It will meet up to six times a year.
iv) The Director-General is responsible for implementing the strategies and actions agreed by the Board, and is appointed by (and accountable to) the Party Chairman. Paul Judge, 'who has a strong business and management background', was appointed in early 1993.
v) Although the Board will establish its strategic aims, the day-to-day running of the professional extra-parliamentary party will remain with the 'directorates' set up by the Brooke Report of 1988. There will, however, be a restructuring of Central Office's 'satellite' headquarters (see Figure 2.6).

**Figure 2.7**  Conservative Board of Management

*Source*: Fowler (1993: 19–20).

divided into 'regions', while the voluntary extra-parliamentary wing is still divided into 'areas', does not immediately seem as 'rational' as Fowler's report would have its readers believe.

Fowler's main aim, however, was to enhance the decision-making structures of CCO while giving the impression that it was becoming more closely integrated with the National Union and, therefore, the membership. The outcome was a new Board of Party Management, ultimately responsible for the conduct of the party outside Parliament (Figure 2.7). It is, in May 1993, rather early to judge the efficiency of this new body. What is clear, however, is that the idea of greater rank-and-file input into CCO is seriously at odds with the structure of the Board.

Its 'Director General' is not to be elected by party members, but appointed by the Party Chairman, who himself remains the appointee of the leader. Of the Board's thirteen members, moreover, only three have some elective connection with the constituency membership.

### An impending storm?

The Conservative Party has customarily been seen as one dominated by its leader and upheld by a membership wedded to the *führerprinzip*. This chapter would suggest that such a view has been weakened since 1979 as vital changes in politics and society found echoes among both back-benchers and constituency activists – none of whom seemed so ready to offer unqualified support to a leader so long as he (or she) was successful. As one constituency chairman warned in 1989, the government's stress upon individualism and self-reliance would only encourage activists to assert their own ideas in party debates and challenge those of senior but distant party figures.

> We have been told, rightly, that the man in Whitehall no longer knows best. Why, then, should we still assume that the man in Central Office or Downing Street knows best when it comes to the ordering of our Party's affairs? (*Charter News*, 1989)

When examining the distribution of power inside the party, such attitudinal changes far outweigh in importance any structural reforms, which have in any case been scarce this century, let alone since 1979. Nevertheless, Fowler's 1993 report, by signally ignoring such shifts in attitude, perpetuates a profoundly undemocratic party structure, apparently in conflict with a new, questioning generation of Tory activists, fortified in their self-belief by the party's electoral triumphs. This may be a recipe for grave internal conflict in the years ahead.

## Conclusion: McKenzie refuted

In the absence of any similarly exhaustive survey, Robert McKenzie's *British Political Parties* of 1955 remains a key reference for students of party organisation. Yet its central point, that the two major parties are essentially oligarchic with constituency activists having only a peripheral influence, merits fresh and critical assessment following developments since 1979.

For the Conservatives, there were signs in the 1980s that the party valued increasingly the support and goodwill of its rank-and-file, and that this could no longer be guaranteed at either its national conferences or more locally-based meetings. That this trend became especially marked after 1983 itself undermines one of McKenzie's side-arguments, namely that a party leadership's dominance would intensify in the wake of electoral success; the Tories' landslide victories in 1983 and 1987 only served to ignite greater degrees of dissent among constituency members, their political self-confidence firmed up by the party's electoral pre-eminence. Alternatively, the position of Labour leader Neil Kinnock – which, according to McKenzie's criteria, should have been crippled by the party's heavy defeat in 1987 – was seemingly enhanced as a result, Kinnock using electoral rejection as the excuse for bracing internal reforms which, on the whole, boosted his own authority. For those students reared on the McKenzie thesis, the 1980s clearly left behind a series of perplexing questions.

Nevertheless, prior to 1992 the case of the Labour Party still offered some corroboration of McKenzie's argument. His belief that the suppression of grass-roots policy preferences was vital to a party's electoral well-being seemed to be confirmed, first, by Labour's disastrous performance in 1983 (when grass-roots preferences largely prevailed) and secondly, in the years that followed, by Labour's recovery as a 'respectable' and 'electable' force (when the leader reimposed his dominance amid alleged violations of 'party democracy'). Yet McKenzie's link between electoral success and top-down organisation looked to have been dealt a mortal blow by Labour's defeat in 1992. One of the most centralised campaigns in Labour's history yielded only a slender increase in its share of the votes, still leaving it much further behind the Tories than at any time between 1945 and 1979 – although on account of its impressive performance in some marginal seats, this is easily obscured by the party's bigger increase in parliamentary representation (Denver, 1992).

That Labour did well, often exceptionally well, in some marginals but not in others provides both a reason for the party's overall failure in 1992 and a bridge between the two areas of political science with which McKenzie was associated: the first, of course, being the locus of power inside the parties, the second being his approach to psephology which, in turn, gave rise to his deployment of the 'swingometer' on BBC TV's pioneering election programmes (and for which, beyond academe, he earned almost cult status). The rationale of the swingometer was that, in the 1950s and 1960s, there seemed to be a uniform pattern of voting behaviour throughout the country (in 1951, for example, not one Labour candidate was able to resist the 1.1 per cent swing to the Tories) which McKenzie also used to bolster his theory of party organisation. Sensing that mass, nationwide media did much to explain the uniformity of swing, McKenzie argued that the role of constituency party workers and the local campaign had been further marginalised: elections were now determined by the national party leaders, fighting national campaigns through the national media (the electronic variety being particularly decisive).

By the 1970s, however, regional variations in voting behaviour had become much more apparent and, by the end of the 1980s, a formidable body of literature had been assembled arguing that elections were decided more and more by regional circumstances (Johnston, 1988). In a sense, this was only to be expected in an economy whose features came to vary so much from area to area during the period after 1979. Yet a number of studies had also suggested that regional variations in voting behaviour might also be affected by variations in the strengths of the local party machines (Miller, 1977). This notion was to receive some support in 1992 when there were remarkable variations of swing not just between, but within, particular regions: in Bolton West there was a swing of 3.2 per cent to Labour, but a swing of only 0.7 per cent in Bolton North East; in Mid-Worcestershire there was a Con–Lab swing of 5 per cent, yet in Worcestershire South a swing of 1 per cent from the Liberal Democrats (formerly Alliance) to the Conservatives.

The oddity here is that such psephological trends do not seem to have been fully accounted for by those reorganising the Labour Party after 1983. Labour became increasingly centralised at a time when the factors affecting voting behaviour seemed increasingly decentralised. Labour's strong emphasis upon the efficacy of its national head-quarters, national advisers and of course national leaders thus appears anachronistic, based upon electoral assumptions that had been tenuous for some time. As noted earlier, between 1983 and 1992 the role of the CLPs was not accredited much more importance by the leadership than twenty years earlier, apart that is from the role 'ordinary' members would play in counteracting the 'negative' images of the trade unions and hard Left.

Seyd and Whiteley's research (1992: 188–89), however, shows that such an approach was profoundly mistaken. In 1987, for example, Labour did particularly badly in constituencies where there was a 'relatively inactive' CLP; in 68 per cent of these, Labour polled less than 20 per cent, well below the national average. On the other hand, Labour fared much better in those constituencies where the CLP was 'very active'; in 59 per cent of these Labour polled over 40 per cent, well above the national average. From this, it was later calculated that if, in 1992, Labour's membership had been 25 per cent greater in the twelve top marginals, Labour would have deprived the Tories of their overall majority.[3] For Seyd and Whiteley (1992: 199), the moral of their study was plain: 'an active party membership is absolutely vital to the electoral performance of the Labour Party . . . since it is clear that local campaigning plays a big part in influencing election outcomes'.

It may be contested that this has always been acknowledged by Tory activists, who claim that their much larger membership (about a million more than Labour's in 1987) is a much neglected factor when explaining their party's electoral success this century; as a former Secretary of the National Union explained, 'Many of our members are not young and many are in a sense apolitical . . . but they can be relied upon to turn out and perform mundane tasks at each election time'.[4] These 'mundane tasks' should not be undervalued if, as seems likely, they help the local party communicate its message to most local electors; in the light of present swing variations, they could make the difference between victory and defeat.

If there is a psephological incentive for local parties to be less reliant upon their national party machines, the practicalities of doing so are also becoming less onerous. The 1980s witnessed a revolution in information technology, which could help local parties to reassert their independence *vis-à-vis* their London-based bureaucracies. As Heffernan and Marqusee (1992: 317) noted of the CLPs, 'Desktop publishing technology had made the production of high quality leaflets possible for local activists, who felt they could dream up more resonant and relevant campaign copy than the hamstrung professionals at Walworth Road.' This point was backed up in Butler and Kavanagh's survey of the 1992 local campaign, observing that improvements in information technology enabled local parties to undertake many of the tasks which hitherto had to be entrusted to national headquarters.

In summary, both electoral studies and the effects of party reorganisation have, since 1979, exposed the dangers of concentrating power and responsibility at the top of modern political parties. Indeed, if one agrees with Seyd and Whiteley that mass membership is vital to a party's success, and that an elitist party structure is inimical to mass membership, then any such concentration threatens a party's survival as an effective political force. It is contested that, hitherto, the Conservatives have been immune to this danger, though for this local Tories can only thank themselves rather than the leadership or Central Office. The 1993 Fowler Report still betrayed, on the part of the Tories' national organisers, a 'McKenzie-esque' view of effective party organisation, apparently blind to the surveys and developments discussed above – hence the frosty reception it received at the activists' 1993 Central Council. Tory activists, however, can at least take heart that the National Union remains highly decentralised and that the constituency associations retain much of their organisational autonomy, in which case they are still free to respond to the challenges which the Fowler and Feldman surveys managed to ignore. But for the Labour Party, whose constituency units have much less financial independence (and therefore less autonomy), and whose organisational 'culture' has become more centralised, the utility and style of successful party activity in the late twentieth century may require a more urgent and explicit examination.

## Notes

1. This idea was confirmed in a working party report to the NEC in February 1993.
2. Author's conversation with Robin Nelder, 5 November 1986.
3. P. Seyd, lecture at Manchester Grammar School, 10 February 1993.
4. Author's conversation with Robin Nelder.

## References

Benn, T. (1980), *Arguments for Democracy*, London, Jonathan Cape.
Butler, D. and Kavanagh, D. (1992), *The British General Election of 1992*, London, Macmillan.
*Charter News*, autumn publications 1986–1992, The Charter Movement, Beckenham, Kent.
Crick, M. (1984), *Militant*, London, Faber.
Critchley, J. (1985), *Westminster Blues*, London, Futura.
Denver, D. (1992), 'The 1992 General Election' *Talking Politics*, Autumn 1992.
Feldman, B. (1993), *Report on the Review of the National Union of Conservative and Unionist Associations*, London, Conservative Central Office.
Fowler, N. (1993), *One Party: Reforming the Conservative Party Organisation*, London, Conservative Central Office.
Gamble, A. (1979), 'The Conservative Party' in Drucker H. (ed.) *Multi Party Britain*, London, Macmillan.
Garner, R. (1990), 'Labour and the Policy Review' *Talking Politics*, Autumn 1990.
Garner, R. and Kelly, R. (1993), *British Political Parties Today*, Manchester, Manchester University Press.
Gilmour, I. (1992) *Dancing with Dogma*, London, Simon & Schuster.
Heffer, S. (1991), 'Thinning Out the Mental Porridge' *Spectator*, 11 May.
Heffernan, R. and Marqusee, M. (1992), *Defeat from The Jaws of Victory*, London, Verso.
Hughes, C. and Wintour, P. (1990), *Labour Rebuilt*, London, Fourth Estate.
Johnston, R.J., Pattie, C.J. and Allsopp, J.G. (1988), *A Nation Dividing?*, London, Longman.
Jones, B. (1993), 'The Labour Leadership Contest 1992', *Talking Politics*, Winter 1993.
Kellner, P. (1988), 'Labour's Leading Problem' *The Independent*, 26 September.
Kelly, R. (1988), 'Party Tricks' *Spectator*, 8 October.
Kelly, R. (1989), *Conservative Party Conferences*, Manchester, Manchester University Press.
King, A. (ed.) (1985), *The British Prime Minister*, London, Macmillan.

Leapman, M. (1987), *Kinnock*, London, Unwin Hyman.

Lovenduski, J., Geddes, A. and Norris, P. (1991), 'Candidate Selection', *Contemporary Record*, Vol. 4, 4.

McKenzie, R.T. (1963), *British Political Parties* 2nd edn, London, Heinemann.

Miller, W. (1977), *Electoral Dynamics*, London, Macmillan.

Minkin, L. (1978), *The Labour Party Conference*, London, Allen Lane.

Pinto-Duschinsky, M. (1972), 'Central Office and "power" in the Conservative Party', *Political Studies*, March 1972.

Pinto-Duschinsky, M. (1990), 'The Funding of Political Parties Since 1945' in Seldon, A. (ed.) *UK Political Parties Since 1945*, Hemel Hempstead, Philip Allan.

Punnett, R.M. (1992), *Selecting The Party Leader*, Hemel Hempstead, Harvester Wheatsheaf.

Seyd, P. (1987), *The Rise and Fall of the Labour Left*, London, Macmillan.

Seyd, P. and Whiteley, P. (1992), *Labour's Grass Roots*, Oxford, Clarendon Press.

Shaw, E. (1988), *Discipline and Discord in the Labour Party*, Manchester, Manchester University Press.

Shepherd, R. (1991), *The Power Brokers*, London, Hutchinson.

Smith, M. and Spear, J. (eds) (1992), *The Changing Labour Party*, London, Routledge.

Tyler, R. (1987), *Campaign!*, London, Grafton.

# 3
# The parties in Parliament

*Philip Norton*

Since 1945, there have been three identifiable periods in parliamentary history. The first, from 1945 to 1970, was a period of quiescence. Both Houses were chamber-oriented institutions, the emphasis being on deliberation on the floor of the House. Both Houses were party dominated, party cohesion being a marked feature of voting in the division lobbies of the House of Commons (Beer, 1969; Norton, 1975). Party ensured that Parliament was an institution essentially 'closed' to any groups and individuals operating outside the context of party (Norton, 1991a). Parliamentarians, not surprisingly therefore, were little troubled by groups and not too often troubled by constituents. The focus of Members of Parliament was predominantly Westminster and, at Westminster, fighting the party battle on the floor of the House. If a Member wished to specialise in a particular sector, or to express disquiet at, or opposition to, a particular policy being pursued by the party's front bench, then the means for so doing were private, party means: party committees and the whips. MPs thus operated at two levels: public and private.

The second period, from 1970 to 1979, saw an erosion of this divide between public and private. The division had never been a complete one, but in the 1970s it became notably blurred. Rather than confining intra-party dissent to private party forums, MPs increasingly made their dissent public. The decade witnessed an unprecedented, and sudden, increase in cross-voting (Norton, 1975, 1980). MPs not only cross-voted in greater numbers than before but also with greater effect. Government defeats as a consequence of cross-voting by government back-benchers, unknown in the preceding quarter-century, were features of all three Parliaments between 1970 and 1979.

The third period is that since 1979. In parliamentary terms, 1979 constitutes an important watershed. The year not only witnessed the return of a new government – a Conservative government under Margaret Thatcher, with a clear working majority – it also saw the creation of the first series of departmental select committees in the House of Commons. It was also the beginning of an era in which demands on MPs from pressure groups and from constituents increased enormously. All these developments have had important consequences for the parties in the House of Commons. The period has been one in which regular party structures have become less significant but members of the party, at least on the Conservative benches, have become relatively more important. Parties in the House of Lords have not been unaffected by some of these developments, but the effect has been less marked than in the Commons.

## The House of Commons

*The Conservative Party*

Since 1979, Conservative MPs have acquired a new power and continued to make use of those powers vested in them as MPs. The new power is that of being able to vote the prime minister out of the party leadership. The existing power for Members on the government benches has been to defy the whips and threaten the government's majority.

*Choosing the leader*   Conservative ministers have sometimes resigned or been eased out of office because they have lost the support of their back-benchers. Dissatisfaction has been channelled through the party whips, through the weekly meetings of the 1922 Committee or the relevant party committee. Occasionally, it has reached the floor of the House, most dramatically in 1940 when the number of Conservative MPs voting against the government signalled to Neville Chamberlain that it was time to go.

Party channels, though, are the most frequently used channels for easing ministers out. The period since 1979 has been notable for the number of ministers who have resigned as a result of losing the confidence of their parliamentary supporters. Lord Carrington resigned as Foreign Secretary in 1982 after Conservative MPs, at a crowded meeting of the 1922 Committee, expressed dissatisfaction with his handling of negotiations over the Falkland Islands. (Two other Foreign Office ministers resigned with him.) In January 1986, Trade and Industry Secretary Leon Brittan encountered extensive criticism of his conduct during the Westland affair at a meeting of the 1922 Committee. He resigned the following day. Edwina Currie resigned as junior Health Minister in 1988 following comments on salmonella in eggs that brought widespread condemnation from poultry farmers and from many Conservative MPs. In September 1992, National Heritage Secretary David Mellor attracted extensive press publicity over his private life, worrying an increasing number of Conservative MPs. Eventually, the chairman of the 1922 Committee telephoned the minister to tell him that he had lost the support of the parliamentary party; within an hour, the minister had resigned. In June 1993, the minister of state for Northern Ireland, Michael Mates, was under pressure to resign following revelations of his links with a fugitive businessman. The Prime Minister came under pressure to dismiss him, but declined to do so. Instead, the minister's fate was left to be decided at a meeting of the 1922 Committee. Mates avoided the embarrassment of being judged in that forum by resigning a matter of hours before the Committee met.

The number of cases of back-bench-induced resignations is not great, but it is much larger than in any preceding post-war decade. Furthermore, there is one important name missing from the list: that of Margaret Thatcher. For the first time in the history of the Conservative Party, the parliamentary party voted the Prime Minister out of the party leadership.

Before 1964, the leader of the Conservative Party 'emerged'. There was no formal procedure for selection, since there was normally an heir presumptive. If the party was in office, the heir would be summoned to Buckingham Palace on the resignation of the incumbent, as was the case, for example, in 1955 when Sir Anthony Eden succeeded the ailing Sir Winston Churchill. However, the 'emergence' was not always problem-free. In 1911, for example, after Arthur Balfour resigned the leadership, there were two contenders for the succession: Austen Chamberlain and Walter Long. A ballot of Conservative MPs appeared necessary in order to decide, but was avoided when the two stood down in favour of a compromise candidate, Andrew Bonar Law. In 1957 and again in 1963, when the party was in power, there was more than one contender to succeed Eden and Macmillan respectively. The battle for the succession ensnared the Queen in political controversy: she had to make a choice who was to be Prime Minister and, therefore, leader of the Conservative Party. It was in order to avoid further such embarrassment that the party leader and parliamentary party in 1964 agreed rules which provided for the election of the party leader.

Under the 1964 rules, election was to take place only when the incumbent gave up the office and the electorate was to comprise solely Conservative MPs. The rules were employed in 1965 on the resignation of Sir Alec Douglas-Home, resulting in the election of Edward Heath as leader. However, in 1974 – following two successive election losses in that year – pressure built up within the parliamentary party for Heath to offer himself for re-election. There was no provision for such an election. The result was that the executive of the 1922 Committee initiated and then agreed a revision of the leadership election rules, providing for the annual election of the leader (the rules are reproduced in Fisher, 1977: 194–7). Believing he would win easily, Heath agreed to the change. A leadership challenge under the new rules took place at the beginning of 1975, with Heath losing to a little-known challenger, Margaret Thatcher.

The rules agreed in 1974 did not confine the annual election to when the party was in opposition. One consequence, not fully recognised at the time the rules were introduced, was that a Conservative Prime Minister was subject to annual election as party leader. Margaret Thatcher in 1979 thus became the first Conservative Prime Minister to be subject to annual election as leader of the party. From 1979 to 1988, the election was a formality. There was only one candidate – Margaret Thatcher. In 1981, back-bench critics of the government's economic policy did contemplate running a candidate against the Prime Minister, but eventually decided against it. However, in 1989 and 1990, there was more than one candidate.

In 1989, Sir Anthony Meyer, a 69-year-old back-bencher who had never held government office, stood against Mrs Thatcher. He did so to express his opposition primarily to the prime minister's stance on the issue of Europe. Though the prime minister won easily in the election, sixty MPs none the less withheld their support from her (Norton, 1993a: 48–51). The following year, the challenge was more serious.

Party divisions over Europe, worsening economic indicators, the introduction of the poll tax and Mrs Thatcher's unwillingness to consider any change to that tax put the Prime Minister in a vulnerable position. Sir Geoffrey Howe's resignation from the government on 1 November and his subsequent resignation speech provided the conditions necessary for a leadership challenge by Michael Heseltine, who had effectively been waging a leadership campaign since resigning from the government during the Westland affair in 1986. In the first ballot, Margaret Thatcher got more votes than Michael Heseltine (Thatcher 204 votes, Heseltine 152, with sixteen abstentions), but not enough to satisfy the rules to be declared elected. (Under the rules, victory in the first ballot requires not only an absolute majority but a majority that constitutes 15 per cent of the parliamentary party. Thatcher was four votes short of fulfilling the 15 per cent requirement.) After deliberating for twenty-four hours, Mrs Thatcher decided not to contest the second ballot. Two new candidates, John Major and Douglas Hurd, entered to challenge Heseltine, with Major emerging victorious (Anderson, 1991; Pearce, 1991; Shepherd, 1991; Norton, 1993: 51–9). Mrs Thatcher went to Buckingham Palace to tender her resignation as Prime Minister, and John Major was summoned to be her successor. The parliamentary party had voted out their leader and, in so doing, removed the incumbent Prime Minister. Heath had been voted out of the party leadership, but he was not Prime Minister at the time. Margaret Thatcher thus occupies a unique place in the history books for the manner of her going, not just for the length and substance of her eleven-and-a-half years in Downing Street.

The explanation for the introduction and the change in the rules for the election of the leader have been detailed already. Both were the product of political expediency. The possibly unintentional result was a leader more dependent than ever before on the confidence of back-benchers. Though the premiership of Margaret Thatcher was often portrayed as epitomising prime ministerial government, it was also a premiership more vulnerable than previous Conservative premierships to the vagaries of back-bench dissension. When the leader pursued policies that looked likely to lead to electoral disaster, the leader was replaced. Her successor has been subject to the same constraints.

*Influencing policy* The period after 1979 has seen a continued willingness on the part of government back-benchers to vote against their own side. In the 1970–74 Parliament, Conservative back-benchers had voted against their own side more often, in greater numbers, and with more effect than ever before in this century (Norton, 1975, 1978). The scale of cross-voting became even greater under the succeeding Labour government (Norton, 1980). The precedent set in the 1970s was continued in the 1980s and beyond.

The first Parliament of the Thatcher government (1979–83) saw a number of serious rifts within the ranks of the parliamentary party. Some were contained within party channels, the government making concessions before the issue reached the floor of the House, while others took public form on the floor of the House. On at least five occasions it retreated under the threat of defeat, with up to 100 back-benchers reportedly threatening to vote against it if it introduced a bill to make sanctions against Iran retrospective (see Norton, 1981: 232). Economic policy came in for serious criticism, not only from back-benchers but from some within the cabinet. Dissent continued in the two subsequent Parliaments. In the 1983–84 session alone, 137 back-benchers cast 416 dissenting votes, a remarkable incidence for the first session of a Parliament (Norton, 1985: 32). Despite a large overall majority – sufficient usually to absorb most incidents of back-bench dissent – the government suffered an embarrassing defeat on the second reading of the Shops Bill in April 1986, when seventy-two back-benchers voted with opposition parties to defeat the bill (Regan, 1988; Bown, 1990). The government came close to defeat on the issue of top people's pay in 1985, defeat being staved off by the whips claiming that the Prime Minister was ready to resign if defeated. It also modified policies under threat of defeat, for instance on the issue of student loans. Indeed, there were several occasions of compromise, with the normal practice of the chief whip being to arrange negotiations between ministers and dissenters in order to avoid an open revolt (*The Economist*, 4.8.84).

This incidence of independence in voting behaviour was continued under the premiership of John Major, and acquired renewed visibility in the Parliament returned in April 1992. With a small overall majority of twenty-one (reduced later by by-election defeats), the government was sensitive to possible cross-voting by its own supporters and in the first session of the Parliament experienced notable dissension on the issue of the Maastricht Treaty, on pit closures, and on House of Commons' issues, including MPs' allowances (Norton, 1993b).

In the period from 1979 onwards, members of the parliamentary party could not be taken for granted in the way they had been before 1970. Their behaviour resembled that of the 1970s, and not that of the decades before 1970. Their independent behaviour, though, did not have the same effect as that of the 1970s. Why, then, the continued independence? And why the limited effect after 1979?

The reasons for the behavioural change is a matter of considerable academic debate, especially for the period of the 1970s (Schwarz, 1980; Franklin, Baxter and Jordan, 1986; Norton, 1987). This writer has advanced the poor leadership hypothesis (Norton, 1978), with Edward Heath's style of leadership in the 1970–74 Parliament – his unwillingness to listen and to make concessions, his isolation of dissenters – acting as a trigger for the public expression of dissent; dissent which otherwise would have been absorbed within party forums. Once backbenchers had tasted blood by imposing a defeat on the government, they found it much easier to do it a second time. By the time of the 1979 Parliament, cross-voting was an accepted feature of parliamentary life. It was not the rule (see Rose, 1983) but it was no longer a rarity. Members knew they could vote against their own side without incurring serious retribution either for themselves or for the government. The old myths that had attached to cross-voting (such as the government having to resign, regardless of the seriousness of the issue, or of dissenters facing serious disciplinary sanctions) had been dispelled and could not be resurrected. Even the perceived threat to promotion prospects had been undermined, first by the experience of the Callaghan government – cross-voting by Labour MPs was so common at the end of the 1974–79 Parliament that posts could only be filled by MPs who had some history of cross-voting – and, second, by the composition of the first Thatcher cabinet in 1979: several senior figures had been significant dissenters in earlier days.

Once released, then, the genie of back-bench independence could not be put back in the bottle. What has been significant about the period of Conservative government from 1979 onwards has been the radical policies that have been pursued. Margaret Thatcher espoused views that collectively were accorded an 'ism' – Thatcherism – and which found expression in a range of policies, not least economic policy. Most Conservative MPs were prepared to support those policies, but their support was contingent, not certain. The parliamentary party was not a Thatcherite party. Most Conservative MPs, newly-returned as well as longer-serving ones, were not identified with any particular ideological disposition (Norton, 1990a, 1990b). Their loyalty was essentially to the party and they could therefore desert the leader if the government's policies looked likely to lead to electoral disaster. Others were identified with a particular disposition, and those of a disposition different from Thatcherite neo-liberalism could and did express dissent. Mrs Thatcher's style, which in later Parliaments began to resemble that of Edward Heath, exacerbated the problem. She removed critical ministers, such as Norman St. John-Stevas, Sir Ian Gilmour and Francis Pym, from the cabinet and in later Parliaments saw relatively little of her back-benchers (Norton, 1993a). When the Prime Minister became wedded to the poll tax and an intractable stance on Europe then, as we have seen, her support in the parliamentary party dropped away. The radical policies of the Thatcher governments thus provided the necessary basis for much back-bench dissent, though not themselves serving to explain why the dissent took the form that it did. The triggering mechanism for public dissent preceded the Thatcher era.

The reasons for the limited effect, at least in terms of public policy, are to be found in the size of the government's overall majorities. The Thatcher government of 1979–83 and the Major government in the 1992 Parliament faced majorities, not unlike Heath in 1970–74, that were vulnerable to cross-voting by fewer than 10 per cent of the parliamentary party. However, in the two Parliaments from 1983 to 1992 the government enjoyed large majorities (144 and 101 respectively at the time of election) that could absorb dissent by even a considerable body of back-benchers. More than fifty back-benchers would need to cross-vote in order even to come close to threatening the government's majority in the division lobbies – hence the limited effect of dissent by one or a small number of back-benchers.

What is remarkable about this period, though, is not that the effect of dissent was limited but that it had the impact that it did. Despite the large overall majorities it enjoyed, the government was variously threatened with defeat and on rare occasions was defeated: most notably, but not exclusively, on the Shops Bill. Every Parliament since, and including, the 1979–83 Parliament has seen the government fail to carry one or more votes in the House.

*Organisation under pressure* The parliamentary party has a well-developed infrastructure. In the nineteenth century, the organisation comprised essentially the party leaders and the whips. In the twentieth century, the party has acquired a regularly-meeting body comprising all Conservative private Members – the 1922 Committee, so-called because it was formed by MPs first returned at the 1922 election (see Goodhart, 1973; Norton 1994) – and a series of back-bench committees, formed and operating independently of the 1922 Committee (Norton, 1994).

The organisation was well developed by the 1930s and has provided important channels through which back-benchers can express their views and specialise in particular policy areas. The committees have served as important conduits for back-bench influence (Norton, 1979; Brand, 1992), the views expressed in them having some impact on occasion on ministers' actions (Norton, 1993c: 62–63).

There are two features of this party organisation that are noteworthy in the period since 1979. One constitutes a notable continuity with previous decades, while the other constitutes a marked departure.

The continuity lies in the fact that both the 1922 Committee and the various subject committees are channels through which back-benchers can influence ministerial actions and policies. We have already noted the importance of the 1922 Committee in determining the fate of a number of ministers. The careers of other ministers, such as that of Cecil Parkinson as Transport Secretary, have been adversely affected by critical comments at committee meetings. The views expressed by committees have also had some policy affect. In 1984, for example, the education committee appeared influential in persuading the Education Secretary to abandon his plans for greater parental contributions for student maintenance (Silk, 1987: 49). Attendance at meetings continues to reflect the importance attached by back-benchers to an issue. Any Conservative MP can attend any committee meeting – there are no fixed memberships – and a large, critical audience sends immediate warning signals to the whips. When the President of the Board of Trade, Michael Heseltine, announced major pit closures in October 1992, more than 150 MPs crowded into a meeting of the Trade and Industry Committee, the critical comments made at the meeting helping to convince him of the need to make some modification to his policy.

The change from past practice is to be found in the time and attention accorded committees by MPs. Before 1979, committees usually met weekly, with a moderate to good attendance. The smaller committees might only draw half-a-dozen MPs but the more important ones – covering subjects such as foreign affairs, finance, and home affairs – would normally draw an attendance in double figures. For an important speaker, the attendance might reach triple figures. Since 1979 attendance has fallen away, although some meetings still attract a good attendance. The Chancellor's address to the finance committee after he has delivered his Budget speech still attracts a crowd. Controversial issues, such as the pit closures in 1992, can still draw a large attendance, as can the occasional celebrity. England football captain, Gary Lineker, drew a good attendance at a meeting of the sports committee, even though it was held on the same evening as one of the leadership ballots in 1990. Such occasions, though, are very much the exception. Even the more important committees have found it difficult to maintain an attendance sufficient to justify weekly meetings. Most committees have moved away from a weekly timetable to a fortnightly one. By the beginning of the 1990s, the foreign affairs committee had ceased inviting ambassadors to address the committee for fear of having an embarrassingly small audience (Norton, 1994). The problem of poor attendance was deemed sufficiently important for it to be discussed at a meeting of the 1922 Committee, but no solution was forthcoming.

The explanation for the declining attendance is to be found in the competing priorities of MPs, whose workload has increased enormously in recent years. Constituents now make more demands of Members than ever before (Norton and Wood, 1993). Pressure groups now lobby MPs extensively (Rush, 1990). Indeed, since 1979, pressure groups have effectively 'discovered' Parliament. The attempt by government to achieve an arm's length relationship with groups, especially peak economic groups, has been one of several factors encouraging groups to utilise Parliament in a way they had not previously done (Norton, 1991b). Demands from constituents and pressure groups have been compounded by the volume of public business. The creation of departmental select committees in 1979 has added considerably to the burdens of more than 150 Members. The growth of all-party groups has also added to the competing attractions for Members (Norton, 1991c: 10–11). The result is that MPs now have to decide priorities in a way that previously they did not have to – finding time to attend party committees comes low on that list.

There is also an alternative attraction. Many Conservative MPs find informal party gatherings more compelling to attend than the formal committees. Informal dining groups have been a feature of the parliamentary party for many years. So too have groups which have an ideological base, such as the Monday Club and the Selsdon Group. Such groupings are formed by like-minded Members who can meet in a congenial environment (especially the dining clubs) and who can determine who joins the group and who does not. The popularity of such groups has grown in recent years. The '92 Group' (named after 92 Cheyne Walk – home of Sir Patrick Wall – where it originally used to meet) comprises MPs on the right of the party and now has just over 100 MPs in its ranks. The equivalent on the left of the party is the 'Lollards', formed originally by Sir William van Straubenzee, who had a flat in the Lollards Tower of Lambeth Palace. These groups, along with others, organise slates of candidates in the annual elections for officerships of the party committees.

Such groups tend to engage the loyalties of Members in a way that the formal subject committees cannot. The same applies to *ad hoc* informal groupings established on particular subjects. On the issue of Europe, for example, opponents of moves towards European integration have tended to organise themselves, with meetings and 'whips'. An informal body was formed in 1972 during the passage of the European

Communities Bill and in 1992 and 1993 during the passage of the European Communities (Amendment) Bill to ratify the Maastricht Treaty.

Within the Conservative parliamentary party, the closed and formalised nature of the party has given way, especially since 1979, to a more open and informal structure, with Members exploiting or creating new opportunities to express themselves. Members are busier than ever before but now have more opportunities to make their voices heard.

## The Labour Party

For the Parliamentary Labour Party (the PLP), the period since 1979 has seen a notable decline, rather than an increase, in influence. That decline has been experienced at two levels.

The first, and most obvious, was at the level of government. In the general election of May 1979, Labour ceased to be the party of government. Labour MPs now occupied the Opposition benches. In the 1974–79 Parliament, Labour back-benchers had been able to wield considerable influence. With a small – and, after April 1976, non-existent – overall majority, the government was vulnerable to defeat either as a result of its own supporters defecting in the division lobbies or, after April 1976, to opposition parties combining against it. In that Parliament, the government suffered forty-two defeats, twenty-three of them as a result of Labour MPs voting in the Opposition lobby (Norton, 1980). A number of the defeats were on major measures, including the Scotland and Wales Bills designed to devolve powers to elected assemblies in Wales and Scotland. After 1979, Labour back-benchers were not in a position to wield such influence. Cross-voting had no effect on the outcome of divisions. Labour MPs who disagreed with their own front bench could force a division, and thus act as an irritant, in cases where the official line was to abstain, but could do little more than that.

The second level was at that of the party. Labour MPs have never enjoyed the proximity to party policy making as have Conservative MPs. In the Conservative party, the formal fount of all policy is the leader (see Norton and Aughey, 1981: Chapter 6). Conservative MPs enjoy the advantages of being proximate to the party leader. In the Labour party, there is a structured policy-making process, with the ultimate power resting with the party conference. The National Executive Committee and its sub-committees have been the most important actors on a regular basis. The PLP is largely detached from that process. However, until the 1980s, it did have an important role to play in electing the leader and deputy leader of the party (Drucker,

1976; Norton, 1979: 52–53). The PLP elected James Callaghan as leader to succeed Harold Wilson in 1976 and Michael Foot to succeed Callaghan in 1980. That power was to be lost in 1981.

Pressure for constitutional change within the Labour Party resulted in a special party conference in January 1981 in which it was agreed that the party leader should be elected by an electoral college, with the PLP having only 30 per cent of the votes. The result of that decision by the party conference was to weaken the PLP, both formally and politically (see Seyd, 1987: chapter 5) – formally, in that it was now only a minority player in the selection process. Leadership candidates were likely to give more of their attentions to the unions, which collectively controlled 40 per cent of the vote. Politically, it weakened the PLP in that the decision acted as a trigger for the formation of the Social Democratic Party (SDP), siphoning off from the parliamentary party a substantial body of defectors. Between 1981 and the 1983 general election, twenty-eight Labour MPs left the party to join the new party.

The decision of the party conference and the formation of the SDP served to demoralise members of the PLP. The decision of the party to introduce mandatory reselection also had a notable effect on the activity of many Labour MPs. It was common for Members, especially those known to be under threat of deselection by their local party, to desert Westminster and spend as much time as possible in their constituencies. A combination of demoralisation and absence meant that the PLP was weakened as a parliamentary body. That demoralisation was exacerbated by the result of the 1983 general election, giving the government an overall majority that was likely to prove impregnable to attack by opposition parties.

The result of these developments was that, for much of the 1980s, the PLP was a relatively disorganised force. Whipping was often poorly organised, with back-benchers left to decide for themselves what to do. On occasion, a combination of Conservative cross-voting and a full turnout of Labour MPs could have embarrassed or even defeated the government, notably on the issue of top people's pay in 1985. In the event, it was only on the Shops Bill that the government suffered a major defeat, thanks to the size of the Conservative dissenting lobby. For most of the 1983–87 Parliament, the PLP was not seen by many MPs as a serious force.

*Organisational decline*  The state of the parliamentary party was reflected in its internal organisation. Like the Parliamentary Conservative Party, the PLP has a weekly meeting and a series of subject committees. The committees have never attracted the same degree of attention, nor exerted the level of influence, of their Conservative counterparts (Norton, 1979) but they have been useful instruments for considering policy and future business. However, the demoralisation and absence of Labour MPs had an impact. The position was well summarised by Labour MP Austin Mitchell (1983: 62) in considering how Labour MPs might have responded to the growing power of the Labour left:

> Only resolute action by the Parliamentary Labour Party could have stopped the takeover. It could have done this by doing what it had done in the past and developing policy through the subject groups of the PLP, urging it in the House in opposition to the measures of Tory government. The lack of confidence of the parliamentary party, the distraction of reselection, the general collapse of morale, the lack of drive from the top and increasing strength of the new orthodoxy of Conference rules OK, all combined to sabotage any counter-attack. The PLP was not an effective force.

Though three subject groups did help develop policy, group meetings were generally badly attended and not tied in to front-bench activity or thinking. Though PLP morale picked up in the 1987–92 Parliament, subject group activity was still limited, with only one or two members of the shadow cabinet taking the groups seriously and engaging in a serious exercise of consultation. Party policy making was essentially concentrated at the top.

*Fragmentation* The parliamentary party also fragmented during this period. From 1976 to 1982, Labour left-wingers were organised in the Tribune Group. The Group had variously dissented from the stance of the leadership and voted accordingly (Norton, 1980: 434; Seyd, 1987: 79–82). However, the early 1980s saw a notable division on the left. The election for the deputy leadership of the party in 1981 revealed a divide between what became known as the 'soft' left and the 'hard' left; the former being prepared, unlike the latter, to consider some change to established socialist policies. The left divided into two principal groupings, the Tribune Group becoming most closely identified with the soft left and the Campaign Group – formed by twenty-three Labour MPs in December 1982 – representing the hard left. Tensions between the two increased in the 1980s, exacerbated in 1984 and 1985 by differences over the miners' strike (Seyd, 1987: 167–8). The right of the party was organised initially in the Manifesto Group, which included peers as well as MPs. About seventy MPs were believed to be in the Group (it never made its membership list public) but it broke up following the defection of a substantial fraction of its membership to the SDP. It was superseded by the Solidarity Group, which sought to encompass MPs of the centre as well as right of the party. However, 'Solidarity had the characteristics of a rump' (Brand, 1989: 150) and had little notable impact. The principal factions in the 1987–92 Parliament were the Tribune and Campaign Groups.

*Recovery?* The 1992 general election resulted in a larger and more energetic PLP. Though still not the party of government, the party was in a position to harry a government with a relatively small majority. A small number of Conservative dissenters voting with the Opposition could threaten the government's majority. The PLP initiated a review of its organisation. Several new Labour MPs also began to organise informally, meeting regularly to discuss issues and to listen to invited speakers (especially on different aspects of parliamentary organisation, though also inviting an expert on stress management). The group eventually called itself the '1992 Group' and in its origins and form bore some resemblance to the Conservative 1922 Committee. Subject groups also provided an outlet for the energies of new MPs, with the chairs of most being taken by members of the new intake.

The PLP after April 1992 thus witnessed some change in its morale and its activity. There was no paradigmatic change, but Members were more involved and relatively more organised than they had been in the preceding decade.

## Other parties

The Conservative and Labour parties dominated Parliament in the period after 1979. During the 1970s, third parties had grown in number and in size. The Ulster Unionists began to sit as a separate party, the Scottish and Welsh Nationalists saw the return of a sufficient number of MPs to form parliamentary parties, the defection of Labour MPs (and one Conservative MP) to the SDP in 1981 saw a new parliamentary party, and the Liberal Party saw an increase in its parliamentary representation from six in 1970 to fourteen in February 1974. During the period of the Lib–Lab Pact from 1977 to 1978, the Liberal parliamentary party had some impact on public policy. So too, though less publicly observable, did the Ulster Unionists.

Third parties were relegated largely to the parliamentary margins in 1979, with the return of a government with an overall working majority. The Liberals, the largest and oldest of the third parties, had difficulty – as they had before 1974 – making an impact. Given that there were only two voting lobbies, they were always subject to the accusation that they were voting with this or the other major party rather than taking a distinctive line of their own. In practice, they most frequently voted in the Opposition lobby (Norton, 1983). They were given a boost by the creation of the SDP in 1981 and the alliance of the SDP and Liberal parties. However, the greater visibility achieved by the alliance in Parliament was overshadowed by the publicity given to the Falklands war in 1982 and the results of the 1983 general election.

Third parties have some organisation. As long as there are two members of the parliamentary party, one serves as a whip – not so much for the purposes of rounding up Members in a vote but in order to liaise with the whips of other parties and the parliamentary business managers. The parties normally have regular weekly meetings, but none has had a membership sufficiently large to sustain a series of party committees.

The Liberal parliamentary party maintained a reputation as a party of individuals, and though a party line was variously followed some Members took a very individualistic line on a number of issues. The SDP MPs also occasionally split, as on the issue of trade union reform. The same characteristic was evident in the new Liberal Democratic Party. David Alton, MP for Liverpool Mossley Hill, signalled that he may leave the party and adopted a semi-detached stance in the parliamentary party. Simon Hughes, MP for Southward and Bermondsey, toyed with the idea of an alliance with the Greens, and after the 1992 election the party – previously united on the issue – even had a Euro-rebel in its ranks in the form of Nick Harvey, the new Member for North Devon.

Third parties, however, achieved some new prominence in the Parliament returned in 1992. So long as the Conservative ranks held firm, third parties had little relevance for government. However, cross-voting by a small number of Conservative MPs could jeopardise the government's majority. That majority might be saved by the support of a third party. During the passage of the European Communities (Amendment) Bill in 1992 and 1993, and on certain related motions, Conservative dissenters were sufficiently numerous for the government to court the support of the Liberal Democrats and also the Scottish Nationalists. However, even though the support of the Nationalists was forthcoming on an amendment concerning the proposed EC Committee of the Regions, it was not enough to save the government from defeat.

For most of the period from 1979 to 1993, then, third parties were essentially marginal actors in the House of Commons, in sharp contrast to the period from 1974 to 1979. They regained some political leverage in the 1992 Parliament, but their influence was, at best, sporadic.

## The House of Lords

The parties are also organised in the House of Lords, though on a less extensive basis than in the Commons.

The Conservative Party in the Upper House – known since the beginning of the 1980s as the Association of Conservative Peers (previously it was the Association of Independent Unionist Peers) – has been organised for more than seventy years (Norton, 1994). It has held weekly, and increasingly well attended, meetings and has its own elected officers. However, its organisation is less developed than in the Commons. It does not have subject committees: instead, peers may participate in the work of the party committees in the Commons and a number do so.

In terms of party organisation, it can be contended that its influence has declined in recent decades. Only between two and four peers serve now in cabinet – and, since the end of the Thatcher era, only two – and peers have less impact now in leadership contests than was the case before 1964. Under the process of 'emergence', some leading peers could play a role in determining the outcome and in 1963 the views of Conservative peers were reported to Macmillan before he offered his advice to the Queen on a successor. However, under the rules agreed in 1964 Conservative peers had no role in the process. In 1974, it was agreed that their views should be reported to the 1922 Committee before the first ballot. In 1975, 1989 and 1990, their views were reported (supporting the leader), but appeared to have no obvious effect in 1975 and 1990, and in 1989 did not matter.

In terms of public policy, however, the Conservative Party in the Lords has had – and continues to have – some influence. There is a preponderance of Conservative peers in the Lords. At the beginning of 1993, among peers with a declared political affiliation, there were 478 Conservatives, 275 cross-benchers, 117 Labour peers, 58 Liberal Democrats and 12 Social Democrats. A Conservative two-line whip is usually sufficient to ensure a majority of peers attending are Conservative.

During the period of Labour government from 1974 to 1979, the Conservative peers used their voting strength to impose 347 defeats on the government. The presumption following the return of a Conservative government in 1979 was that the Upper House would not be a particular irritant. In the event, Conservative peers continued to use their voting power to defeat the government. In the 1979–83 Parliament alone, the government lost forty-five votes (Norton, 1985: 14) and by 1990 had lost no less than 156 (Drewry and Brock, 1993: 87). The defeats were almost always on amendments to bills, some of them of some import (see Baldwin, 1985). The defeat of the government in 1984 on a central clause of the paving bill for the abolition of the Greater London Council attracted particular attention, signalling the willingness of a Conservative Upper House to go against a Conservative government on central issues of public policy.

The period also saw the development of an axis between Conservative dissenters in the Commons and in the Lords. If there was a sizeable dissenting lobby in the Commons, Conservative peers would then take their cue from their Commons' counterparts and take their dissent into the division lobbies. If the parliamentary party in the Commons was united behind the government on an issue, then peers were less willing to take their dissent to the lobbies.

The nature of the House of Lords has also given some significance to the other parties. There is normally a Conservative majority present in the House, but not always. Conservative peers are not subject to the same political influences (not least constituency pressure) as their counterparts in the Commons and, in any event, may not be able to give the amount of time to parliamentary activity as MPs. Divisions may be held when the opposition parties can muster more peers than the government. On occasion, Conservative peers may vote with opposition Members. The creation of several London-based Labour 'working peers' – peers ennobled in order to spend time in the House – in the late 1980s and early 1990s considerably strengthened the Labour party in the House, sufficient to worry the government and to encourage it to think about similar creations in order to maintain its position in the House.

The explanation for the independence of the House, especially that of Conservative peers, during this period is to be found in the confluence of four developments. One, longer-term, development has been the creation of life peers. They bring new life to the House (Shell, 1993: 7–10), with life peers constituting a disproportionate element of the working peerage. The second development was the failure of the Parliament (No. 2) Bill in 1969, which was designed to reform the House. When it failed, peers realised that reform was unlikely in the near future and so had to make the most of what existed (Baldwin, 1985). Those developments clearly preceded 1979. However, the third feature is specific to the period from 1979 to 1990, namely, the government of Margaret Thatcher.

As it was among Conservative MPs, Thatcherism was, or certainly appeared to be, a minority taste among Conservative peers. Many of the peers appeared to be drawn from the Tory rather than the Whig strand of Conservatism (see Norton and Aughey, 1981) and were sceptical of the general direction taken by the government. Lacking the restraints of their Commons counterparts, they were willing to take their scepticism on occasion to the voting lobbies. That scepticism was retained beyond 1990.

The final feature is one already noted in respect of the House of Commons. Since 1979, pressure groups have discovered the House of Lords as well as the House of Commons. Indeed, for lobbyists, making contact with a peer is as popular an action as contacting an MP (Rush, 1990). Peers are inundated with material. If it is in an area in which they take an interest, it can add considerably to their store of knowledge and serve to make them less dependent on party or government for information. A greater range of information potentially reinforces their Lordships' critical capacity and, allied with the other developments, it has served to generate a more active House of Lords.

## Conclusion

Parliamentary parties in the period since 1979 are very different from those which existing before 1979. In the House of Commons, they are less closed, less structured and less predictable than before. In the House of Lords, they are a more significant influence on government than could be anticipated from the political composition of the House. For members of a parliamentary party, be it in government or opposition, in the Commons or the Lords, the freedom of action is now greater than at any time previously in post-war history.

## References

Anderson, B. (1991), *John Major: The Making of a Prime Minister*, London, Fourth Estate.

Baldwin, N. (1985), 'The House of Lords: Behavioural Changes', in P. Norton (ed.), *Parliament in the 1980s*, Oxford, Basil Blackwell.

Beer, S.H. (1969), *Modern British Politics*, (revised edn), London, Faber.

Bown, F.A.C.S. (1990), 'The Shops Bill', in M. Rush (ed.), *Parliament and Pressure Politics*, Oxford, Oxford University Press.

Brand, J. (1989), 'Faction as its own Reward: Groups in the British Parliament 1945–86', *Parliamentary Affairs*, 42: 148–64.

Brand, J. (1992), *British Parliamentary Parties*, Oxford, Oxford University Press.

Drewry, G. and Brock, J. (1993), 'Government Legislation: An Overview', in D. Shell and D. Beamish (eds), *The House of Lords at Work*, Oxford, Oxford University Press.

Drucker, H.M. (1976), 'Leadership Selection in the Labour Party', *Parliamentary Affairs*, 29.

Fisher, N. (1977), *The Tory Leaders*, London, Weidenfeld and Nicolson.

Franklin, M., Baxter, A. and Jordan, M. (1986), 'Who Were The Rebels? Dissent in the House of Commons 1970–74', *Legislative Studies Quarterly*, 11: 143–59.

Goodhart, P., (1973), *The 1922*, London, Macmillan.

Mitchell, A. (1983), *Four Years in the Death of the Labour Party*, London, Methuen.

Norton, P. (1975), *Dissension in the House of Commons 1945–74*, London, Macmillan.

Norton, P. (1978), *Conservative Dissidents*, London, Temple Smith.

Norton, P. (1979), 'The Organization of Parliamentary Parties', in S.A. Walkland (ed.), *The House of Commons in the Twentieth Century*, Oxford, Oxford University Press.

Norton, P. (1980), *Dissension in the House of Commons 1974–1979*, Oxford, Oxford University Press.

Norton, P. (1981), *The Commons in Perspective*, Oxford, Martin Robertson.

Norton, P. (1983), 'The Liberal Party in Parliament', in V. Bogdanor (ed.), *Liberal Party Politics*, Oxford, Oxford University Press.

Norton, P. (1985), (ed.) *Parliament in the 1980s*, Oxford, Basil Blackwell.

Norton, P. (1987), 'Dissent in the House of Commons: Rejoinder to Franklin, Baxter, Jordan', *Legislative Studies Quarterly*, 12: 143–52.

Norton, P. (1990a), '"The Lady's Not for Turning": But What About the Rest? Margaret Thatcher and the Conservative Party 1979–89', *Parliamentary Affairs*, 43: 41–58.

Norton, P. (1990b), 'Choosing a Leader: Margaret Thatcher and the Parliamentary Conservative Party', *Parliamentary Affairs*, 43: 249–59.

Norton, P. (1991a), 'Parliament Since 1945: A More Open Institution?' *Contemporary Record*, 5 (2): 217–34.

Norton, P. (1991b), 'The Changing Face of the House of Commons: Lobbying and its Consequences', in P. Norton (ed.), *New Directions in British Politics?* Aldershot, Edward Elgar.

Norton, P. (1991c), 'Committees in the House of Commons', *Politics Review*, 1: 5–11.

Norton, P. (1993a), 'The Conservative Party from Thatcher to Major', in A. King (ed.), *Britain at the Polls 1992*, Chatham NJ, Chatham House.

Norton, P. (1993b), 'Parliament', in P. Catterall (ed.), *Contemporary Britain: An Annual Review 1993*, Oxford, Basil Blackwell.

Norton, P. (1993c), *Does Parliament Matter?*, Hemel Hempstead, Harvester Wheatsheaf.

Norton, P. (1994), 'The Party in Parliament', in A. Seldon (ed.), *The Conservative Party in the Twentieth Century*, Oxford, Oxford University Press.

Norton, P. and Aughey, A. (1981), *Conservatives and Conservatism*, London, Temple Smith.

Norton, P. and Wood, D. (1993), *Back from Westminster*, Lexington KY, University Press of Kentucky.

Pearce, E. (1991), *The Quiet Rise of John Major*, London, Weidenfeld and Nicolson.

Regan, P. (1988), 'The 1986 Shops Bill', *Parliamentary Affairs*, 421: 218–35.

Rose, R. (1983), 'Still the Era of Party Government', *Parliamentary Affairs*, 36: 282–99.

Rush, M. (1990), (ed.) *Parliament and Pressure Politics*, Oxford, Oxford University Press.

Shell, D. (1993), 'The House of Lords in Context', in D. Shell and D. Beamish (eds), *The House of Lords at Work*, Oxford, Oxford University Press.

Shepherd, R. (1991), *The Power Brokers*, London, Hutchinson.

Schwarz, J.E. (1980), 'Exploring a New Role in Policy Making: The British House of Commons in the 1970s', *American Political Science Review*, 74: 23–37.

Seyd, P. (1987), *The Rise and Fall of the Labour Left*, London, Macmillan.

Silk, P. (1987), *How Parliament Works*, London, Longman.

# 4
# Parties, ideologies and issues: the case of the European Community

*Alistair Jones*

The current debate on the Maastricht Treaty has brought to the fore more clearly than ever a set of divisions that very rarely surfaces in British politics. Instead of the two major parties opposing each other, a different type of conflict has appeared; within each party, there is a significant minority opposed to the Maastricht Treaty. On their own, these groups have little chance of achieving anything, being overwhelmed by the majority responding to the party whips. This chapter examines these groups for evidence of joint organisation in pursuit of their seemingly common goals. The idea of cross-party networking is an unusual phenomenon in British politics. Only the issue of the European Community appears capable of developing such a response for no other issue divides individual MPs of similar ideological backgrounds while at the same time uniting those of the most diverse.

Britain applied twice for membership of the then-called Common Market in the 1960s before eventually joining in 1973. Between 1974 and 1976, Wilson's cabinet was divided over the issue of Community membership. The referendum held in 1975 on EC membership was fought beyond party lines. That is, there were no strict party political stances. Enoch Powell and Tony Benn were both on the anti-membership platform, while the party leaderships of each of the major parties were tacitly in favour. Despite this, 1979 is still a convenient starting point as in that year, Margaret Thatcher became Prime Minister, and the first direct elections to the European Parliament were held. Thatcher's approach to dealing with Britain's Community partners was significantly different from all of her predecessors; she argued the position of the UK in a far more aggressive fashion. What must also be noted at this point, which complicates matters more than a little, is that the European Community is a unique issue in that it has largely failed to divide into a neat two-party problem. Yet, at the same time, within both the

Conservative and Labour parties there have been stark divisions between pro- and anti-Community Members and, more recently, between pro- and anti-Maastricht Members. This does overstate the issue a little as the majority of Members in both major parties simply toe the line of their respective leaderships. Failure to do so could possibly impede their future political careers: the best possible way to gain promotion as a Member of Parliament is *not* to upset your party leadership.

The 1983 general election is the only example of a clear division between the stances of the two major parties on the issue of the European Community. In all other general elections, the European Community has either been ignored or there has been some general reference to continued membership. In the most recent general election of 9 April 1992 there was further evidence of this, with all the major parties stating their support for the European Community and the Maastricht Treaty.

However, this situation has created a major problem. Basically, there is no clear party political outlet for anti-Maastricht or anti-Community campaigners to voice their opinions. With the different party leaderships all broadly in favour of Community membership and with a commitment to the Maastricht Treaty, inter-party debate has effectively been stifled. The result of this has been the development of a cross-party anti-Maastricht coalition or alliance not dissimilar to that which evolved in the 1975 Referendum on European Community membership. This has occurred not as a result of a political agreement but rather for tactical purposes: the common objective is to derail the Maastricht Treaty. The reasons for doing so are very different. The right wing of the Conservative Party envisage what Margaret Thatcher termed 'a Socialist superstate', with 'some sort of identikit European personality' (*The Times*, 13.5.89) and the further growth of government and the public sector. They adopt a traditional, nationalistic, British position. Compared with this, those on the left of the Labour Party see the result of the Maastricht Treaty as being essentially monetarist, a capitalist club with a 'fortress Europe' mentality that will further drain Britain's resources. In sum, they oppose the idea of the Maastricht Treaty because of the economic argument. Therefore, although the fears of each group are almost diametrically opposed, the objective is the same – to destroy the Maastricht Treaty, whatever it takes. As Lord Tebbit, in a speech to a press gallery luncheon, stated: 'Frankly as any amendment would wreck the treaty I would cheerfully vote for one saying that the moon was made of blue cheese if it had a chance of being carried.'

Bad news makes news, and the divisions within the two major parties present the media with an opportunity to publicise the ineptitude of each of the parties to form a coherent party line. With the Conservatives in power, the media have largely focused on their problems. There has been a negligible focus upon the Labour Party, except for events that are in tandem with the Conservatives. This is in contrast with the early 1980s, when the media exposed the divisions within the Labour Party and presented the Conservatives as united on the issue.

## 1979–84: divided policies

It is with this in mind that 1979 can be viewed as a convenient starting point; Margaret Thatcher becoming Prime Minister marked a significant change in the way that Britain dealt with its Community partners. It was also the year of the first direct elections to the European Parliament. The significance of this is not lost on Butler and Kavanagh (1980: 173), who neatly summed up the importance of both the European Community and the direct elections to the European Parliament in the 1979 general election: 'Despite the impending European elections, virtually no news from the Common Market or its members impinged on British consciousness during the election.' Not only did the issue of the direct elections fail to raise any interest during the general election, but the elections themselves demonstrated a near total lack of interest on the part of either major party.

However, it is here that there is some evidence of intra-party problems for the Labour Party. Many of the Labour Party candidates contested the Euro-election on an anti-membership platform. This, though, was not a uniform position. The party leadership were what may be termed pragmatically pro-European. That is, they were in favour of membership of this loose organisation of states termed the European Economic Community – with much emphasis upon the 'economic'. There was negligible support for any 'political' developments, such as federalism. However, the party manifesto for the Euro-elections was written by anti-Europeans. The anti-Europeans themselves were in a different position – opposed to a directly elected European Parliament, while at the same time wanting anti-Community representation at Strasbourg (Butler and Marquand, 1981). With such a disjointed position, it is not surprising that Labour fared very badly in the Euro-elections. The overall national turnout was a mere 32.1 per cent, with Labour gaining 33 per cent of that vote for a return of seventeen seats out of the seventy-eight mainland seats that they contested.

At this stage there was very little evidence of any anti-European feeling in the Conservative Party. Indeed, their image was that of being the party of Europe. There was only one prominent Conservative Party member, Neil Marten, who voiced any opposition to the direct elections. He was vigorously supported by Enoch Powell (by then a former Conservative Party member). This made Marten's task of trying to find anti-European support far more difficult, as Powell was anything but popular with the Conservative Party. Hence there was no clear example of a cross-party anti-European Community coalition or alliance. However, the divisions within the Labour Party presaged the subsequent formation and emergence of the Social Democratic Party (SDP). It was in the aftermath of the two election defeats in 1979 that the Labour Party increased the intensity of factional in-fighting.

With the Labour Party looking more and more likely to adopt an anti-Community policy, Bill Rodgers, Shirley Williams and David Owen issued a statement urging Britain to stay in the EC. There was also a reference to the possibility of a new party being formed if the Labour Party decided to adopt a policy of withdrawal. In tandem with this, Roy Jenkins, former deputy leader of the Labour Party in the early 1970s, started to express an interest in rejoining British party politics. He had been President of the European Commission, but this post was to end in January 1981. It was highly unlikely that Jenkins would rejoin the anti-Community Labour Party. At the 1980 Labour Party conference, it was decided that the policy on the European Community would be one of withdrawal. This was updated the following year to withdrawal without a referendum to consult the public. The effect of these two decisions was to reopen the old wounds of the 1979 European elections.

In January 1981, Jenkins joined Rodgers, Williams and Owen to form 'The Gang of Four', and later that month the 'Limehouse Declaration' was issued. This led to the formation of the Social Democratic Party (SDP). The new party appealed to many Labour MPs, particularly on the right of the party. In the final count thirteen Labour MPs defected to the SDP. (The SDP also attracted a solitary Conservative MP, Christopher Brocklebank-Fowler.) With Jenkins as leader, a strong pro-community policy was developed. This attitude was to prove very helpful, along with several others, in the eventual development of the Alliance between the SDP and the Liberal Party.

During the 1983 general election, the issue of the European Community barely raised its head. The Labour Party's manifesto announced that Britain would leave the European Community within the lifetime of the next Parliament. However, this policy proposal barely impinged upon the consciousness of the electorate. The Conservatives did not need to address the issue because Thatcher had stood up to Britain's Community partners and got some of 'our money back'. As a result, the issue of the European Community did not arise during the campaign.

With Neil Kinnock elected as party leader Labour's transformation was set in motion, and the hard-line opposition to the European Community was watered down. By the 1984 direct elections to the European Parliament, although the option of withdrawing from membership was retained, the general attitude towards the Community was somewhat more positive. Such an attitude was aided by the development of a European social policy by, among others, Jacques

Delors. This policy, in conjunction with all other directives from the Community, provided an important component of Labour's strategy to counter Thatcherite market economics.

The campaign itself for the 1984 direct elections, although more inspiring than that of 1979, could still be described as unenthusiastic. In fact, voter turnout barely rose. Both of the major parties attempted to demonstrate that the other was internally divided. The Conservatives attempted to attack Labour's commitment to Europe by 'challenging each Labour candidate individually to declare him/herself as a "pro" or an "anti"' (Hearl, 1986: 245). Labour retaliated by trying to show that many within the Conservative Party disagreed with Thatcher's attitude towards Europe. Despite these 'European' issues, the campaign itself focused largely upon national concerns. Each party sought to demonstrate that the other was divided on the issue. However, neither succeeded.

## 1984–90: two parties; similar policies

Since 1984, Labour's leadership has become increasingly enthusiastic about Community membership. Opposition to the European Community was viewed as being unpopular with the general public, therefore Kinnock gradually reversed the policy as part of his modernisation of the party. (Kinnock himself now a convert to the European cause.) By 1987, party policy had become rather ambiguous, but thereafter the Labour front bench became passionately pro-European. This was followed through the whole party to such an extent that the Labour Party became the most pro-European of either of the major parties (Austin Mitchell, personnel communication).

As the Labour Party became more in favour of the European Community, it appeared that the Conservative Party became less enthused. The Westland affair, which was partially linked to Europe, was the only clear-cut example of any division. The consequence of this incident was that when the debate on the Single European Act commenced a few months later, the Conservative Party, to all intents and purposes, put on a veneer of unity. This was most clearly highlighted by the role of John Biffen, then Leader of the House. An avowed Euro-sceptic, Biffen not only followed the majority in the cabinet in favour of the act, but he also had the unenviable honour of guillotining the debate in the Commons before the three-line whipped division.

During the late 1980s, there were no clear unambiguous internal divisions within either of the two major parties. The only significant differences of opinion appeared to be at the leadership level; and more particularly to do with Margaret Thatcher. Thomas (1992: 13) has commented that during the latter stages of her dominance, the Conservative Party 'reflected a dichotomy between her public pronouncements of scepticism and her government's record of compliance with EC legislation and directives.' Moran (1991: 574) has also noted the ambiguity of Thatcher's position, 'for while she used the language of a confederal Europe, it was her own administration which ensured the passage of the Single European Act through the British Parliament'.

Another example of the Thatcher position was her speech to the College of Europe in Bruges on 20 September 1988. The speech established Thatcher as one of the most ardent Euro-sceptics in the Conservative Party. In comparison with the commitment in the Single European Act to extend majority voting in the Council of Ministers, endorse the single market and embrace the idea of social cohesion (Wallace, 1990), Thatcher's Bruges speech reversed this position. Having rolled back the frontiers of the state within Britain, she did not want them reimposed from Brussels. This, in conjunction with the party's poor performance in the 1989 European Elections, demonstrated just how far Thatcher had removed herself from the mainstream of thought within her own party. It left her open to attacks from a number of former colleagues, including her predecessor Edward Heath. However, the most damning comments of all were to come from Geoffrey Howe, in his resignation speech to the House of Commons on 13 November 1990.

Very simply, Howe put forward the stark realities as to the way in which the Conservative Party was approaching the issue of Europe. At the same time, he rounded on Mrs Thatcher, condemning her role.

> We commit a serious error if we think always in terms of 'surrendering' sovereignty and seek to stand pat for all time on a given deal of proclaiming, as my Right Hon. Friend the Prime Minister did two weeks ago, that we have 'surrendered enough' (*Hansard*, 1990, Vol. 1537: 463).

Howe did not just attack Thatcher's position, but also her style. Once pilloried by Labour's Denis Healey as being like a 'dead sheep', now one of his Conservative Party colleagues, Peter Rost, was quoted as calling him: 'A dead sheep that turned out to be a rottweiler in drag' (*The Times*, 14.11.90). The speech was the final part of the catalyst that eventually led to Thatcher's downfall.

## The Maastricht Summit

With John Major replacing Thatcher as Prime Minister, the party's position on European issues changed significantly. However, during the period from Major becoming Prime Minister until the signing of the Maastricht Treaty, if not until the general election of April 1992, there were very few overt divisions within either of the major parties. It was all part of the build up to the general election, with party discipline stifling internal debate, both public and private. Even by the eve of the Maastricht Summit, very little had been done to open up debate on the issue. Michael White (1991) reported:

> One Cabinet minister, less pro-European than he was before entering office in 1979, surmises: 'If John [Major] can get a deal in Maastricht which can be supported by Norman [Lamont], Michael [Howard] and Peter [Lilley] on one side and Ken Clarke, David Hunt and John Gummer on the other, that will permeate the party. A revolt next spring involving 20–30 rebels is manageable, 60–70 including big names is serious.' (*Guardian*, 6.11.91)

As debate on the Maastricht Summit and its potential consequences intensified, there were calls for a referendum on the issue of membership of a federal Europe. Some even questioned whether Britain should sign the Maastricht Treaty. Such debate was quickly squashed by Conservative Party managers who saw the potential damage of such debate on the election campaign. Beyond this, there were rumours that the Euro-sceptics, Lilley and Howard, would resign from the cabinet if a federalist compromise was struck at Maastricht. Both later denied making such statements. Regardless of the accuracy of this particular report, the issue was potentially very divisive. Both major parties, and more particularly the Euro-factions within each, realised the damage that debate and division would do, not only for their party's electoral chances, but also for Britain's negotiating position at the summit itself.

These postures of party unity continued on Major's return from Maastricht, with 'Conservative MPs of all European persuasions' rushing 'to proclaim the Maastricht summit a negotiating triumph for John Major' (*Guardian*, 12.12.91). Pro-European Conservative MPs commented on Britain leading the European Community, while those of an anti-Maastricht persuasion described the result as successful damage limitation. The Labour Party repeatedly commented on the omission of the Social Chapter, but appeared to give at least tacit approval to the rest of the agreement. Again, on both sides, there was near total unity. Few spoke out against Major's 'triumph' on the Conservative benches. Even Margaret Thatcher remained silent.

The rigid party stances continued from the Maastricht Summit through the general election and beyond. During the campaign itself, there were no keynote speeches by either Major or Kinnock on the issue of the European Community or, more specifically, the Maastricht Treaty. Even the pledges in the manifestoes were suitably vague and non-divisive. In January 1991, Bill Cash was asked by Douglas Hurd, in front of the Conservative Manifesto Committee, to conduct some research into the future of Europe (William Cash, personnel communication). Cash's research was then ignored by the manifesto committee. The issue itself was a potential election loser and was thus to be avoided at almost any cost.

It is really at this stage that the divisions within the two major parties started to become more prominent. At the same time, the networking between parties also started to surface publicly. What is clear is that there are sections within both the Labour and Conservative parties that are opposed to the Maastricht Treaty. At the same time, there are also sections within each party that strongly support the idea of greater economic and monetary union across Europe. Yet these are not two cohesive blocs within each party – although the media tended to simplify it down to such a level. While this simplification can be useful it is important to note potential factionalisation: within each so-called bloc, there are sub-groups which have particular attitudes towards Europe, and Britain's involvement in the future of Europe.

## Positional breakdowns

Norton (1992: 41–2) breaks the Conservative Party down into four fairly clear-cut groups: anti-Europeans; Euro-sceptics; Euro-fanatics; and Euro-agnostics. The anti-Europeans are opposed to membership of the Community. This can be compared with the Euro-sceptics, who are opposed to greater centralisation within the European Community, but at the same time support the idea of an 'economic' European Community. The Euro-fanatics are quite simply the strongest supporters of greater political and economic union. The largest of all the groups are the Euro-agnostics, which quite possibly make up a majority within the Conservative Party. They accept the reality of entry, and generally toe the party line on issues concerned with the European Community.

The problem with Norton's breakdown is that the blocs are still too clear-cut, too stark. The Euro-sceptics, in particular, cover too broad a range of viewpoints on Community membership. Many Euro-sceptics have actually demonstrated that they are pro-European (Cash, 1992a). Therefore, it might be useful to consider an alternative classification, that presented by Ashford (1992). He breaks the Conservative Party down into six areas, some of which overlap to some degree. Firstly, there are the anti-marketeers, who oppose membership. Secondly, there are the Tory Gaullists; this group emphasises the importance of each member state within the Community. There is a commitment to the European Community, but not at the expense of Britain's interests. Similar to this is the position of the Tory modernisers, who also wish to protect Britain's interests within the Community. However, the way they see this as being done is through Britain playing a more active role in the Community. The fourth group is, again, quite similar. Ashford terms them as free market neo-liberals. This group approves of the idea of the Treaty of Rome and its free-market principles and, in return, is willing to sacrifice some sovereignty. Next are the federalists, who form a distinct minority within the Conservative Party. As their label suggests, they are committed to a federal Europe. Finally, there is the largest group of all – the common-sense Europeans. These are the passive supporters of the European Community, and of Britain's membership. Although not committed in any particular direction, this group simply acknowledges that Britain's future lies with the Community, and that Britain should therefore make the most of it.

Ashford also develops a similar typology for the Labour Party (1992). There is the anti-European left, who view the European Community as a capitalistic, militaristic bloc. A similar position is adopted by the nationalistic right of the party, who are also anti-Community because of the loss of sovereignty involved in membership. A third group views the idea of membership as increasing the possibility of achieving socialist goals at a European level, as opposed to simply at a national level. Then there are the committed Europeans. Many of these drifted off to join the Social Democratic Party in the early 1980s. Finally, there is the largest of all the groups: the pragmatic centre. This group, like their Conservative counterparts, accepts membership without enthusiasm, while tending to accept the party line. These are the 'soggy middle' (Austin Mitchell, personal communication) which follow the party leadership. Bryan Gould describes them as 'the ballast in the ship that wobbles' (Gould, personal communication) because if the party leadership changes its perspective, this mass changes position with it.

In theory, at least, it is possible to envisage potential lines of communication and organisation between the different sections of both the Conservative and Labour parties. For example, the anti-marketeers of the Conservative Party might conceivably join forces with the nationalistic right of the Labour Party. Similarly, the Tory Gaullists might also have some linkages with this inter-party line of communication. Within the pro-European branches, Labour's committed Europeans might well develop dialogue with the Tory modernisers or the Tory federalists. Throughout the 1980s, much of this potential would not have been realised: only with the debate over the Maastricht Treaty did the need for such cross-party links develop.

## Internal divisions; cross-party links?

The Danish Referendum of June 1992, and its subsequent 'no' vote, in conjunction with Britain taking over the Presidency of the European

Community in July 1992, brought prominent divisions within both the Conservative and Labour parties to the fore. Within this was also the first clear-cut evidence of there being a cross-party axis against Maastricht. The first and second readings of the Maastricht Bill (formerly called the European Communities (Amendment) Bill) were both passed in May. Debate had been stifled, especially since the Labour Party was not voting against the government on the bill. The result of the Second Reading was 336 ayes to 92 noes. It was with Labour's withdrawal of their tacit support for the bill, shortly afterwards, that opportunities arose for ways and means in which it could be defeated.

The 'no' vote in the Danish referendum brought a series of conflicting demands upon John Major. There were calls for a referendum in Britain on the issue, from both sides of the House of Commons, as well as calls to abandon the Maastricht Treaty. Major resisted these demands, and, with regard to the latter, was supported in this stance by both Neil Kinnock and Paddy Ashdown. Anti-Maastricht campaigners claimed that the Danes had successfully scuppered the Treaty. Both Conservative and Labour party leaderships acknowledged that such a referendum would split each of the major parties and were therefore not willing to take such a risk. Neither party leadership made any attempt to stifle the demands for a referendum within their party. Opponents of the Maastricht Bill argued that a referendum was 'absolutely essential', as there was to be no free vote on the legislation, and no white paper (William Cash, personal communication). The surprise, however, was the eventual U-turn by both. From having refused to even consider a referendum, it was announced that one could not be ruled out (*Guardian*, 17.6.92). Sceptics argued that this U-turn could not be taken seriously.

Thatcher's maiden speech to the House of Lords was the most prominent of these early demands for a referendum. She pointed out that a referendum was needed because all three major parties supported Maastricht, and the electorate had no way of expressing opposition. This received no comment from the front bench of either major party.

The party political positions were restated at the party conferences in September and October 1992. Speakers at each conference tacitly acknowledged that their party was split on the issue of the Maastricht Treaty, and warned of the dire consequences for their own party. Gerald Kaufman informed the Labour Party conference that 'Maastricht is the Tories' problem. We should not turn it into Labour's problem. To push for a referendum is a diversion which would only help the Tories' (*Guardian*, 29.9.92). The tone was set and the eventual outcome was that the Labour Party would not call for a referendum.

The Conservatives did not have such a straightforward problem. Euro-sceptics such as Lord Tebbit paraded their colours for all to see, despite Douglas Hurd's warning that the Conservative Party could break itself over Europe. Rarely at a party conference had the Conservatives appeared so divided.

What both conferences demonstrated was the lengths that party managers would go to in an attempt to prevent inter-party alliances being formed against the Maastricht Treaty. However, these were only partially successful. Those who were opposed to the Maastricht Treaty simply became more firmly entrenched in their opposition, but without any obvious links with the other political parties. The waverers, on the other hand, were given nothing to push them in either direction. Those in favour of the Treaty needed very little for them to maintain that support. The first litmus test of the success of this politicking was to be the paving motion.

The objective of the paving motion was to speed up the ratification of the Maastricht Treaty. However, John Major had stated that the Maastricht Bill would not return to the House of Commons for a third reading until the Danes had changed their minds and voted for the Treaty. This gave Labour the opportunity to oppose the paving motion without damaging their pro-European credentials. Therefore, with the Euro-sceptics within the Conservative Party likely to oppose the motion as well, it appeared that the motion would be defeated. However, one aspect that was favourable for Major was that the Liberal Democrats were likely to support it.

Another favourable aspect was that the actual wording of the paving motion omitted the word 'Maastricht'. The objective here appeared to be to make the wording more attractive to those waverers on the Conservative back benches. There was very little body to the text of the motion. 'It was so bland that even the ultra-sceptic, Bill Cash, conceded that he might be able to vote for it' (*Guardian*, 31.10.92). Paddy Ashdown committed the Liberals to support the motion, while the shadow cabinet agreed to vote against it, and on a three-line whip. Ashdown argued that the motion was to do with the Maastricht Treaty and the European Community, and since the Liberal Democrats were firmly committed to Europe, they could not be reasonably expected to vote against it. The Labour Party argued the opposite, saying it had nothing to do with Europe, but was to do with the Major style of government. In fact many on the front bench of the Labour Party argued that it was almost a vote of confidence in the Major government, despite the fact that it was not a substantive motion. Were the government to be defeated on the motion, it would not be a fatal blow. There would simply be a vote of confidence the following day, in which even the most ardent anti-Europeans would support the government.

The end result of the paving motion was a government majority of six – 319 votes to 313. This was no thanks to the many Conservative MPs who had voted against the motion, but rather a result of Liberal

Democrat support. The consequence of this action earned the Liberal Democrats much derision for being closet Tories.

The Edinburgh Summit in December 1992 was the next opportunity for both pro- and anti-Maastricht campaigners to leave their mark. Yet very little was achieved by the Summit, and there was no evidence of cross-party networking. Agreeable terms of reference were set for a second Danish referendum, and Britain was set a deadline of 30 June 1993 by which the Maastricht Treaty had to be ratified. This was in return for concessions on social and environmental policy.

The upshot of this was that the Conservative Euro-sceptics announced their intentions of fighting the legislation even harder (*Observer*, 13.12.92). Shortly afterwards, the shadow Foreign Secretary, Dr Jack Cunningham, announced that he would not commit the Labour Party to supporting the Third Reading of the Maastricht Bill, while the Liberal Democrats threatened to withhold support unless the Thatcherite faction was brought under control. Thus, with regard to the domestic situation, the Edinburgh Summit changed little. The thirty or so Conservative rebels were going to fight on, leaving Major dependent upon a Labour Party abstention for the Third Reading, or having to concede a referendum to gain Liberal Democrat support. If neither option was forthcoming, the Maastricht Bill looked doomed.

In an attempt to save the situation, Major announced his refusal to accept the 30 June 1993 deadline for ratification of the Maastricht Treaty which had been set at the Edinburgh Summit. This had limited success, with pro-Maastricht Labour MPs urging their leader to help Major ratify the Maastricht legislation. It was an opportunity, they argued, for Smith and the Labour Party to seize the initiative. There was no evidence to suggest any Conservative involvement in this statement from the Labour MPs.

The networking that has gone on between those MPs opposed to the Maastricht Treaty on both sides of the House is difficult to establish with certainty. Support for the treaty has also tended to be more tacit than real. MPs themselves are very cautious as to how they conduct themselves. There have been suggestions that, particularly among the Conservatives, a party has been developing within the party. The anti-Maastricht campaigners have many of the trappings of a political party – for example, party whips. However, there was no clear leader among those in the Commons. Michael Spicer is seen as the chairperson of this group, but it has been in a very low-key role. There appears to be nothing similar in the Labour Party; no chairperson, and no pseudo-party whips.

There is, however, some evidence of inter-party networking. It tends to be spasmodic, suggesting a degree of opportunism on the part of the anti-Maastricht groups. One of the better publicised examples was the Campaign for a British Referendum which marched on Trafalgar Square on 17 January 1993. On the platform were Bill Cash, Teddy Taylor, Richard Shepherd and Teresa Gorman from the Conservative Party; Tony Benn, Peter Shore, Austin Mitchell, Lord Stoddart and Lord Jay from the Labour Party; and the Liberal Democrat Nick Harvey.

There were further cross-party demands for a referendum, taking the form of a far more public appeal. A telephone hotline was developed in early February for people to phone in their support or opposition to Maastricht. The media publicity included Bryan Gould, Peter Shore and Lady Thatcher encouraging people to participate – and preferably to voice their opposition to the Maastricht legislation!

Of course, some of those who called for a referendum did not believe that it would necessarily be successful. Several MPs were of the mind that it would not be fought on a level playing field. The government, in conjunction with the Opposition front bench, would present their line of argument as the voice of reason and moderation – as had happened in the 1975 referendum. Most of those in favour of a referendum have the objective of trying to inform the public. With an apathetic public, it is argued, the government can pass whatever legislation it likes. A referendum would at least kindle some interest, even if it did result in public endorsement of the Maastricht Treaty.

Apart from some very public stunts, then, there has been very little overt networking between the anti-Maastricht campaigners. Part of the problem was that the Labour opponents of the Maastricht Treaty gained very little media coverage, unless they were doing something in tandem with a Conservative counterpart. The consequences for those Labour MPs were not always pleasant. Bryan Gould, for example, received much flak from his own party colleagues for daring to enter a publicity stunt with Margaret Thatcher about the Maastricht hotline (Bryan Gould, personal communication). Others were simply dismissive of the idea, and of Gould's involvement.

Much of the problem is that the sceptics on both sides of the House are not truly cohesive. Those on the Conservative side are split between pro- and anti-referendum supporters, pro- and anti-Europe supporters. For example, John Biffen declined to be involved in the telephone referendum and the Maastricht Referendum Campaign since he is not overly keen on the use of such devices. His position was accepted by those in favour of a referendum, such as Bill Cash, and the campaign against Maastricht continued. They are simply members of the awkward squad: 'It is very much a collection of individualists, and because they're individualists it's absurd to try and have the disciplined party structure for the sceptic group within the Conservative Party' (John Biffen, personal communication).

Despite this, the sceptics do maintain formal links with the other political parties at the House of Commons. In particular, they keep up their relations with the Ulster Unionists. At the same time, the

Conservative sceptics established a link with the Labour whips, to find out how the Labour Party's strategies were developing. This has been of particular importance during the committee stage of the bill, when Labour withdrew its tacit support of the legislation. What is of note is that prominent sceptics play down any links with their Labour counterparts; emphasising coincidence and convenience as to why they occasionally fight together.

Labour anti-Maastricht campaigners tend to espouse a similar line. Links between the major parties are for tactical purposes; there is too much disagreement for a clearer development of the relationship into an alliance or a coalition.

It is simply dissent within the political parties that tends to come to the fore. Within the Conservative Party, the divisions are numerous. In June 1992, Major compelled the Euro-sceptics within the cabinet, Lilley and Portillo, to give statements of loyalty to the government's defence of the Maastricht Treaty (*Guardian*, 11 June 1992). Both obliged immediately. However, there was something of a backlash against each of them. Budgen has described their actions as 'slightly dishonourable' (Nicholas Budgen, personal communication), suggesting that possibly both ministers should reconsider their positions. Other Conservative sceptics tend to follow a similar line, except that they feel neither minister should consider resigning. According to Marlow, it is better for the sceptics' cause if they remain where they are. It is not worth sacrificing their positions if they are not going to achieve anything (Tony Marlow, personal communication).

During the committee stage of the Maastricht Bill's progression through the House of Commons, party divisions became very clear cut. The amount of contact between the different groups was impossible to ascertain. With over 400 amendments tabled, the Speaker and Deputy Speakers of the House had to decide which amendments would be debated. This in itself caused much grievance for pro- and anti-Maastricht campaigners alike. One of the most important amendments was number 27, which contained seven troublesome words. Its objective was to remove Britain's opt-out of the Social Chapter by deleting the words 'with the exception of the United Kingdom'. The consequence of this would be that Britain would become a signatory of the Social Chapter. For the Labour Party, the largest of all stumbling blocks would be removed; for the Conservative Euro-sceptics, it was the golden opportunity to kill off the Maastricht Treaty. However, the *Observer* (14.2.93) reported that 'John Major plans to ratify the Maastricht Treaty without the Social Chapter – however Parliament votes'. The threat here was to ignore the wishes of Parliament because of the bizarre coalition to pass Amendment 27.

In the end, all of this furore appeared to come to nothing when the Deputy Speaker, Michael Morris, refused debate on the amendment.

This led to outcries from the Conservative Euro-sceptics, as well as from the vast majority of the Labour Party, that the will of Parliament was being subverted. However, the government later dropped another vote on Maastricht as it realised that it would lose (*Guardian*, 12.3.93). With the Newbury by-election approaching, the government wanted to incur as little damage as possible. As a consequence, several Labour Party amendments to the legislative proposals were accepted without parliamentary divisions being held. The most significant change was the reversal of the decision on amendment 27. The Speaker of the House, Betty Boothroyd, overturned her deputy's decision and permitted a division on the amendment, renamed amendment 2. The government, fearing the worst, simply accepted the amendment. It was generally acknowledged that the fight would continue in the courts.

What is of note here is the attitude of the anti-Maastricht MPs, from both sides of the House, towards the Social Chapter. Sir Teddy Taylor has pointed out that the chapter is of little importance: 'It is neither a Communist conspiracy, as the Government seems to think, nor a great charter for workers' rights, as Labour imagines. The whole row is bogus' (*Observer*, 25.4.93). Austin Mitchell has expressed similar sentiments, calling the chapter 'Labour's fig leaf', and adding that it is 'a list of good things which we should do but nobody helps us or subsidises us to do them' (Austin Mitchell, personal communication). Therefore, the whole debate on the Social Chapter can be reduced to yet another opportunity for defeating the Maastricht Bill. Norman Tebbit has pointed out:

> The social chapter is not within the main text of the treaty. Britain, therefore, does not have an opt-out clause. There is, however, a protocol to which we agreed allowing the other eleven to use the institutions of the Community to enforce the Charter on each other.
>
> That clearly increases to near certainty that our failure to implement its provisions will sooner or later be ruled illegal by the Court of Justice (Speech, Press Gallery Luncheon 10.2.93).

So with all of these different perspectives being put forward by the anti-Maastricht campaigners in Parliament, it is no wonder that many MPs are simply willing to follow their party's line.

It was with this final decision on the part of the Conservative Party front bench, to accept the final Labour amendment, that the report stage of the Maastricht Treaty was completed. The Third Reading was a formality, with the Labour shadow cabinet agreeing to abstain on the vote. The bill was passed comfortably, and the debate moved on to the House of Lords.

The vote of confidence and the Labour amendment were both won by the government by significant margins, 40 and 38 respectively. Many of the rebels decided to vote with the government on this occasion for the simple reason that it was not so bad to have the Maastricht Treaty when the alternative was a probable general election defeat, followed by the ratification of the Maastricht Treaty with the Social Chapter included in the document.

## Conclusion

The European issue in general and Maastricht in particular are capable of generating numerous specific issues, all contentious. The narrow parameters were set between 1979 and 1993. However, the broader issue of European Community membership has been around in some form or another since the 1950s. Added to this, the consequences of the Maastricht legislation will be around until the turn of the century, if not longer.

The objective of this chapter was an exploration of inter-party networking on the issue of the European Community/Maastricht Treaty. In the early 1980s, the focus was the rift in the Labour Party which helped lead to the formation of the Social Democratic Party. In the early 1990s, it has been the divisions within the Conservative Party that have caught the attention of the media. There is little overt evidence to demonstrate that there have been alliances or coalitions formed between the parties. Rather, what have been highlighted are the divisions within the parties. There was no evidence of a 'party within a party' operating on either side, still less of like-minded factions organising to form new party-like bodies. The most visible structure of opinion was, in fact, one of 'factions within a faction'.

There has been interlinking between those opposed to the Maastricht legislation on both sides of the House. However, it is not some sort of unholy coalition. Their activities are labelled by Euro-fanatics as sheer opportunism and sensationalism, or alternatively as harking back to the days when Britannia ruled the waves. This is to take the issue a little too far. John Biffen has described the Conservative Euro-sceptics as members of the awkward squad. They stand by their beliefs, and have been consistent in doing so.

For Euro-sceptics, working with members of another party is not an impossibility. A mutual interest, and a cross-party amalgam in favour of membership, has left them with little option. Many realised that the cause, if not lost, was not very winnable. Nevertheless, there has been more of this networking over the last year than at almost any other time, on any issue to do with the European Community. However, what has been overlooked is the unholy alliance between both front benches in *support* of the Maastricht Treaty. To supporters of the Treaty, this is not unethical; but for opponents to do something similar results in cries of outrage from both front benches.

The networking both for and against the Maastricht Treaty will continue. Sceptics acknowledge that, for the moment at least, their position has been weakened. However, there are many more battles to be fought. The next may well be the Euro-elections of June 1994. Both sceptics and fanatics from each party are already working together in developing their strategies. Without an overt opposition party standing against the Maastricht Treaty, British democracy requires someone to present an alternative perspective to the government's position. No opposition party is willing to oppose the treaty, nor to give total support to it, as the consequences might well be catastrophic. Therefore, it is left to a small band of individuals who are willing to work together, to oppose the Maastricht Treaty, in the name of democracy.

Finally, a point worth noting is that possibly one should not be searching for a party within a party, but rather for the party being imposed upon another. Conservative MEPs are now members of the European People's Party at the European Parliament. This party is largely made up of Christian Democrats. It is, however, committed to a single proportional electoral system and, eventually, a single political entity within Europe. This would appear to be counter to the stance adopted by John Major and his front bench, if not the vast majority within the Conservative Party. Alternatively, there is some sort of hidden agenda that the front bench of the Conservative Party has adopted. The final option is that joining the European People's Party was an inept move made by some individuals who did not have a full grasp of either the situation or the implications of their actions.

## Acknowledgements

I wish to thank all the Members of the House of Commons and House of Lords who gave up their valuable time to assist me in this chapter. Particularly, I would like to mention: John Biffen, Bryan Gould, William Cash, Austin Mitchell, Tony Marlow, Nicholas Budgen, Lord Tebbit, and Tony Benn. I would also like to thank Clive Gray and Stephen Ingle for their valuable comments.

## References

Ashford, N. (1992), 'The Political Parties' in S. George (ed.) *Britain and the European Community: The Politics of Semi-Detachment*, Oxford, Clarendon Press.

Butler, D. and Marquand, D. (1981), *European Elections and British Politics*, Harlow, Longman.

Butler, D. and Kavanagh, D. (1980), *The British General Election of 1979*, London, Macmillan.

Butler, D. and Kavanagh, D. (1984), *The British General Election of 1983*, London, Macmillan.

Butler, D. and Kavanagh, D. (1992), *The British General Election of 1992*, London, Macmillan.

Cash, W. (1992a), 'Federation and the Political Engineers', *New European* 5.

Cash, W. (1992b), *Europe: The Crunch*, London, Duckworth.

Hearl, D. (1986), 'The United Kingdom' in J. Lodge (ed.) *Direct Elections to the European Parliament, 1984*, London, Macmillan.

Moran, M. (1991), 'Britain and the European Community' in B. Jones (ed.) *Politics UK*, Hemel Hempstead, Philip Allen.

Norton, P. (1992), 'The Conservative Party from Thatcher to Major' in A. King, I. Crewe, D. Denver, K. Newton, P. Norton, D. Sanders and P. Seyd, *Britain at the Polls 1992*, Chatham, Chatham House.

Parliamentary Debates (Hansard) (1990) Sixth Series, volume 180, London, HMSO.

Parliamentary Debates (Hansard) (1993) Sixth Series, volume 227, London, HMSO.

Rosamond, B. (1990), 'Labour and the European Community: Learning to be European?', *Politics*, 10.

Tebbit, Lord (1993), Speech – Press Gallery Luncheon 10 February 1993.

Thomas, S. (1992), 'Assessing MEP Influence on British EC Policy', *Government and Opposition*, 27.

Wallace, H. (1990), 'Britain and Europe' in P. Dunleavy, A. Gamble and G. Peele, *Developments in British Politics 3*, London, Macmillan.

# 5
# Britain's third party

*Stephen Ingle*

The period since 1979 has probably been the most eventful for third parties in Britain since the 1920s, when the struggle between the energetic and growing Labour Party and the divided and declining Liberals for the status of the major anti-Conservative force dominated politics at Westminster. It will be useful before considering post-1979 in some detail if we answer a prior question: if Britain was supposed to be, after New Zealand, the best example of a two-party system, why was there, in 1979, a third party at all?

In 1962 the Liberal Party, which had held on to a declining handful of seats in the 'Celtic fringe' since 1945, won an incredible by-electoral victory in the previously safe suburban Conservative seat of Orpington; in the same year they made sweeping gains in the local government elections. Commentators began to talk of a Liberal 'revival' (Ingle, 1966) and with some justice because the Liberals had all but disappeared as a national party in 1950. The political background to this revival included a jaded and unpopular Conservative government and a Labour opposition whose leader was at odds with the left wing of his party. Research showed that the Liberals were largely supported by protest votes, but not entirely negative ones; the simplest form of protest, after all, is not to vote at all. To some extent at least the Liberals were benefiting from a new kind of voter who did not feel the need to justify his/her voting allegiance by reference to class. The British middle class had been growing steadily if unspectacularly at the expense of the working class over a long period and this process accelerated during the 1950s as a result of better secondary education[1] and better conditions of life generally for the urban working class. When Labour had suffered a third consecutive electoral defeat in 1959, Gaitskell had analysed the political implications of these trends, finding clear signs of 'a breaking up of the traditional political loyalties' (Abrams, 1961). It was clear at the time, and made clearer by subsequent events, that these voters were not lost for ever, but were no longer Labour's for the asking (Marsden and Jackson, 1962). It was chiefly this new kind of voter, 'Orpington Man', who had decided to vote for the Liberal Party, and the party itself, unencumbered by traditional class images or by links with either of the great battalions of industry, seemed to be an appropriate vehicle for his aspirations.

The Liberal revival, however, was to prove short-lived and did not re-emerge until the Conservatives were in office again, in 1970. When the government became unpopular and the Labour opposition appeared ineffectual, the Liberals enjoyed another surge of support and won several notable by-elections. Again, however, the Liberal revival was undermined by a Labour victory in the ensuring general election. So the pattern indicates that in periods of unpopular Conservative government, disunity among Labour ranks is punished by disillusioned supporters of both parties voting for what they see to be a middle-of-the-road party, but that when Labour heals (or hides) its wounds a sufficient number return to the camps to allow the two-party struggle to continue at the next general election. To this must be added the rider that the numbers who do not return to camp continued to grow and, more generally, tribal allegiances to decline.

Another factor worth mentioning before we approach the 1980s is the considerable debate during the early 1960s about the possible formation of a 'Lib–Lab' pact. Such a pact was, of course, impossible given Labour's commitment to nationalisation but that it was discussed at least by some on the right of the Labour party is significant (Wyatt, 1962; Marquand, 1962). For their part the Liberals (or at least their leader) were committed to a realignment left-of-centre. As early as 1959, Liberal leader Jo Grimond looked forward to the creation of a strong non-socialist left-of-centre party and added significantly that he 'didn't give a tinker's cuss what such a party shall be called'. The quest for a realignment among centrists and left-of-centrists, nurtured periodically on a diet of Tory failure in office and Labour disunity, was to remain a theme for the following thirty-three years. Hence Britain's third party.

In some respects the 1979 election seemed to have reversed the trends of dealignment, in that the Conservatives were elected on a 7 per cent swing, the highest in post-war history. Yet Butler and Kavanagh show that the process of dealignment had not been reversed. There had been a swing of 11.5 per cent of manual workers and 9 per cent unskilled workers to the Conservatives. By 1979 Labour held only 45 per cent of the working-class vote and indeed only half of the trade union vote; overall it attracted only 36.9 per cent of votes cast, its lowest since 1931. Moreover, the victorious Conservative Party's share was only average. The Liberals, meanwhile, secured a respectable if unspectacular 15.2 per cent (Butler and Kavanagh, 1980). Behind the apparent return to 'business as usual' for the two-party system in 1979, then, lay the reality of a continued and more general decline. The break-up of old allegiances which Gaitskell had noticed twenty years before had not been reversed.

Moreover, and underlining another fear of Gaitskell's, the Labour party came increasingly under the influence of the left wing. After the 1979 election, the left felt bitterly thwarted, and the coming to power of a right-wing Conservative administration bent upon radically restructuring the balance of power in the British economy presented the left with an opportunity to 'democratise' the party structure and challenge the right-wing leadership. At the 1980 conference decisions were taken to explore ways to relieve the parliamentary leadership of control of the manifesto, to require all MPs to seek reselection and to broaden substantially the base from which the party leader was to be elected. Moreover, on Callaghan's resignation as leader the ensuing election in November 1980 brought defeat for the acknowledged leader of the right, Denis Healey, and victory for Michael Foot, a man with leftist views on major issues such as unilateralism and the EEC. Worse followed when Tony Benn made it known that he intended to challenge Healey for the deputy leadership. All proved too much for three members of the previous Labour government, Shirley Williams, David Owen, and William Rodgers, who together with another ex-Labour cabinet minister, Roy Jenkins, issued the Limehouse Declaration (25 January 1981) giving notice of their intention of leaving the Labour Party. Within two months the Social Democratic Party (SDP) had been formed.

What was the SDP and what did it hope to achieve? The party's first leader, Roy Jenkins, in the Dimbleby Lecture of 1979, provided the clearest answer to these questions. He argued that the two great parties were coalitions but that no real community of interests existed within them any longer. He argued for the building up, through a proportional electoral system, of 'living' coalitions. He dismissed the counter argument that such coalitions could not provide the effective and coherent government which the first-past-the-post system (however unfairly) tended to produce: 'Do we really believe that we have been more effectively and coherently governed over the past two decades than have the Germans . . .?' He spoke of the Labour left as a small group of activists with the power of political life or death over an MP elected by twenty to thirty thousand voters. He suggested prophetically that Labour's NEC would prepare for the next election 'a totally different sort of manifesto, one on which the majority of those now elected by the people would not wish to fight . . .'. Jenkins argued that Britain suffered from an inability to adapt consistently, and too great a capacity to change inconsistently. Britain needed to harness the 'innovating stimulus of the free market' and yet avoid the brutality of 'untrammelled distribution of rewards' or 'indifference to unemployment'. Jenkins clearly saw a role for state intervention, but his social democratic state would know its place. It was important, he continued, to devolve decision making, giving parents a voice in the school system, patients a voice in the health system, residents a voice in neighbourhood councils and so on. Social Democrats would be unequivocally committed to ending the class system but had no wish to replace it with a brash meritocracy. Above all, Jenkins believed it to be necessary somehow to involve in politics at a variety of levels the considerable and growing number of people presently alienated from the business of government.

For the Liberals the sudden appearance and almost meteoric rise of the SDP must have seemed at best a mixed blessing. A competitor in the centre ground, especially one that seemed capable of capturing the support of so many so quickly, could scarcely have been seen as an advantage. For the Liberals the choice was to stand by and applaud the achievements of a group who were (Liberals believed) capitalising on investments made by Liberals over the years, to compete with the group and try to 'strangle it at birth' (Cyril Smith's original option) or to make overtures to the SDP to join in a formal association. That they chose the latter, and that they managed to dominate and not be dominated by the SDP in the ensuing alliance, owes much to the vision and political skills of David Steel. This point wants emphasising: in 1981 the SDP posed a graver threat to the continued success of the Liberals than had either of the major parties for more than a decade. Yet Steel's game plan turned out to be a failure. For the greatest advantage to the Liberals of forming an Alliance was to capitalise on the SDP's capacity, clearly demonstrated by Jenkin's near-miss in the Warrington by-election of 1981, to do what the Liberals in their previous revivals had seldom managed to do: win over Labour voters in numbers. An alliance between the Liberals and a separate SDP could enable Steel, or so he thought, to fulfil the vision he had inherited from his mentor and former party leader Jo Grimond: a non-socialist realignment of the centre-left. No wonder the Liberals supported the idea of alliance.

The Alliance was launched on 16 June 1981; to be more accurate, the 'basis for a working alliance' was officially established on that day, for it had to be accepted formally by both parties at their autumn gatherings. The embryo alliance set out its objectives in a short document entitled *A Fresh Start for Britain*. In order to flesh out their joint approach into policy commitments the would-be allies planned to establish joint commissions on major areas of policy – for example, on constitutional reform, on employment and industrial recovery. The SDP broke away from Labour because it believed that the Labour Party had deserted the majority of non-ideological but progressive-minded voters. It found much in common with the Liberals in that both sought to emphasise the importance of maximising citizen participation and decentralising decision making. Like the Liberals, the SDP sought to 'break the mould' of British politics. And between 1981 and 1983 it appeared that they might succeed. Who would have thought that the two Alliance partners would have been able to divide 650 parliamentary seats with so few disagreements? (The successful outcome of that enterprise has tended to disguise its awesome difficulty.) Who would have thought that the parties could have agreed on a joint manifesto for an election only two years after the formation of the Alliance? Those were remarkable – if not generally remarked upon – developments. On the other hand, the massive early gains which the Alliance made in terms of declared support in opinion polls – which put them ahead of the major parties – subsided. Yet the Alliance became a definite part of the political landscape for most voters. But did it have something distinctive to say?

The Liberals would claim to have developed a distinctive ideology and approach to politics long before, and the SDP tended to align itself to this ideology; after all, like the Liberals, it claimed to be a non-socialist, left-of-centre party. What was Liberal ideology? Liberals claimed to believe in a society in which the individual was able to *participate* to a greater extent than at present in the decisions which shaped his or her own life. The attempt to build such a society was an essentially radical exercise, though it also represented one of the basic tenets of traditional liberal faith: man's rationality. The objective of liberalism, then, for the modern Liberal was the creation of opportunities for men and women to become self-directing responsible persons.

Liberals had never been happy with the label of 'centrists', or 'middle-of-the-roaders'. 'By any strict language Liberals are the true Left, the real progressives', said Elliot Dodds (Dodds, 1959). There are only two senses in which the Liberals (and their SDP allies) may be said to have been unequivocally centrist: first, their attitude to the 'public' versus 'private' debate was chiefly pragmatic and, second, they enjoyed substantial support from the middle classes. Liberals supported the nationalisation of coal and opposed that of steel, they supported the sale of council houses in some areas and opposed it in others. As for middle-class support, it was after all chiefly though by no means entirely this sector which currently sought to participate, that is, to shape the decisions affecting society. All the same, the involvement of many more citizens in the shaping of decisions, the extension downwards and outwards of decision-making machinery along the lines and for the reasons advocated by J.S. Mill, were hardly middle-of-the-road policies.

Participation then, was the carat of modern liberal and (by extension) Alliance politics (Ingle, 1987) and it stood in contradistinction to the bureaucratic elitism of socialism and the social elitism of the major strands of Conservatism. But equally important to the understanding of modern Alliance belief was the context of participation. At the grass-roots level the context was provided by the community. Community politics was both a means and an end. It was a means of creating a less unequal society superior to public ownership, and it was an end in so far as giving as many citizens as possible a say in the decisions affecting their lives was a goal of traditional liberalism. Participation was a basic ingredient of the policy of decentralising government, of giving more not fewer powers to democratically elected local authorities, of inserting a regional tier into the British system of government which required devolving executive powers to assemblies in Scotland and Wales. Again these were hardly middle-of-the-road policies: they would radically shift the balance of power in Britain away from London.

More important to Alliance strategy, though, was the parliamentary and electoral context of participation politics, for both Alliance parties were firmly committed to electoral reform. The constitutional impact of electoral reform, certainly in the long term, could be considerable. Not only would it be likely to produce coalition or minority government but as a direct concomitant would result in the weakening of party influence, with voting in the House less easily controlled by the whips and with back-benchers consequently seeing their parliamentary careers more in terms of active membership of committees than of party loyalty. Parliament would become a much more important body and its select committee system far more competent, in terms of scrutinising government policy and eventually of actually making policy. With a weakened party system and a strengthened committee system the pressure for more open government would be much more difficult to resist and a change in the nature of the relationship between back-benchers and the civil service might well have ensued, thus affording better protection for the individual citizen (another traditional liberal aim). In short, given time, a proportionately representative House of Commons could revolutionise British parliamentary practice. This prospect may be seen as enticing or terrifying but it cannot, surely, be considered middle-of-the-road. So much for the Alliance's ideology.

Before moving on to consider the Alliance's performance in its first election (1983) it is necessary to say just a word about its record in Parliament. How well did the parties hold together? Figures for their first Parliament show that of 283 important divisions in the House of Commons between 1981 and 1983, all Liberal and SDP members voted the same way in 227. On no occasion did the parties oppose each other. The Alliance was to secure a higher parliamentary profile after 1985 when the leader of the Liberal Party, by formal arrangement, was given the right to choose the topic for debate in three of the twenty 'opposition days'. The Liberals also obtained the right to raise their own amendments to the Queen's speech at the opening of each parliamentary session. From its early days there were around fifty Alliance peers, most of them hereditary Liberals. The number of regular attenders was much smaller, however, although they did have the support of an administrative secretary and a research assistant (Baldwin, 1985).

The 1983 general election was, predictably, both a triumph and a disaster for the Alliance: a triumph because of the 7.8 million votes gained (compared with 4.3 for the Liberals in 1979), and because in more than half the seats contested the Alliance candidate came in second (only eleven deposits lost compared to Labour's 119); a disaster because the Alliance won only twenty-three seats, because of the twenty-six SDP Members who stood after defecting from Labour (one from the Conservatives) only four survived. In general terms the Alliance suffered from what was referred to as the 'plateau effect'; its share of the vote increased least where it was already strong, probably because the Labour vote had already been squeezed dry. It was most certainly for this reason that so few of the apparently most winnable seats actually fell to the Alliance.[2]

There could be no disguising the deep disappointment of the Alliance leadership; indeed David Steel took a year's 'sabbatical' leave from active politics. In the period 1983–87 the Alliance slipped back in the opinion polls, lost much of its self-confidence, and yet benefited from the high profile of new SDP leader David Owen. When it entered the general election of 1987 its expectations were far less optimistic than in 1983. It had become an established force in British politics but had not made a breakthrough; conversely it had surrendered the substantial advantage of being a novelty. In addition the party had come to realise that even if it managed to improve upon its 1983 performance at the next election, the net result of its efforts would be to establish Mr Kinnock in 10 Downing Street. (In fact a strong Alliance performance was thought to be Mr Kinnock's only chance of electoral victory.) If Labour were to make a success of government then the Alliance's prospect of major party status, that of eating into the Labour vote, would have gone. In other words, short-term success would imply longer-term failure. On the other hand, what if the Alliance held the balance of power in the next Parliament? Whom would it support? Soundings on the issue among its supporters gave no encouragement to Alliance leaders: approximately one-third were pro-Labour and strongly anti-Conservative, approximately one-third were pro-Conservative and strongly anti-Labour and approximately one-third were against making an arrangement with either party. In other words, whatever course Alliance leaders opted for, they would be opposed by two-thirds of their members. All that can be said is that for the Alliance actually to have to confront this, its most fundamental problem, would imply that it had solved all of the others; to put things mildly, in 1987 this was a very long way off. Indeed, it still was in 1993.

The Alliance election campaign of 1987 was a comparative failure; indeed managers at Alliance headquarters were convinced from the beginning that no breakthrough would be achieved and saw the campaign largely as an exercise in damage limitation. In securing 23 per cent of votes cast and returning twenty-two MPs, the Alliance did less well than in 1983. More significant than the results, though, was the obvious failure of the 'dual leadership' strategy. After all, the Alliance claimed to be offering the voters something new – partnership. And partnership proved to be a hostage which fortune seized with both hands. Pictured by the media as Tweedledum and Tweedledee, the two leaders were clearly at odds during the campaign – for example, on whether they would be prepared to form a coalition with the Conservatives under Mrs Thatcher – and, like those two young gentlemen, they agreed immediately after the campaign to 'have a battle'.

Within a week of Mrs Thatcher's third successive electoral victory David Steel, the leader of the Liberal party, publicly called for a merger between his own party and its Alliance partner. This signalled the end of the Alliance which Steel had helped to forge amidst such euphoria in 1981. Although for Steel merger could be seen as a logical end to the developments initiated in 1981, he could have had no illusions that his opposite number, David Owen, would feel the same way. For that matter Owen could have had no illusions that his own preferred option, of retaining the parties' separate identities but continuing to work together, would receive any support from the Liberal leader or his senior colleagues. The end of the Alliance then was inevitable and acrimony likely; under discussion was what, if anything, should take its place. Why did Steel choose to plunge the Alliance into such bitter controversy?

By 1987 two developments had begun to reshape the Alliance. At ground level most, though not all, Liberal and SDP local groups were cooperating fully and acting more or less as a united party. Joint open selection of candidates took place in seventy-eight constituencies and in a further sixty allocated to the SDP, Liberals were permitted to share in the selection process. At the leadership level precisely the opposite was happening. Owen's position was becoming increasingly clear; after a brief period when he appeared to be moving towards reluctant acceptance of some form of merger he reverted to his former hostility and firmly opposed the growing local cooperation as 'merger by the back door'.

Owen's coolness towards the Liberals needs some explanation. He had himself moved perceptibly from the centre-left to the centre-right. Butler and Kavanagh argue (1986: 75): '. . . he appeared more out of sympathy with Labour than most Liberal MPs and . . . had moved further away from Labour than other members of the SDP's founding Gang of Four'. He was not alone in distancing himself from Labour; one of his former Labour and SDP MP colleagues, John Horam, announced his 'conversion' to Conservatism in 1987 whilst another, Neville Sandelson, urged Alliance voters to vote Conservative in that election. Owen's position, though, was much more crucial. Through his domination of the SDP's coordinating committee he was able to keep a rein on party policy making and where his writ did not run, for example in the joint Liberal–SDP policy commissions, he was able to use his personal authority to undermine the credibility of those bodies. (Thus he had belittled the report of the 1986 commission on defence as 'unacceptable fudge and mudge'.) At the parliamentary level Owen was also responsible for delaying the appointment of joint Alliance policy spokespersons virtually until the end of the Parliament.

A second aspect was Owen's growing hostility towards the Liberal's policy-making structure. The Liberal rank-and-file (though not the leaders) were mostly proud of what they saw as their 'bottom-up' procedures. Their administrative machine had, in accordance with party principles, been decentralised in 1983 (Ingle, 1987); to Owen the reforms only reinforced the Liberal's tendency to anarchy. He despaired of Steel's being able to make stick any agreements between the two of them. The defeat of the Liberal Executive's defence resolution at the 1986 conference, when it appeared that everybody who happened to be present (including party stall-minders) might vote, seemed to bear out Owen's worst fears.

A third aspect of Owen's coolness was more personal. He knew that in any long-term arrangement between the partners after the general election there would be moves towards a unified leadership. The leader would, in natural justice, be the head of the larger of the parliamentary parties and that was certain to be David Steel.

Fourth and finally, Owen had great misgivings about a number of Liberal policy stances (not just on defence) though, for obvious reasons, he did not articulate them until the merger debate. Owen chose to remind colleagues that from the earliest days his preferred strategy had been for an electoral pact with the Liberals with one prime objective: securing electoral reform. Thereafter there would be no need for the parties to merge. The move towards a structured relationship with the Liberals came from Owen's colleagues who, he believed, saw the SDP, from its very inception, as merely a stepping-stone to merger.

From the Liberal perspective there was probably much in Owen's criticisms that Steel and those close to him would have accepted, but they would still have found Owen's rightwards ideological shift anathema. Moreover, the shift was clearly beginning to have ramifications in terms of SDP support. Rosie Barnes's victory in the Greenwich by-election in 1987, for example, was based in good part on the support of the academic and professional middle class. By the time of the general election of that year, far from bringing the Alliance cause the great additional advantage of disenchanted working-class ex-Labour voters, the SDP could be characterised as a predominantly middle-class Home Counties party with 'more members in Camden than in all of Yorkshire' (Butler and Kavanagh, 1988: 78).

If the SDP anti-merger group was dominated by Owen, others shared his misgivings. The only Conservative MP to defect to the SDP had been Christopher Brocklebank-Fowler. The setting up of the new party, he wrote, 'excited all of us who made such personal sacrifices to join the SDP. None of us would have done the same to join the Liberals' (*The Independent*, 19.6.87). He believed that allying with the Liberals had only obscured the new party's message and identity. 'The SDP was not founded to promote the Liberal party . . . nor indeed was it intended to be an anvil on which the Liberal party's outdated constitution should be refashioned.' To the observer and indeed to the voter, however, there seemed much that was common to both Liberal and Social Democratic traditions. This view was shared by many Social Democrats such as ex-Labour MP David Marquand, who saw nothing incompatible between the two traditions. He was forced to wonder, consequently, what distinctive policies an independent SDP would promote and concluded: 'So what will an Owenite splinter party stand for' . . . the answer is embarrassingly simple. Owen' (Ingle, 1988: 47–51).

There were Liberal opponents of merger, though they were relatively few. They felt themselves to be representatives of the north of England radical Liberal tradition nurtured in the nonconformist textile belt, and were opposed to what they saw to be a watering down of the party's traditional radicalism. 'We have no hesitation' wrote one, 'in stating that the only possible basis for a merged party is as a Liberal party whatever it is called' (Ingle, 1987: 189).

Turning now to more general arguments concerning 'the Alliance's' role in the future of British party politics, David Marquand, writing in *The Independent* (16.7.87) posed three questions: could the Labour Party capture the Alliance vote; could the parties of the Alliance conceivably overtake Labour as the main opponents of the Conservatives; and could the Alliance parties make common cause with Labour? In addressing these questions Marquand pointed out that the Alliance vote had become a definable constituency yet not automatically the Alliance's. Labour could win that constituency but only by breaking with the unions and abandoning state socialism – in other words, by ceasing to be the Labour Party. As for the Alliance overtaking Labour, this seemed an even more remote possibility. The inhabitants of the forlorn council estates and bedraggled terraces had an almost instinctive loyalty to Labour. So if Thatcherite Conservatism was successfully to be opposed, Marquand concluded, there would have to be an understanding between Labour and the Alliance parties as a permanent feature of the political system. Marquand indicated that this would only be possible if the Alliance parties merged rather than remain as Grimond's 'panto-mime animal with two heads and two humps'.

It was between these competing views that the membership of both parties had to decide. In a postal ballot in which 78 per cent of the membership participated, the SDP decided to negotiate for merger by 57 per cent to 43 per cent. Later, at their annual conference at Harrogate, the Liberals, too, decided on negotiations by 998 votes to 21. David

Owen resigned as SDP leader; Robert Maclennan, erstwhile opponent of merger, now put himself forward as SDP leader on a very cautious pro-merger platform. The game was on.

Before the year was out the storm clouds began to break. First, over the issue of the new party's name. An inordinately lengthy and often acrimonious debate eventually led to the compromise proposal of the Union of Liberals and Social Democrats. This disagreement was nothing compared with the howls of anguish from nearly all Liberals and most Social Democrats which greeted the leaders' joint policy declaration in January 1988. Even hardened commentators were incredulous at a document which contained proposals for the introduction of VAT on children's clothing and the abolition of mortgage tax relief. One can say no more of the document than this; it effectively signalled the demise of both party leaders. A fresh team of negotiators was assembled and a new document, less radical in every sense, was prepared. It was considered to be sufficiently acceptable to be put, together with a new constitution, to both parties for a decision. Finally, almost nine months after the election, the Liberal and Social Democratic parties merged to form the Social and Liberal Democrats. The journey appeared finally to have been successfully accomplished, but many bodies littered the way.

The Owenite SDP lived on, however, to cause considerable confusion in the public mind and to split the already diminished third-party vote. In July 1988, for example, the parties contested a by-election at Kensington. The Conservatives held the seat with a greatly reduced majority but the SLD secured a mere 10.8 per cent of the votes and finished a poor third. The SDP only narrowly avoided losing its deposit. Even combined, the votes of both parties were fewer than had been obtained by the Liberals or the Alliance at any by-election outside Scotland since 1979. Moreover, when NOP asked a sample of Kensington voters whether they could name the new party only 37 per cent were correct. Even among those who had voted SLD as many as 40 per cent either could not remember the party's name or got it wrong.

In the meantime the SLD had become engaged in a leadership contest. A leadership election is at best a double-edged weapon: it can keep a party in the public eye but its very nature is divisive; there has to be something to choose between. In this case, the campaign unfolded, it became clear that Beith was portraying himself as the custodian of the radical Liberal tradition, prepared if necessary to come to some mutually beneficial accommodation with Labour, whereas Ashdown was more pragmatic, more interested in modernising the party, and strategically committed to replacing Labour. When the result was declared it was seen that Beith had been decisively beaten. He nevertheless pledged his unqualified support for the new leader.

What of the SDP? When Owen resigned as party leader he was gambling on the failure of merger negotiations. His hand was forced by a genuine belief that the Liberals would swallow his party and nullify the distinctive contribution which he believed the SDP had to make to the development of British politics. Owen's decision was a great blow for he was, in the public's mind, the Alliance's greatest single asset. Owen's gamble failed; the negotiations succeeded and created a party which is not simply the Liberal Party writ large. These were dramatic, indeed traumatic, times. Not only did the merger result in the loss of David Owen, but the parties which had claimed to represent a new approach to politics based upon cooperation were now divided by bitterness and recrimination and intent upon internecine war to the death, and their image was tarnished beyond recognition.

The nadir of the Liberal Democrats' (having now changed their name from the Social and Liberal Democrats) fortunes came in the European parliamentary elections of 1989, when the party secured only 6 per cent of the popular vote, less than half the Green Party vote. This public humiliation was partly the consequence of a less well-known but more deep-seated problem: the party was back in financial crisis with a projected year-end deficit of £600,000 and no credible plan to restore the deficit to historical proportions. Morale could hardly have been lower in 1990 (which was thought to be the pre-election year) with the party still at 6 per cent in the polls in March.

Ashdown took over the party when it was 'confused, demoralised, starved of money and in the grip of a deep identity crisis' (*The Independent*, 7.9.91). He presided over not only a remarkable transformation of the party's public image – and indeed of its self-image – but also over a palpably significant improvement in the party's policy-making machinery, with tangible and immediate benefits for the subsequent shaping of strategy. Party morale was further boosted by the dramatic by-election victories of Eastbourne and Ribble Valley.[3] Almost incredibly at the beginning of 1991 the deficit was back to historic proportions (£250,000) and an election fund of £500,000 had additionally been raised. In fact, when the election eventually came the party had a budget at its disposal of £1.96 million, raised almost entirely by the membership.[4]

The next election was looming and it became clear that Ashdown was to be played as a trump card. All Liberal Democrat research showed that he enjoyed a remarkably favourable image with their target voters, and indeed with the general public. Though Ashdown himself railed against the cult of personality he recognised his own worth to the party. The Gulf War had enabled him to exhibit the benefits of military experience (and indeed sound political judgement). 'By the end of it', said *The Independent* (17.9.91) 'he had succeeded in adding a gravitas to his political image that went beyond his political weight.'

Liberal Democrat strategy in 1992 was constructed around the 'Big Idea' of constitutional reform. The issue was held to be a vote winner.

On the other hand, an NOP survey on electoral reform in January showed that only 51 per cent were in favour of PR (*The Independent*, 18.1.92). It was a mistake, surely, for the Liberal Democrats to convince themselves that constitutional reform, especially proportional representation, was the Big Idea that set the works canteens ablaze or, for that matter, the staffroom of the local comprehensive school. Moreover, the issue of hung parliaments and potential coalitions came more and more to dominate the later stages of the campaign, and not in such a way as to give the Liberal Democrats any advantage.

Charter 88 had decided there would be a Democracy Day during the campaign, and it sponsored debates in many major cities. All three parties responded. In a sense this was what the Liberal Democrats, the Alliance and the Liberals had always wanted: that their own favoured policy should become a central electoral issue. The Liberal Democrats and Labour took the opportunity to express their support for the main planks of Charter's electoral policy, the former more wholeheartedly. The Conservatives, decisively, saw this as an opportunity not only to pin their own flag of uncompromising opposition to PR and to Scottish devolution very firmly to the mast but also to link Labour and the Liberal Democrats almost indissolubly. Major was adamant: 'So I don't favour PR, I wouldn't introduce PR and there are no circumstances in which I would introduce PR. I hope that is clear.' It was.[5] What became equally clear and substantially more damaging was his identification of the Liberal Democrats as 'Labour's Trojan horse'. Suddenly the entire platform of constitutional reform, in all its complexity, had been reduced to an electoral gimmick for getting Mr Kinnock into Downing Street. So much for over thirty years of policy promotion.

There were other ways in which the constitutional issue backfired for the Liberal Democrats. The two issues of PR and Scottish devolution came into conflict when Labour hinted that in its first Queen's Speech it would include legislation to set up a Parliament in Edinburgh but not introduce PR. Would Liberal Democrats vote against such a speech in the event of a hung parliament? Ashdown had been consistently clear on this: no deal without PR. Malcolm Bruce, leader of the Scottish Liberal Democrats, Sir David Steel and others were equally clearly of a different mind. Would the party be whipped to vote against a legislative programme including devolution, increased spending on education, a stronger commitment to Europe and a Freedom of Information Act simply because Labour's Plant committee on electoral reform was still deliberating? What would have happened to Scottish Liberal Democrats in a second election brought about by their having voted down a programme including a parliament for Scotland? In fact the party in Scotland had, like Labour, come dangerously close to espousing independence and it is by no means clear that the national party would have survived such a dispute.

And what of Banquo's ghost, a hung parliament? Ashdown's repeated position was that his party would respect the democratic wish of the British people, and try to reach an accommodation with the larger of the two major parties in the event of an indecisive election. The perennial problem of the Liberal Democrats' divided support on this issue was as perplexing as ever. A poll in February 1992 indicated that the traditional divisions were as clearly marked as ever: 60 per cent of 'Lib Dem' supporters would be opposed to a deal with either party, with 31 per cent opposed to pacts or coalitions in principle and the remainder split almost equally between those opposed to a pact with the Conservatives and those opposed to a pact with Labour (BBC *Panorama*, 3.2.92). But as Hugo Young made clear, a pact with the Conservatives was not feasible. Major's opposition to constitutional reform was unambiguous and so the Scottish Liberal Democrats would find an alliance with the Conservatives insupportable. A hung parliament represented both the Liberal Democrats' best opportunity and greatest threat. It offered, in Hugo Young's words, the prospect of a deal with Labour providing a 'post-socialist, post-Thatcherite radical government achieved in one adventurous vault, from the springboard of a public desire for stability as evidenced in an inclusive election result' (*Guardian*, 6.2.92). It also posed the threat of imminent break-up of the party if it became too closely associated with Labour. The party needed to avoid discussion of hung parliaments to maximise its vote and yet 'how to use their modest manpower in a variety of situations has to be their only abiding interest'.

David Marquand described the 1992 election as representing the triumph of fear over hope. For the Liberal Democrats twenty seats were held or won on a national vote of six million: no breakthrough, no balance of power. 'After much agonized dithering', Marquand wrote, 'a bemused and troubled nation decided, at the last moment, to cling to the nurse' (*Guardian*, 11.4.92). He described the party as a left-of-centre party masquerading as a centre party but it might be better described as a party with a preponderance of left-of-centre policies supported preponderantly by centre and right-of-centre voters. Putting the paradox in these terms rather than Marquand's helps to explain why it was simply not possible for the Liberal Democrats to do what Marquand wanted: to campaign openly 'as part of a broad-based progressive coalition, essentially social-democratic in inspiration'. The Liberal Democrats may indeed rely upon Labour's support for any realistic prospect of power; but they rely on Conservative support (defecting Conservatives) for the electoral success upon which they could hope to bargain with Labour about power.

There is a certain justice in Marquand's characterisation. But there is surely another observation to be argued. For the average voter an election represents the opportunity to pass judgement on the performance (chiefly economic) of a government and more especially on the quality of its leadership. If the government or its leaders are seen to have failed then they will usually be replaced. In a real sense there had been an election in 1990 when the Thatcher government was deemed to have failed and it was, to all intents and purposes, replaced. In their way the events of that autumn had proved just as exciting and as uncertain as a general election, and equally cathartic. The pressure for change, building up to a powerful head towards the end of 1990, had succeeded in toppling a government; thereafter it had been dissipated. For the Liberal Democrats, as ever, the necessary and, to be somewhat cynical, probably sufficient condition for electoral advance was what it had always been: a jaded and unpopular Conservative government and a divided Labour opposition. No campaign strategy, however professionally executed, could disguise the fact that in 1992 they were deprived of both.

Just over a decade after the formation of the Alliance, the Liberal Democrats were in a far stronger position than the Liberals had been in 1979, with twenty MPs and not far short of 20 per cent of the vote, with a strong record of by-electoral victories, with electoral reform (their most important and distinctive policy) much further up the political agenda, with a strong leadership and organisation, a paid-up membership of over 100,000 and stable finances, and with over 3,500 local councillors. And yet the Alliance had promised so much more. The story of the Alliance tells of achievements against the odds; of the successful division of parliamentary seats (thought by most commentators at the time to be impossible) not once but twice, of electoral support measured at above 40 per cent for more than six months, of a combined membership of over 200,000, of pushing Labour close for second place in a general election (1983) in terms of votes won. Ultimately though the story is one of failure: failure actually to break through in 1983 and failure of the two parties to merge without serious fracture after the general election of 1987. Failure to 'break the mould'.

The first-past-the-post system thwarts the Liberal Democrats today as effectively as it always thwarted the Liberals. Within the constraints that it imposes, the Liberals and their allies have in fact done remarkably well. Indeed perhaps their electoral successes have been even greater than is acknowledged, for the successes of the Alliance have surely been partly instrumental in Labour's remarkable reforms. If Jo Grimond's original intention, back in 1959, was to create a non-socialist radical alternative to the Conservative Party, then perhaps he and his colleagues were finally successful. He did not, we remember, give a tinker's cuss what such a party should be called: perhaps it is called the Labour Party. Now for Labour to achieve electoral victory, an understanding, an electoral agreement, with the Liberal Democrats seems essential. For this to be acceptable to the majority of voters

Labour's rehabilitation as a radical, non-socialist party would have to be complete and be generally perceived to be complete. Logically, if that were the case, there would be no need of a Liberal Democratic Party. Voting, however, is not the most logical of activities and it remains true that Labour's and the Liberal Democrats' best chance of achieving power is for the former to encourage about fifty selected constituency parties not to fight the next election. The realignment of the centre-left has already progressed substantially; it might yet be completed; in that event Britain might yet be governed by a Lib–Lab coalition.

## Notes

1. The *Crowther Report* (1959), London, HMSO, indicated that the children of skilled manual, semi-skilled and unskilled workers formed 51 per cent of the grammar school population of England and Wales.
2. There were thirty-one seats in which the Liberals did particularly well in 1979. Only three were allocated to the SDP.
3. At Eastbourne on 18 October a Conservative majority over the Liberal/Alliance candidate of 17,000 was overturned and the Liberal Democrat was returned with a majority of nearly 5,000. In the Ribble Valley on March 7th, 1991 a Conservative majority of almost 20,000 over the SDP/Alliance was overturned and the Liberal Democrat won, again, by nearly 5,000.
4. This money was raised almost entirely by the membership. There were, however, a number of personal donations of tens of thousands of pounds from a number of small businessmen, including Asians (one of whom had shrewdly donated to each of the major parties!). The comedian John Cleese had also donated.
5. After the events of 'Black Wednesday' of September 1992 Mr Major's emphatic pronouncements were treated with far more scepticism. At this time, however, none doubted his resolve.

## References

Abrams, M. (1961), 'Class and Politics: Another Look at the British Electorate', *Encounter*, October: 14–20.

Baldwin, N. (1985), 'The House of Lords: Behavioural Changes', in Norton, P. (ed.), *Parliament in the 1980s*, Oxford, Blackwell.

Butler, D. and Kavanagh, D. (1980), *The British General Election of 1979*, London, Macmillan, especially the concluding chapter, 'A Watershed Election'.

Butler, D. and Kavanagh, D. (1988), *The British General Election of 1987*, London, Macmillan: 75.

Dodds, E. (1959), 'Liberty and Welfare', *The Unservile State Papers*, London, Allen and Unwin: 15.

Ingle, S.J. (1966), 'Recent Revival of the Liberal Party', *Political Science*, 18: 39–49.

Ingle, S. (1987), *The British Party System*, Oxford, Blackwell.

Ingle, S. (1987), 'Six Years on: The Liberal/SDP Alliance', *Teaching Politics*, 6: 204–22.

Ingle, S. (1988), 'Liberals and Social Democrats: End of a Chapter or End of the Book', *Talking Politics*, 2: 47–51.

Marquand, D. (1962), 'Has Lib-Lab a Future?', *Encounter*, April: 34–37.

Marsden, D. and Jackson, B. (1962), *Education and the Working Class*, London, Routledge, passim.

Wyatt, W. (1962), 'My Plea for a Lib–Lab Pact', *New Statesman*, January, 1-22-24.

# 6

# Party politics in local government

*John Gyford*

The presence of party politics in British local government has expanded relentlessly during the twentieth century. By 1992 86 per cent of all councillors were representatives of the Conservative, Labour or Liberal Democrat parties: with the inclusion of Scottish and Welsh nationalists the figure rose to 87 per cent. The overall picture conceals some variations: the party presence is highest in England at 90 per cent; including the nationalists, the Scottish and Welsh figures are 76 per cent and 67 per cent respectively. It is in the urban areas that party politicisation has proceeded furthest: 99 per cent of seats on the English metropolitan district councils are held by the three main party groups, who also hold 96 per cent of the London borough seats. In the English shire districts, their share falls to 86 per cent while in the Welsh districts the same three parties plus Plaid Cymru can claim 66 per cent of all councillors – representing the lowest ratio of party to non-party councillors of any type of local authority.

With a presence thus ranging from two-thirds to almost 100 per cent in terms of occupancy of seats on different types of local authority, the political parties are clearly a major feature of British local government. Their role within local government has traditionally been described as comprising a number of elements (e.g. Gyford, 1985a): they have acted as a channel of recruitment for new councillors and as the funders and organisers of local election campaigns; they have represented particular social groups and interests within the local community; they have, by operating as organised party groups within the council, provided a means of giving coherence to the sometimes diffuse decision-making structure of councils, committees and sub-committees; and they have espoused and promoted particular patterns of local authority spending, with Labour councils, for example, tending to spend more on redistributive and ameliorative services than their Conservative counterparts. That, at least, is the broad picture: but inevitably it obscures or overlooks certain features. In particular, although that broad picture of the role of parties in local government contains some essential truths, it does not adequately illustrate the changes that have come about in the way that the role has been interpreted and performed since the 1970s. In order to understand these changes, it will be helpful to utilise three concepts previously employed by Hill (1972) and to apply them to the recent history of party politics in local government.

In the course of comparing local government in Britain and the United States, Hill distinguished between three styles of politics – administrative, ideological and bargaining politics. Although these three styles were not seen by Hill as being characterised by absolutely clear-cut distinctions, they do represent very different approaches to political decision making. *Administrative politics* occurs where decision making is, in practice, dominated by the administrators, that is to say by the officials or bureaucrats, rather than by the politicians. The politicians are not entirely excluded from the decision-making process: they will be recognised by the administrators 'as representatives of the public, or of particular interest groups' and administrators will normally try 'to take their views into account and generally sell policies to them'; the right of politicians to 'legitimate' administrative actions through formal democratic procedures will be acknowledged; and some politicians may be 'in effect, co-opted into the ranks of the administrators' (Hill, 1972: 231).

*Ideological politics* is found where 'political parties compete . . . by submitting distinct programmes between which the electorate can choose'. Here the running is being made by the politicians who have clearly formulated policies and programmes which they expect the administrators to implement. One consequence of this is that it 'puts a great strain upon administrators' who find themselves faced with the need 'to devote themselves wholeheartedly to the service of a particular party without at the same time compromising themselves' in the event of a subsequent change of political power (Hill, 1972: 211, 216). As for *bargaining politics*, this is associated with 'the dispersion of power', where 'the only way to achieve effective action is . . . by a very extensive bargaining process', so that effective action occurs as a result 'of deals and reciprocal commitments rather than as a consequence of shared ideals' (Hill, 1972: 210, 217). In what follows, we shall suggest that the recent history of local party politics in Britain has witnessed, first, an escalation of ideological politics and, second, the emergence of certain forms of bargaining politics, both these developments having occurred within a system traditionally dominated by administrative politics. In considering this history it is appropriate to identify three phases of development: the pre-1979 period; the first half of the 1980s; and the latter 1980s and beyond.

## Before 1979: administrative politics

The emergence of newly reorganised local authorities in 1974 (1975 in Scotland) witnessed a marked increase in the extent of party politics in local government. In the newly created authorities Labour had reached out electorally from its urban strongholds to contest adjoining areas with which they had now been amalgamated, while Conservative Central Office had been encouraging its supporters to wear the party label rather than serve as Independents.

Despite the advance of party, however, there was little sense of any immediate sharpening of ideological conflict at the time of reorganisation. The new councils were, in fact, emerging into the twilight of the post-1945 consensus about both the welfare state and the role of local government within it. For some three decades local party politicians had operated within a broad common understanding which assumed the permanence of the welfare state and the mixed economy, which looked to continued economic growth to fund otherwise competing demands on public services and which saw a key role for local government in the provision of those services. Certainly, there were differences of opinion on specific topics such as council house rents or selective education, but there were few sharp ideological disputes between or within the parties on local government issues. Within this broad consensus it was none too difficult for politicians and administrators to agree on the rules of the game, to read one another's minds to some extent and to operate broadly within the style of administrative politics. An increasingly professionalised local government service was relied upon for its expertise, its integrity and its ability to 'deliver the goods' in policy terms subject only to a measure of scrutiny and perhaps modification by the politicians.

By the mid-1970s, however, such arrangements were already beginning to come under strain. In 1974 unprecedented increases in the year's rate demands sparked off a 'ratepayers' revolt', thereby setting in train a debate about local taxation which was to culminate in the end of domestic rates, the disaster of the poll tax and the introduction of the council tax. In 1975 the Secretary of State for the Environment, Anthony Crosland, warned local authorities that 'the party is over' as far as spending was concerned. Then in June 1976, after a Treasury-managed devaluation of sterling ran out of control, major public spending cuts of £1 billion were added to those already in train, to be followed by further cuts later in the year as the International Monetary Fund was called in to rescue the pound: in the same year the public sector unions launched a National Steering Committee Against the Cuts. Increasingly local politicians found themselves 'beset on one side by apparently impossible-to-achieve central government demands and on the other by increasingly more militant and powerful unions' (Steel and Stanyer, 1979: 424).

In addition to conflict over levels of local authority spending, there also emerged criticism of the scale and remoteness of some of the newly reorganised authorities – symbolised by Harold Wilson's 1975 complaint about too many chiefs and not enough Indians – and a growing willingness to challenge the assumptions and presumptions of the local government professionals on whose expertise politicians had relied for the translation of party principles into practical policies and who had underpinned the workings of administrative politics.

Public debate about the financial, bureaucratic and professional aspects of local government was accompanied also by grass-roots action, for 'a new activism was afoot among middle-class residents' groups'; (Marwick, 1982: 176) while in the inner cities it had become common to see 'people in deprived areas looking at their own problems and seeking their own solutions' (Baine, 1975: 17). As the 1970s wore on the established pattern of local politics was undergoing active reappraisal. By the end of the decade the administrative politics which had hitherto prevailed alongside a growing party politicisation was to find itself under serious challenge from a new ideological politics.

## The early 1980s: the onset of ideological politics

From the point of view of local party politics this period is framed by the introduction by the Conservative government of the Local Government, Planning and Land Act of 1980 and by the passage of the Local Government Act of 1985, which abolished the Greater London Council (GLC) and the six metropolitan county councils; it also saw the height of the battle generated by the Rates Act 1984 over rate-capping. The 1980 Act heralded the government's determination to take tighter control over local spending, while rate-capping provoked a major political controversy; both measures also saw the emergence of a phenomenon that was to recur in subsequent years – the willingness of local party politicians to unite in criticism of central government policy regardless of their own party affiliations. As for the 1985 Act, it displayed very clearly the government's eager determination to destroy the local strongholds of its chief ideological enemies. The Acts of 1980, 1984 and 1985 were, of course, items on the national political agenda, but the vigorous debate that they provoked at the national level had its parallels at the local level as new ideological perspectives were brought to bear on the workings of individual local authorities, through the emergence of what came to be called the new urban left (NUL) and the new suburban right (NSR) (Gyford, 1983 and 1985b; Holliday 1991).

The NUL and NSR represented the local expression of a process of ideological polarisation undergone by both the Labour Party and the Conservative Party during the early 1980s: radicals of both left and right offered their own alternatives to the assumptions which had underlain the post-war consensus. In the context of local government something of the nature of the competing alternatives is caught in this summary by Holliday (1991: 48).

> . . . the NUL developed local economic strategies and socialist forms of participatory democracy, [while] the NSR took up the hallowed Trinity of Economy, Efficiency and Effectiveness . . . and sought to withdraw the local authority from sectors in which its involvement was considered improper and/or ineffectual.

Despite the clear differences between their approaches, the NUL and NSR in some ways shared certain common preoccupations, at least by way of problems identified rather than solutions proposed. Both of them saw local government in terms of its relationship to a capitalist economy. The radicals of the right saw it as an unnecessary obstacle to the fullest effective workings of a market economy and also as an unjustified 'no-go area' for market relations. Radicals of the left saw it as caught up in the social conflicts generated by the fiscal crisis of capitalism and as thereby providing a major battleground for struggle against the capitalist system. Both the NUL and the NSR shared a considerable suspicion of the professional bureaucracies around which local authorities were structured. From the right Michael Forsyth (1981), later to become a key figure in introducing the poll tax as a junior minister, complained about the 'impersonal, sneering professionals' of local government: on the left the then leader of the GLC, Ken Livingstone, celebrated the willingness of 'people with a basic radical contempt for existing bureaucratic structures . . . to kick a lot of backsides' (*Evening Standard*, 23.3.84). On both of the radical wings there was a desire to open up local government to new pressures and new forces. The right sought to invigorate local authorities through the introduction of market forces, privatisation and the wider employment of commercial management techniques. The left sought to devise more participatory forms of local politics, to mobilise as political actors those who had hitherto been excluded or marginalised by virtue of their gender, race, disability or sexual orientation and to revive local economies debilitated through deindustrialisation.

The origins of this ideological party politics at local level were undoubtedly linked to broader changes happening elsewhere in the British political system. Yet they did also have some roots in specifically local concerns. The NSR, for example, in its concern with economy and efficiency in local government, was echoing views originally articulated by the militant National Association of Ratepayers Action Groups formed in 1974 at the time of the ratepayers' revolt. As for the NUL, many of its own concerns, and indeed some of its more active members, could be traced back to local community action campaigns in working-class areas of the major cities in the late 1960s and the 1970s. In terms of its occurrence or incidence this ideological style of politics was by no means universal throughout local government. Thus the NUL operated largely, as its name implies, in mainly urban localities – the GLC, certain London boroughs, Manchester, Sheffield and some of the metropolitan counties – but with outliers including Derbyshire and Stirling: Liverpool, with its particular story of Militant infiltration of the Labour Party, tended to stand somewhat apart from the main body of the NUL, advocating a strategy of outright resistance to Conservative government policy whilst eschewing any involvement in the NUL 'rainbow' politics of ethnicity, feminism and alternative lifestyles. As for the NSR, Holliday (1991: 49) suggests that its true suburbanism lay in 'its value system . . . of thrift, economy, hard work, just rewards, etc. . . . built on the various "housewifely" homilies which Mrs Thatcher was fond of giving': the councils which gave most enthusiastic attention to these values included Wandsworth and Westminster but also some genuine representatives of suburbia such as Merton (until it fell to the Liberal Democrats).

Councils which embraced the doctrines of the NUL and the NSR often saw themselves as pioneers, showing the way ahead for their party as a whole: they were identified by the media as fit topics for news coverage and for the apportionment of praise or blame according to political preference. Their leading figures gained 'name recognition', notably Eric Pickles of Bradford and Shirley Porter of Westminster on the right and Ken Livingstone of the GLC, David Blunkett of Sheffield, Margaret Hodge of Islington and Derek Hatton of Liverpool on the left. Levels of publicity for some local party leaders reached new heights, yet paradoxically their higher public profile did not necessarily mean that they could be seen as unquestioned 'bosses' in the manner of an earlier generation of council leaders. Increasingly councillors expected their leadership to operate in a democratic, or at least consultative, style and to respond to the views expressed by their group. Moreover, the party organisation outside the council was increasingly taking an interest in the work of its elected councillors.

Not only did leaders have to have regard to the views of their group, but both the leader and the group found it necessary to take account of the wishes of local party activists, most notably in the case of the Labour Party where 'manifesto monitoring groups' were sometimes set up in order to ensure that party councillors were giving due attention to the implementation of manifesto undertakings. The attention thus being paid to manifesto commitments was in itself symbolic of the growing importance attached to the local party manifesto. A survey carried out in

1985 found that 52 per cent of councillors agreed that manifesto implementation was the 'first concern' of elected members, a view held more strongly by Labour councillors (79 per cent) than by their Conservative (49 per cent) or Liberal (33 per cent) counterparts (Widdicombe, 1986: 76–9). Manifesto-based local elections have now become particularly common in urban areas, being found in four out of five urban districts under party control (Young and Davies, 1990: 22).

Distinctive manifesto policies, based on radical ideological stances, spearheaded by high-profile council leaders, backed by local party organisations giving a new degree of importance to local government work – all these taken together represented a considerable polarisation of local party politics with a far wider range of policy prescriptions being generated than was common under the ambit of administrative politics. Moreover, these new policy initiatives were most decidedly not being generated by the councils' officers and then 'sold' to or legitimated by the politicians as under the administrative political model. The new generation of ideological politicians knew what they wanted and they expected the officers to comply or get out: as one chief officer in an NUL council described it to the present writer in tones of reluctant admiration: 'My God, you should have seen them. They hit the beaches running and they took no prisoners.' For local government officers who are 'professionals with a strong sense of their right to expect a measure of professional autonomy' there could thus be a strong sense of being 'significantly threatened by ideological politics' (Hill, 1972: 215). This was particularly the case where leading councillors insisted on the right to intervene in the day-to-day affairs of council departments in order to ensure that policy decisions were being implemented on the ground: they were unwilling to rely on 'Yes, Councillor' as a sufficient assurance in all cases.

If an ideological party politics thus produced tensions between officers and councillors, it could do the same between councillors of different parties and between councils and members of the public. Within the council chamber there could be open inter-party hostility which might well carry on into the corridors or the members' lounge, with no quarter given and no room for socialising over post-meeting drinks: and from the public gallery heckling and demonstrations might challenge the orderly conduct of business. A polarisation of party politics was thus accompanied by a degree of intensification of the party battle.

The government professed itself concerned with some of the manifestations of a polarised and intensified party politics at local level and in 1985 established a Committee of Inquiry into the Conduct of Local Authority Business, among whose terms of reference were to be 'clarifying the status and role of party groups in decision-taking' and 'studying officers' relationships . . . with elected members and political groups' (Widdicombe, 1986: 17). The provisions of the legislation which followed the inquiry in the Local Government and Housing Act 1989 included measures to ensure that all party groups secured representation on council committees in proportion to their overall strength on the council, thereby ending the practice of one-party committees; to regulate the practice of appointing council staff to act as political assistants to party groups; and to place certain restrictions on the political activities of senior council officers.

Yet the polarisation and intensification of local party politics was not the whole story, for not all councillors, or party groups or local authorities, aligned themselves with the radical left or the radical right. There still remained councillors immune to the call of the NSR or the NUL; 'wet' Conservatives and moderate Labour members might well carry on as before, ignoring the ideological prescriptions of their more radical party colleagues or adopting or adapting them selectively and carefully. Moreover, Liberals and their successors in the Alliance and the Liberal Democrats had their own ideological remedies, under the banner of community politics, stressing more open government, more consultation and participation and a greater concern for environmental issues (Pinkney, 1984). In these respects the menu of available policies had become a more variegated one right across a broadened political spectrum: local party politics had in this sense become diversified as well as intensified and polarised under the impact of ideology.

Amongst the competing brands of ideological politics on offer, however, the NSR had one crucial advantage denied to its competitors: it had the enthusiastic backing of the government of the day. Ultimately this backing had major implications for the outcome of ideological party conflict at the local level, spelled out most clearly and brutally by Norman Tebbit in his explanation in 1984 of why the government was proposing to abolish the GLC: 'The Greater London Council is typical of this new, modern, divisive version of socialism. It must be defeated. So we shall abolish the Greater London Council' (quoted in Livingstone, 1987: 286). In the last analysis the government had the inclination, the power and the will to ensure that the scope for the pursuit of NUL policies was progressively reduced. By the abolition legislation, by the use of legislation restricting the powers and duties of local authorities and by increasing central controls over council spending the room for manoeuvre of the NUL was gradually whittled away. Perhaps most crucially of all, the eventual victory of the government over the councils who threatened rebellion and non-compliance over rate-capping in 1985–86 called into question the ability of the NUL to mount an effective long-term resistance to Thatcherism. At the same time the prescriptions of the NSR were increasingly translated into central government policy and legislation through such devices as compulsory competitive tendering, the encouragement of grant-maintained schools and the virtual cessation of the council house building programme.

Yet the battle between the NUL and the NSR did not end entirely one-sidedly: in some fields of local authority activity NUL ideas percolated, albeit in modified form, beyond their points of origin. A concern for equal opportunities, for more decentralised and participatory structures and for more proactive local economic strategies, for example, gradually became part of the repertoire of a growing number of councils even if in doing so they sometimes lost their more radical overtones. As for the NSR, one of its triumphs, that of securing the implementation in 1990 of the poll tax (in 1989 in Scotland) as a device for securing the greater financial accountability of local councils, was to prove to be perhaps the greatest public policy disaster in Britain since 1945 by the time its abolition was announced in 1991. By then the headier days of local ideological politics had passed, though the style now seemed set to continue alongside the administrative politics inherited from an earlier period as part of the stock from which party politicians could draw their strategies and tactics. Meanwhile, however, that stock had been further supplemented and variegated – some might say complicated – by the emergence of bargaining politics.

## The latter 1980s and after: coping with bargaining

At the 1985 county council elections in England and Wales, no fewer than twenty-five of the forty-five councils were left with no party having an overall majority. The figure fell to twelve out of forty-five at the next county elections in 1989 but in 1991 the non-metropolitan district elections produced no fewer than 108 councils out of 333 where no single party obtained overall control. At the county elections in 1993 the number of county councils with no overall majority rose to twenty-eight surpassing the figure reached eight years previously. Hung councils had existed before 1985 but it was the county elections of that year that first made them headline news, with the overall number of such hung authorities reaching somewhere around fifty-five. By 1993 there were 153 councils with no overall majority control out of 513 authorities in England, Scotland and Wales, over a quarter of the total number: the great bulk of them were in the non-metropolitan areas. This growth in the incidence of hung councils was largely a reflection of the electoral success of the Liberal/Alliance/Liberal Democrat parties whose councillors rose in number from just over 1,000 in 1979 to over 4,300 in 1993. Councils such as these were soon seen to require new modes of working if business were to be conducted effectively, and this in turn often required effective inter-party bargaining. As Leach and Stewart (1988: 51) express it: 'In hung authorities, the predominant style of politics and policy-making which develops is based on bargaining, negotiation and consensus-seeking, at least between two of the parties.'

The sorts of outcome which might result from a hung council election have been helpfully categorised by Leach and Stewart (1987: 3ff). They identify five main types of hung arrangement:

1.  Low partisanship, where party politics has traditionally been fairly low-key and senior political posts such as chairs of committees have been shared out on a seniority or territorial basis: in these conditions political life may go on much as before;
2.  The formal coalition where two or more parties combine to provide a joint administration;
3.  The minority administration, where one party is allowed to form an administration with the tacit agreement or explicit support of another party: this is the commonest hung council arrangement;
4.  'Knife-edge' control where one party, with exactly half of the seats, relies on the casting vote of the mayor or chair to sustain an administration; and
5.  No administration, where there is no ongoing party-based administration but only some more or less stable *ad hoc* arrangements which may sometimes involve the sharing of committee chairs and/ or the redistribution of the powers of chairs amongst party group spokespersons.

All of these arrangements, but especially the last four, might require considerable negotiation, either to set them up in the first place or to maintain them on a day-to-day basis. In some cases, the agreements negotiated might take the shape of formal conventions or ground rules signed by the relevant party leaders and designed to clarify inter-party arrangements. As to the factors which might influence the prospects for, and the workings of, such arrangements, a number have been suggested by Leach and Stewart (1987) and Mellors (1983). They include the exact political arithmetic produced by the election; the likelihood of any change in this arithmetic through by-elections or where elections are held three years out of four; the previous history and intensity of party conflict; the internal stability and cohesion of individual party groups; the attitudes of, and mutual relationship between, local party group leaders; and the ability of the council's chief executive to act as a broker between the parties in the process of devising new inter-party arrangements.

The attitudes of the political parties themselves to the need for this bargaining about the exercise of power in hung authorities has varied. To the Conservatives it might come as an unfortunate necessity, since in the non-metropolitan districts and counties it was often they who were dislodged from majority control, sometimes after a considerable period: in Kent, Norfolk and Surrey in 1993, for example, they lost outright control after over a hundred years in office. Indeed, in some cases the desire of Labour and Liberal councillors to maximise their political gains after so long in the wilderness could sometimes lead to the exclusion of the Conservatives from the bargaining process as the former opposition parties tried to devise their own arrangements.

For the Liberals and their successors, responding to the hung council situation represented a genuine opportunity, not only to have some real influence and a share of power but also to give expression to a commitment to the very idea of power sharing and an end to adversarial politics. For Labour, however, such situations presented not only an opportunity but also a problem, arising from the party's suspicion of coalitions and its desire to maintain its distinctive political identity. The party's guidelines for hung councils have always ruled out the establishment of formal coalition administrations and the sharing of committee chairs unless the latter were stripped of all political functions, with political tasks devolving to group spokespersons. In practice the existence of such restrictions has not prevented some Labour groups from ignoring them and working out arrangements, some formal, some informal, with Liberal Democrats, even to the extent of standing down from contesting particular seats where Liberal Democrats might beat Conservatives in a straight fight. Indeed, from some Labour groups in hung authorities there was growing pressure on party headquarters in the early 1990s to take a more relaxed view on such matters, but in 1993 although the National Executive clarified a range of options it stopped short of approving formal coalitions or electoral pacts.

The fact that inter-party bargaining can produce not only formal but also informal arrangements can sometimes create a degree of ambiguity. A formal agreement on hung council procedures may very well not extend to any agreement about policy for example. Thus a set of ground rules adopted by one hung council, Braintree, in 1991 goes so far as to make it clear that they 'are not designed to stifle or temper any genuine disagreements about policy or strategy' but are only intended 'to clarify the mechanics of running the Council'. Questions of policy and strategy thus become matters requiring further resolution. In some cases this resolution may depend upon issue-specific party deals, the nature and outcome of which are not clear until the key vote is taken: in these situations, as one chief officer expressed it, 'We are playing Blind Man's Buff!' On the other hand two parties might well enter into an informal understanding, or their leaders might at least confer regularly, in such a way that, although there is no formal coalition, an effective majority can be summoned up on key issues. Such tacit arrangements may be the subject of differing interpretations: in the run-up to the 1993 county council elections, for example, there was considerable controversy between the Conservatives and the Liberal Democrats over the question of how many, and which, county councils were, or were not, being run in effect by implicit Labour and Liberal Democrat coalitions. In some cases, no doubt such 'coalitions' had never been formally announced; in politics, as in other walks of life, there are sometimes things which may be better left unsaid. Such arrangements may, however, thereby create their own problems of political accountability and responsibility.

Bargaining politics in hung councils is thus by no means confined solely to establishing procedures for running the council in the absence of a clear majority party. It also extends to the resolution of questions of policy, with majorities having to be constructed to secure the passage or defeat of particular proposals, whether on an issue-by-issue basis or as part of some broader agreement between particular parties. Bargaining in this area reaches its apogee in the making of the council's annual budget, with its fundamental implications for both spending and taxing.

Leach and Stewart (1992: 130–32) have identified two different types of budgetary process within hung councils. In some cases, the bargaining process over the budget is *structured*, with inter-party discussions taking place in the months leading up to the council budget meeting. Such talks may be both formal, through all-party working groups or sub-committees, and informal, through personal discussions amongst group leaders or their representatives. At their conclusion the likelihood is that at least the main areas of disagreement will have been clarified or even narrowed down; possibly some overall agreement will have been reached or a political majority constructed for a particular budgetary strategy in time for the council budget meeting itself. In other cases the budgetary process is best described as *unstructured*, with little or no attempt to narrow differences or to secure agreement before the final budget meeting. Here oppositional or opportunistic strategies on the part of at least one party preclude a structured bargaining process. This can leave the outcome very much dependent on what Leach and Stewart (1992: 131–32) describe as the 'superior use of tactics' in the 'hothouse atmosphere' of a 'highly-charged adjournment period during a long budget-fixing meeting' at the eleventh hour, or indeed into the small hours of the morning.

In the case of budget making at least, such bargaining politics has emphasised the pivotal position of the Liberal Democrats and their predecessors. The work of Mellors (1989) and of Leach and Stewart (1992) revealed a successful track-record for the Alliance parties in the second half of the 1980s in respect of the relationship between original party proposals and eventual domestic rate increases agreed by hung county councils. Leaving aside questions of bargaining expertise or tactical superiority, some degree of such Alliance success did of course reflect the fact that its own initial budgetary proposals were likely to be somewhere between those of the Labour and Conservative parties. As a result, under 'the normal pattern of bargaining, which is that actors move from extremes towards a compromise position between them, it is hardly surprising that the Alliance performed well' (Leach and Stewart, 1992: 128); or alternatively, as one participant in such procedures described it rather wearily to the present writer, 'we end up with Liberal proposals for Labour policies at Conservative prices'.

The need for bargaining in the absence of a stable political majority does, of course, extend beyond council procedures and budget making into the broader field of policies for service provision. Here much may depend on whether there is any measure of agreement, either explicit or implicit, between individual parties as to priorities or initiatives. Where there is, then, as with the 'structured' form of budgetary bargaining, it may be possible to achieve a degree of stability in the policy-making process with both councillors and officers having some sense of overall direction and of the way the policy agenda is likely to develop. In other circumstances, however, the situation may be much more uncertain, with unforeseen proposals emerging and with policy decisions very much dependent on the outcome of individual debates at committee and council meetings.

For local party politicians the need to cope with bargaining politics can present itself as both a chore and a challenge. The chores arise through the tendency of bargaining politics to demand more meetings and therefore more time, both for inter-party and intra-party purposes. Leaders can find themselves at times having to bargain in two directions, with their opposite numbers in other parties and with the members of their own party group, and perhaps also with the local party outside the council, in order to secure necessary agreement. On the other hand, these operational chores are a means of confronting the more substantial challenge of finding new ways of working and thereby of exploring the scope for ingenuity and innovation within local political systems.

## Party politics and local governance

Innovation in local political systems has not been confined to bargaining politics. Ideological politics also brought its own innovations as a range of new policies came to be applied from differing points across the whole party spectrum. In these respects the history of party politics in local government since 1979 is one which combines a continued growth in its extent with an increased diversity of policies and practices under the impact of ideological and bargaining politics. Such a history suggests that local party politics has now become both securely entrenched in its occurrence and increasingly creative in its responses to a range of challenges to its traditional ways of working. Moreover, there have been times when party politicians of virtually all persuasions at the local level have united in vigorous and informed criticism of central government policy, suggesting a recognition of their own mutual interests as political actors. Yet there remains one major question about its future, one associated with the emergence of what has become known as a new form of 'local governance'.

The notion of local governance recognises the development of a system of local policy making and service delivery in which local authorities now find themselves joined by a variety of other bodies from the public, private and voluntary sectors, instead of being themselves the sole or dominant providers and decision makers. This move towards a municipal pluralism of multi-sector, multi-agency provision of local services, a move much encouraged by the Thatcher and Major governments, may or may not be a Trojan horse for the advancing forces of privatisation (cf. Gyford, 1991: 147–51). It does, however, have serious implications for local party politics and more widely for local democracy as a whole.

A key characteristic of many of the new non-local authority institutions of local governance is their insulation from electoral accountability. Bodies such as urban development corporations, city challenge boards, training and enterprise councils, housing associations, joint boards and committees (such as those replacing the GLC and metropolitan county councils) and the governing bodies of opted-out schools and further education colleges all have an increasingly tenuous link with the world of representative democracy and electoral politics. Their proliferation and the composition of their ruling bodies has given rise to fears of an emerging 'new magistracy' of appointees, evoking memories of the way in which much administration in the counties was once controlled by appointed magistrates until the creation of elected county councils in 1888 (Stewart, 1993). Under such conditions, the future of party politics at the local level may seem uncertain, despite (or possibly because of?) its strength, resilience and liveliness in the years since 1979. The rise of the new magistracy certainly lends itself to the interpretation that it is a way of rolling back party politics in local government, thereby ridding central government of the sources of power of some of its most persistent critics. If such an interpretation is in any way correct, then it suggests that the future of party politics in local government may yet become bound up with the wider question of the future of local democracy.

## References

Baine, S. (1975), *Community Action and Local Government*, Occasional Papers on Social Administration No. 59, London School of Economics.
Forsyth, M. (1981), *Re-servicing Britain*, London, Adam Smith Institute.
Gyford, J. (1983), 'The New Urban Left: A Local Road to Socialism?' *New Society*, 21 April: 91–93.

Gyford, J. (1985a), 'The Politicization of Local Government', in M. Loughlin, M.D. Gelfand and K. Young (eds) *Half a Century of Municipal Decline 1935–1985*, London, George Allen and Unwin.

Gyford, J. (1985b), *The Politics of Local Socialism*, London, George Allen and Unwin.

Gyford, J. (1991), *Citizens, Consumers and Councils: Local Government and the Public*, London, Macmillan.

Hill, M.J. (1972), *The Sociology of Public Administration*, London, Weidenfeld and Nicolson.

Holliday, I. (1991), 'The New Suburban Right in British Local Government – Conservative Views of the Local', *Local Government Studies* 17 (6): 45–62.

Leach, S. and Stewart, J. (1987), *The Changing Patterns of Hung Authorities: A Report of a New Survey*, Luton, Local Government Training Board.

Leach, S. and Stewart, J. (1988), 'The Politics and Management of Hung Authorities', *Public Administration*, 66: 35–55.

Leach, S. and Stewart, J. (1992), *The Politics of Hung Authorities*, London, Macmillan.

Livingstone, K. (1987), *If Voting Changed Anything They'd Abolish It*, London, Collins.

Marwick, A. (1982), *British Society Since 1945*, Harmondsworth, Penguin.

Mellors, C. (1983), 'Coalition strategies: the case of British local government' in V. Bogdanor (ed.), *Coalition Government in Western Europe*, London, Heinemann.

Mellors, C. (1989), 'Non-Majority British Local Authorities in a Majority Setting', in C. Mellors and B. Pijnenburg (eds) *Political Parties and Coalitions in European Local Government*, London, Routledge.

Pinkney, R. (1984), 'An Alternative Political Strategy? Liberals in Power in English Local Government', *Local Government Studies*, 10 (3): 69–84.

Steel, D.R. and Stanyer, J. (1979), 'Administrative developments in 1977 and 1978: a survey', *Public Administration*, 57: 407–56.

Stewart, J. (1993), *The Rebuilding of Public Accountability*, London, European Policy Forum.

Widdicombe, D. (1986), *Report of the Committee of Inquiry into the Conduct of Local Authority Business*, London, HMSO.

Young, K. and Davies, L. (1990), *The Politics of Local Government Since Widdicombe*, York, Joseph Rowntree Foundation.

# 7
# The recruitment of parliamentary candidates

*Joni Lovenduski and Pippa Norris*

Candidate selection is one of the most important activities of modern political parties. It is an activity which may be both complicated and sensitive. When a political party recruits its prospective legislators it must balance considerations of power within the party against the desired outcome of qualified, able and electable candidates. Political parties are diverse organisations which are affected by the context in which they operate. The external or political context includes the political and legal constraints of electoral fortunes and laws, the degree of party competition etc., while the internal or party context includes the formal and informal rules governing the selection of candidates and the party culture in which it takes place. The political and party contexts shape the process of selection, which is the series of steps involved in choosing a parliamentary candidate. In Britain the process is almost entirely determined within parties and each party has developed distinctive selection mechanisms. Nevertheless there are important similarities in the procedures, which in recent years have been subject to considerable reform.

One reason for reform is concern about their outcome. A common observation about the British House of Commons is how different is its social composition from that of the electorate. The average MP, of whatever political party, is much more likely to be white, male, middle-class and highly educated than is the average voter. This social bias has been carefully documented in studies of social backgrounds of MPs; W. Guttsman (1968), Colin Mellors (1978), Martin Burch and Michael Moran (1985) have all shown conclusively that the House of Commons, in common with legislatures in other Western Liberal Democracies, is socially unrepresentative of the general electorate in terms of class, education, gender and race.

Why does this social bias exist? One explanation is that it reflects the choices of voters, who prefer their candidates to be middle-class white men. But studies of voting behaviour indicate that voters are much more motivated by party preferences. They do not, for example, penalise women candidates (Rasmussen, 1983; Hills, 1981). Recognising this, some political scientists blame political parties for offering too narrow a range of candidates, thus denying voters the opportunity to return a socially diverse parliament (Castles, 1981; Hills, 1981; Vallance, 1981). But Bochel and Denver (1983) argue that Labour selectors did not discriminate against women candidates, rather that they simply chose from among those who put themselves forward. In fact there has been little systematic research into why the social bias of parliament exists. The elements of candidate selection have long been a puzzle, a process once referred to as the 'secret garden of British politics'.

In safe seats the key decisions about who becomes an MP are taken not by the electorate but by the 'selectorate', the group of party activists and members who choose candidates. To understand the reasons for the social bias of parliament we need to understand how the system of candidate selection works. Accordingly, in this chapter we investigate the rules, procedures and practices employed by the Labour and Conservative parties when they select their prospective parliamentary candidates. For reasons of space we confine our account to the two major parties, which between them return more than 90 per cent of all MPs.[1] We draw on the results of the British Candidate Study[2] to explore two major questions: (i) Who selects and how? and (ii) Who gets selected and why?

## Who selects and how?

Electoral laws set only minimal qualifications for MPs. To be eligible candidates must meet certain criteria; undischarged bankrupts, clergy of the Established Church, aliens and certain office holders, such as civil servants, judges and members of the police and armed forces, are not legally eligible to become MPs. Most British adults are formally eligible, but to get into Parliament an individual must complete a set of procedures determined by his or her political party.

These procedures may be complicated and prolonged. Despite periodic attempts to streamline selection, reformers have come up against many obstacles when they have tried to simplify procedures. Imagine that rational party actors were given *carte blanche* to set up procedures for selection that were entirely functional for their party. How would they define their task? Clearly many of their aims would be the same. They would want a system that was easy to administer; one that facilitated the selection of the 'best' candidates, which preserved party unity. It would be important to have a procedural consensus amongst party members. This would almost certainly entail agreement that the procedures were 'fair' and 'democratic'. In most British political

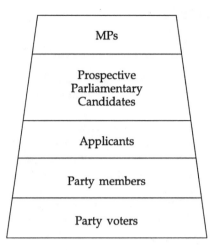

**Figure 7.1** Ladder of recruitment

parties the division of responsibility between the centre and the constituency would need to be acceptable. Other aims would be specific to the particular parties but functionally similar. Thus the procedures should reflect a party's ideas about political representation and their obligations to key groups of supporters. Of course party reformers never have *carte blanche*. They operate in complex organisations constrained by traditions. Reformers are not design engineers with the opportunity to make brand new products, but political actors. The selection mechanisms reflect this. They are not 'streamlined, graceful machines' but more like bulging, eccentric-looking Heath-Robinson contraptions with wires hanging out and extensions tied on with bits of string – they are products of incremental *ad hoc* adaptions to changing circumstances.

It is useful to think of candidate selection as a multi-step ladder of recruitment as illustrated in Figure 7.1, which shows at each step who is eligible to climb to the next step. At the bottom of the ladder are party voters. Next are party members. On the step above, applicants are those on party lists seeking a parliamentary career. Near the top of the ladder are the Prospective Parliamentary Candidates (PPCs) who have been adopted by a constituency and at the top are MPs. The ladder of recruitment is steep. Many never begin the climb, and of those who do, very few reach the top. Selecting candidates is largely a process of elimination according to methods which are sometimes the subject of intense political struggle. Frequently under review, over the years the methods have changed considerably.

## Conservative selection

*The process*

A Conservative candidate of the 1950s or 1960s, observing the selection process today, would find much of it familiar. The process continues to involve four main stages: formal vetting by Conservative Central Office, application to individual constituencies, shortlisting by the local selection committee and formal approval by party members. Nevertheless, when Conservatives choose their prospective parliamentary candidates they do so according to procedures that were developed in three reforms: the Maxwell-Fyfe reforms of party finance, approved in 1949, the Chelmer reforms of 1972 and the introduction of selection boards in 1980. Reformers were concerned to increase the party's 'representativeness', both in terms of the social profile of the parliamentary party and the role played by party members. The current Conservative selection procedures were devised at the beginning of the 1970s and made more rigorous in the 1980s. Following demands for a democratisation of the party, the Chelmer Committee was established in 1969 with a brief which included candidate selection. The Chelmer Report led to the adoption of new 'model rules' for constituency selection. These rules are not obligatory, but almost all constituency associations follow them closely.

Conservatives regard the search for a candidate as a search for the 'best' person. The member is to be a representative, not a delegate. The official 'Notes on Procedure', which are issued as advice to selecting constituencies, assert: 'Ultimately, the party's capacity to govern the country must depend on the calibre of its representatives in Parliament.'[3] The procedures themselves were designed to rationalise as far as possible the means by which party selectors seek their high-calibre representatives.

Conservative selection decisions are shared between the National Union whose interests are administered from Central Office in Smith Square, London and local constituency associations. Aspirant candidates must get on the 'Approved List' which means they must first be accepted by the party vice-chairman with responsibility for candidates, then get through a residential selection board. Finally they have to win the nomination in a particular constituency. These steps are illustrated in Figure 7.2

*Application to Central Office*

The role of the party vice-chairman is pivotal. Formally, the selection of parliamentary candidates in England and Wales is overseen by the

**Central Office**
approval
↓
Application form
References
Vice-Chairman interview
↓
Selection Board
↓
Approved Candidates List
↓
**Constituency Association**
↓
Constituency Selection Committee
shortlist
↓
Constituency Executive Council
interviews
↓
Constituency Special General Meeting
selects/confirms

**Figure 7.2**   The selection process in the Conservative Party

Standing Advisory Committee on Candidates (SACC).[4] The SACC is empowered to examine the qualifications and records of all those who apply to be a Conservative candidate.[5] The day-to-day work is done by the party vice-chairman with responsibility for candidates, a post filled from 1983 to 1992 by Sir Tom Arnold and currently held by Angela Rumbold MP.

*The Central Office interview*

Individuals complete a six-page form which requires information about their personal circumstances, education background, employment history and political experience. They must state the type of constituency they are seeking and name three referees (sponsors) 'if possible one MP and a constituency chairman' and another person the applicant has known well for ten years. The sponsors are then sent standard forms to complete and the applicant is invited for an interview with the Central Office Agent, who is the paid representative of Central Office in that locality. The agent will make a report which will cover, *inter alia*, the accuracy of the applicant's details. Once the four reports are in, the vice-chairman assesses them and decides whether to proceed by inviting the applicant to Central Office for an interview. In the past this interview was the main hurdle to getting onto the approved list; the vice-chairman, helped by two or three MPs, evaluated the applicant's personal qualities, speaking ability, political experience and educational qualifications. This initial vetting seeks to eliminate applicants who are not legally qualified and those who might prove an embarrassment – for example, if they have a criminal record or have been members of extremist political parties such as the National Front. A politically unsuitable applicant might be, in the words of one party manager, someone 'wearing a Union Jack under his shirt'. Applicants should be in the 'appropriate' age range – some in their early twenties have been told to reapply after gaining more local party experience. A women in her mid-forties was warned that she was almost on the political shelf: 'another few months and you'll be what we could consider past it'. Applicants are also warned to consider the financial costs of nursing a constituency. The interview continues to be a significant hurdle, but applicants considered it quite straightfoward and fair. During Sir Tom Arnold's term of office, about 25 per cent of applicants did not get beyond this stage.

*Selection boards*

The next stage is the residential selection boards, which are two-day recruitment exercises during which applicants are judged on their intellectual, personal and political skills. The exercise was especially designed for the party by Brigadier Sir Nicholas Somerville, who reorganised the officer recruitment process for the British army. It first came into use in 1980, so it has not been experienced by all current Conservative MPs. Passing the residential selection board is a requirement for inclusion on the party's approved list. Moreover, anyone who has been on the list for ten years without being selected by a constituency must go through the residential selection board. By the mid-1990s virtually all of the candidates on the approved list will have been through the board, as will the majority of sitting MPs.

The precise procedures of the boards are confidential, as are the assessments of any individual applicant. Boards are held at regular intervals. A set of forty-eight applicants is divided into six groups of eight, each with a group leader. They participate in various exercises modelled on the work of an average MP; for example, the groups argue policy, prepare press releases and act out television interviews. Two assessors divide their attention between two groups. Assessment is by existing MPs, senior party activists and party officials. The exercises are designed to test character, leadership, intelligence and confidence, and to be sufficiently diverse so that an applicant might make up lost ground in one exercise by performing well in another. The pressure on applicants is high, and increases over the weekend. Aspirant candidates have mixed feelings about the selection boards:

> Then I was told you will now have to go on to this parliamentary weekend which is totally ghastly . . . it is so awful, you make good friends out of it . . .[6]

> It was an experience that I don't think anyone who's interested in politics should ever miss.[7]

> I was very irritated when they had the section where you had a mock parliamentary debate . . . someone . . . felt that part of the exercise involved making braying noises . . . you feel, my god, if you've got to behave like this to get on, do I want to do it?[8]

The process is fair in the sense that it treats all applicants equally and attempts to assess qualifications in an objective manner. Moreover, assessors are inclined to give applicants the benefit of the doubt, making allowances for such factors as youth or nervousness. A range of abilities are sought so that, for example, poor speaking skills would not necessarily disqualify someone. There is some sensitivity to gender – for example, care is taken so that a woman is not placed alone in a group of men. About 50 per cent, perhaps slightly more, of those who attend the residential boards are approved straightaway, while a further 15 per cent are deferred but get through eventually. Some 1,500 people had been through this process by the middle of 1991.

Through its interviews and the selection boards, the candidates office accredits the approved list. The list has grown steadily more important, largely because the authority of Central Office has been legitimated by the introduction of selection boards. The aim of the office is to make available a pool of well-qualified 'high-calibre' potential candidates. Sir Tom Arnold likened his role to that of a marriage broker and spoke of the need for 'horses for courses' when considering different constituencies. Of course the party centre also aims to place individuals whom the leadership would like to see in parliament in winnable seats. However, although a few such individuals may be placed in each round of selection, this power of placement is not reliable, and the most important power of central office is its control of the pool of eligibles.

*Adoption by a constituency*

Once on the approved list, individuals are notified of, and can apply for, vacant seats. Although constituencies do consider other, normally local, applicants, since the Chelmer Report the trend is to choose candidates from the approved list. The elements of the process are the same for all constituencies; what differs is the level of competition. The approximately 800 people who may be on the approved list must engage in fierce competition for desirable seats. Once a vacancy is notified individuals inform the party vice-chairman that they wish to be considered for the seat. He passes their names and biographical details on to the constituency officers. As many as 300 people may apply for a good seat.

For constituency associations the selection is an elaborate process of elimination. A great deal of information is generated and must be assessed. The way the constituency does this a matter for each association, but most follow the guidelines set out in the party's 'Model Rules'. All applications, which are in the form of curriculum vitae, are 'sifted' by a shortlisting committee which may choose as many as twenty-five people for a brief interview. Most constituencies also make a point of seeing all local applicants. Often the interviews take place over a weekend, and time will be allowed for social contact with applicants and their spouses. At least three applicants will be selected by exhaustive ballot to go forward to the next stage; in good seats selectors usually opt to send at least six names forward. These candidates face selection by the constituency's executive council, which may consist of a hundred or more delegates from constituency branches and committees. If one candidate gets over 50 per cent of the vote at this stage the others are eliminated, and the next stage becomes a formality. This is becoming less common in good seats, where the trend is for at least three names to go forward to the last stage, a vote by the special general meeting of the constituency association.

Shortlisting is a vital hurdle. The constituency shortlisting committee is briefed before the process begins in order that members have a clear idea of their responsibilities. Often the briefing will be followed by a discussion of guidelines about the kind of person they seek. For example, they may decide that they want an experienced middle-aged candidate with a strong local background. Such guidelines help the committee members to sift through the large number of applications they must process and choose those who are to be invited for interview. Most applicants are very skilled at selling themselves and it is difficult for shortlisters to choose. Often quite arbitrary scorings are made:

I marked the CVs out of 100, on the basis of education, profession, age, political experience, a person who had been an MP got marks. Or one who had fought elections . . . family, personality, willingness to live locally . . . [got marks] . . . The cut-off point was 74 per cent.[9]

I selected x because his wife was in the photo . . . [he] seemed a caring young person because it said married with three children and gave their ages.[10]

Once the long shortlist is agreed the constituency chair, accompanied by the area agent, will pay a visit to the party vice-chairman. Central Office may offer advice. Constituencies are enjoined to choose the best candidate, but they might also be told to bear in mind the wider needs of the party in Parliament and give special consideration to female, ethnic minority or trade union applicants. Central Office intervention does not always take place. It needs to be carefully judged, as some constituencies will not accept it. During the visit the vice-chairman might draw attention to a likely candidate who has been overlooked by the shortlisters. At this stage important details – for example, the chronic poor health of an applicant – which do not appear on CVs will come out. Our interviews with party officials suggest that generally they can help people to get interviews with a selection committee, and occasionally they may be able to stop someone from being interviewed. However, once the interview process begins, applicants are on their own. Most applicants regard getting an interview as the critical hurdle to getting selected. An interview gives them a chance to get on the shortlist; without an interview they can get no further.

The feature of the process that provides its 'democratic' character is successive ballots conducted among selectors whose number increases at each stage in the process, from the selection committee, to the executive council and finally to a special general meeting which may involve up to 500 people. Increasing the number of selectors is appropriate – once selected, the candidate must win the support of a still larger group: the voting electorate. Moreover, the process probably increases the commitment of participating party activists to their Prospective Parliamentary Candidate.

*Conservative selectors*

Constituency association selectors are local party members, active enough to attend selection meetings. Selectors must be party members in good standing for at least six months. It is possible to identify a 'core selectorate' of those who serve on selection committees. Normally these are officers of the constituency association, chairpersons and representatives of association committees. The rules and conventions about the composition of shortlisting committees make for a large committee, normally of fifteen to twenty members. Shortlisting takes place under the close procedural supervision of the Area Agent or their Deputy. Shortlisters are chosen to be representative of the constituency association, rather than because they have particular relevant recruitment experience. Only 12 per cent of selectors had taken part in selections in 1987. The more important the selection is, the less likely it is that selectors are experienced. Safe seats may select as infrequently as once in twenty-five years, while hopeless seats will select for each election. Even where selectors are experienced, there will be a large element of

**Table 7.1** Class, education, gender, race, age and union membership of Conservative Party MPs, candidates, applicants, selectors and voters (%)

|  | 1 | 2 | 3 | 4 Selectors/ party members | 5 |
|  | MPs | PPCs | Applicants | members | Voters |
|---|---|---|---|---|---|
| **Class** | | | | | |
| Professional/ technical | 44 | 46 | 41 | 33 | 20 |
| Managerial/ administrative | 54 | 46 | 56 | 39 | 16 |
| Clerical/sales | 1 | 6 | 1 | 22 | 30 |
| Skilled manual | 0 | 1 | 1 | 4 | 15 |
| Semi-skilled manual | 0 | 1 | 1 | 2 | 19 |
| **Education** | | | | | |
| Graduate/ | 69 | 66 | 70 | 28 | 6 |
| non-graduate | 31 | 33 | 30 | 72 | 94 |
| Oxbridge/ public school | 26 | 13 | 15 | – | – |
| **Gender** | | | | | |
| Male | 94 | 85 | 87 | 48 | 48 |
| Female | 6 | 15 | 13 | 52 | 52 |
| **Race** | | | | | |
| White | 100 | 99 | 98 | – | 99 |
| Non-white | 0 | 1 | 2 | – | 1 |
| **Age** | | | | | |
| over 60 | 17 | 0 | 1 | 44 | 14 |
| fifties | 33 | 9 | 16 | 23 | 17 |
| forties | 43 | 28 | 47 | 17 | 20 |
| thirties | 6 | 43 | 32 | 7 | 17 |
| under 30 | 1 | 20 | 5 | 9 | 33 |
| **Trade union or staff association** | 8 | 14 | 17 | 14 | 19 |
| **Number** | 142 | 222 | 225 | 601 | 1,405 |

*Sources*: British Election Study 1987; British Candidate Study 1992.

guesswork in their decision making because, as one agent put it, 'you are asking them to make a judgement about quite a unique job'.

## Labour selection

*The process*

More formalised than the process in the Conservative Party, Labour's procedures are also more complicated and have more often been the subject of party debate. Because the Labour Party is a federal organisation of individual members, trade unions and other affiliated branches, its procedures are designed not only to select the best candidate but also to give roles to the component parts of the organisation. Nevertheless there are some similarities between the two parties. Like the Conservative Party, Labour maintains national candidate lists: the 'A' list of trade union sponsored candidates, the 'B' list of names put forward by constituency parties, the 'C' list of names approved by the Cooperative Party, which is an affiliated organisation and the 'W' list of names of eligible women. When a selection begins the constituency draws up a timetable and 'freezes' its membership, to prevent packing of selection meetings. Constituency organisations, including party branches, women's sections and trade union branches, are invited to nominate candidates. They may choose names from one of the national lists, but they are free to nominate other candidates who must be party members in good standing. Branches vary in their nomination practices; some 'interview' several hopefuls, while others make nominations without seeing their candidate. For Labour applicants, the difficulty of getting a nomination is the most important obstacle to selection. Labour constituency parties have an average of twenty-three nominating bodies, each of which may put forward only one name. These are forwarded to the constituency executive committees, which draw up a shortlist from amongst those nominated and presents it to the General Management Committee (GMC) of the constituency party. The GMC, which in large constituencies might consist of hundreds of members, is a committee of delegates from all the party and affiliate branches in the constituency. It approves, or amends and then approves the shortlist. Until 1987 the GMC then 'interviewed' the nominees by hearing short speeches and conducting a question and answer session, after which it elected the candidate by 'exhaustive ballot'.

Once the candidate is chosen, approval from the National Executive Committee (NEC) of the party is required before he or she may be adopted by the constituency. In this system decisions are firmly local, and, by comparison to the Conservative's procedures, the powers of the leadership are particularly limited. The party leadership does not have

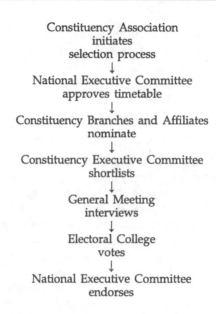

Constituency Association
initiates
selection process
↓
National Executive Committee
approves timetable
↓
Constituency Branches and Affiliates
nominate
↓
Constituency Executive Committee
shortlists
↓
General Meeting
interviews
↓
Electoral College
votes
↓
National Executive Committee
endorses

**Figure 7.3**   Interim Labour selection process 1987–92

the power to manage the choice of candidates through control of the lists. Labour lists are indicative; inclusion on them neither constrains branch choices nor commits the NEC to approving a nomination. Moreover, Labour selectors have less choice. The pool of applicants from which a shortlist is drawn is rarely larger than a few dozen, by contrast to the 300 applicants Conservative selectors may consider.

In 1988 the shortlisting and balloting procedures were modified as the result of a number of debates and arguments in the party. Struggles between the left and the right for control of the party during the 1980s highlighted the candidate selection mechanism as in need of reform (Seyd, 1987; Lovenduski and Norris, 1991). While the left, particularly in its campaign for compulsory reselection of MPs during each parliamentary term, sought to increase the powers of activists in the GMCs, the right and the centre supported the aim of leader Neil Kinnock to modernise the party. Part of his strategy was to bypass activists in favour of individual members. The debates were further complicated by the trade unions, who sought to maintain the considerable influence over selection they derived from their domination of many GMCs. These struggles coincided with efforts by party feminists to increase the representation of women in the Parliamentary Labour Party. The result of these cross-cutting intra-party debates was a set of interim reforms introduced in 1988 which were to be reconsidered in 1990.

The interim reforms determined the method used in the selections for the 1992 general election. Reform covered the shortlisting rules and the method of choosing from the shortlist. The nomination process remained a matter for the local party and affiliated branches, and other societies which make up a constituency party organisation. Shortlisting continued to be a matter for the executive committee, but there now were certain rules the committee had to follow. If a woman was nominated, then there had to be at least one woman on the shortlist. Shortlists were to contain at least five nominees, provided five people had been nominated. Sitting MPs who wished to stand again had to be shortlisted and any nominee with 25 per cent of the nominations had to be shortlisted. Shortlists of one were acceptable only where there was a sitting MP, and exceptional cases had to be approved by the NEC. This reform proved controversial, largely because it resulted in numerous 'token' shortlistings of women aspirants in seats where they had no real chance.

More controversial still was the mechanism for choosing the candidate from the shortlist. The GMC lost its powers of selection to an electoral college which consisted of individual members and affiliated organisations in proportion to their share of constituency membership. There was a ceiling of 40 per cent on the proportion of votes affiliates could cast, and individual members had the right to apply for a postal ballot. The electoral college was widely regarded to be a temporary expedient as the party moved to selection by votes of individual members. The system proved complicated, and considerable effort was expended by party agents and NEC representatives ensuring it was properly implemented.

Labour's system favoured local candidates who could more easily learn when a selection was likely to take place and who were known to local activists and members. A rule banning canvassing placed outsiders at a further disadvantage. Applicants for the last round of selections suggested that the key to securing nominations was good networking among local members: 'I think you'd have to make a spectacular impression on the Labour Party if you were coming from outside to be able to get on the shortlist . . .'[11] Many good applicants failed to get nominations, hence were not considered for shortlists. Others lacked the vital support of trade unions, who controlled more than half of the nominations in most seats. Their favoured applicants were active trade unionists with local party experience.

The role of the unions attracted unfavourable comments both from the national and local press and from rejected applicants. There were some allegations of abuse, particularly by trade union branches whose method of determining their nominations and votes was neither regulated nor scrutinised. In September 1990 the party conference voted to abolish the interim procedure and introduce a one member one vote (OMOV) system in candidate selection. But in 1993 unions mobilised in opposition to their loss of selection power, calling for a system which continued to allow members of affiliated union branches to vote in candidate selections. Proposed moves toward OMOV, reducing the power of the affiliated unions, were under consideration from then until the autumn of 1993. The OMOV debate is more than a procedural technicality. Both trade union and party leaders regard the issue as central to the historic party–union relationship. In early 1992 a Trade Union Links Review Group was established. The group reported to the NEC in February 1993, proposing five options for the arrangements for parliamentary selection, of which two were the subject of widespread discussion: (i) candidates should be selected only by individual members of the party on the basis of one member one vote; (ii) a form of electoral college in which registered party supporters who were members of affiliated unions and resident in the constituency were entitled to a share of the vote. Supporters of the first option, who included many MPs and some of the leadership, argued that union influence over candidate selection was undemocratic and contributed to the party's unpopularity with important sections of the electorate. Party leader John Smith supported the first option as an interim measure, asserting that the second option could not be implemented in time for the next round of selections (*Guardian* 18.5.93). He offered a discounted membership rate for political levy payers, but the suggestion was rebuffed by most of the larger unions. By the time of the 1993 Annual Conference at Brighton John Smith was fully committed to these proposals. With NEC backing he gained the support of conference by a narrow vote. Constituency parties will choose their candidates on the basis of the votes of individual members from January 1994.

*Labour selectors*

There are two categories of Labour selectors: constituency activists and members, who are described in Table 7.2, and activists in trade unions and other affiliated organisations. Less is known about the affiliated trade unionists, whose votes and nominations are weighted according to the number of union branches who have members resident in a constituency and have paid affiliation fees. In practice, if a union branch has only one member living in a constituency it has been able to affiliate all of those branch members to the party, through the simple means of paying a membership affiliation fee. In the past this has entitled the union branch to forward a nomination to the constituency executive committee, to send delegates to the GMC and to participate in the electoral college. It is difficult to generalise about union practices. There is considerable evidence that in some constituencies unions have exploited their position (Back and Solomos, 1992) while in others their nomination and voting procedures have been models of democratic

**Table 7.2** Class, education, gender, ethnicity, age and union membership of Labour Party MPs, candidates, applicants, selectors and voters (%)

| | 1 | 2 | 3 | 4 Selectors/ party members | 5 |
| --- | --- | --- | --- | --- | --- |
| | MPs | PPCs | Applicants | members | Voters |
| **Class** | | | | | |
| Professional/ technical | 61 | 66 | 56 | 46 | 13 |
| Managerial/ administrative | 24 | 24 | 23 | 19 | 4 |
| Clerical/sales | 1 | 5 | 11 | 14 | 19 |
| Skilled manual | 11 | 5 | 6 | 12 | 19 |
| Semi-skilled manual | 3 | 1 | 3 | 9 | 45 |
| **Education** | | | | | |
| Graduate/ | 71 | 72 | 62 | 44 | 6 |
| non-graduate | 29 | 28 | 38 | 56 | 94 |
| Oxbridge/ public school | 3 | 2 | 2 | – | – |
| **Gender** | | | | | |
| Male | 91 | 74 | 63 | 60 | 48 |
| Female | 9 | 26 | 37 | 40 | 52 |
| **Race** | | | | | |
| White | 98 | 99 | 96 | 96 | 93 |
| Non-white | 2 | 1 | 4 | 4 | 7 |
| **Age** | | | | | |
| over 60 | 14 | 3 | 2 | 21 | 22 |
| fifties | 34 | 11 | 12 | 16 | 19 |
| forties | 43 | 39 | 49 | 24 | 17 |
| thirties | 8 | 40 | 31 | 24 | 16 |
| under 30 | 0 | 6 | 6 | 15 | 26 |
| **Trade union or staff association** | 99 | 97 | 91 | 78 | 34 |
| **Number** | 97 | 318 | 127 | 885 | 1,000 |

*Sources*: British Election Study 1987; British Candidate Study 1992.

deportment. A further source of union power is their practice of sponsoring candidates, paying some of their election expenses and often assisting with other constituency costs. The 'A' list of candidates is drawn up by the unions, who devise their own methods for scrutinising and choosing the individuals they will sponsor.

Unions are often accused of imposing their candidates on reluctant constituency parties. In 1992 complaints were made that the electoral college votes of union branches were often cast by officials who had not consulted their members, and that unions combined to make deals to support each others' candidates. Another common complaint was that the electoral college gave members of unions who were not party supporters influence over the choice of candidates.

Union-sponsored candidates tend to be selected for the best seats, hence their rates of election to Parliament are high. In 1992 the trade unions sponsored 173 Labour candidates of whom 143 were elected, the largest number to become MPs in any election. The success rate for union-sponsored candidates was 83 per cent, compared to 17 per cent for unsponsored candidates (Criddle 1993; Minkin, 1992). Supporters of sponsorship argue that it enables working-class applicants to stand for election who otherwise might not be able to afford it. Although constituencies are barred from considering costs in making their decision, and party rules place limits on the amount which may be contributed, selectors know who will be sponsored and it is hard to see how they can avoid taking it into account.

## Who gets selected and why

In both parties selection procedures involve application, shortlisting and interviewing. In both selectors ask applicants to speak in public, to answer questions and to invest in learning about the constituency. But the procedures differ from the point of view of the applicant. Compared with the Labour Party, the Conservative process is more meritocratic, efficient and competition for seats is more national. In the Conservative Party the process is very like applying for a management job. Individuals whose names are on the approved list are informed of coming selections and send off their CVs to constituencies. The 'trick', they told us, is to get an interview. Labour aspirants face greater difficulties. First they must learn of a coming selection, then apply to various branches in the hope of securing a nomination. The Labour system favours local applicants who will more easily learn about upcoming selections and are known to selectors, while the Conservative system draws potential candidates from all over the country.

To return to our initial concern with the social bias of the House of Commons, we can see from the data in Tables 7.1 and 7.2 that the background of MPs is similar, although not identical, to that of candidates. MPs and candidates are more likely to be male and middle-class than are the electorate. There are two possible reasons for this: (i) demand, that is, selectors may be prejudiced in favour of such applicants and therefore discriminate against others, or, (ii) supply, which suggests only certain kinds of applicants come forward, hence selectors have little choice. If demand-side factors are important we would expect to see a significant difference in the characteristics of applicants (columns 3) and candidates (columns 2), while if supply-side factors are important we would expect to see a significant difference in the characteristics of party members (columns 4), who form the pool of those formally eligible to become candidates, and applicants (columns 3).

*Class*

Within each party the socio-economic status of applicants is nearly identical to that of MPs and candidates. The similarities between columns 1, 2 and 3 of our tables is striking. If all the incumbents resigned and all applicants took their place the social composition of the House of Commons would hardly be affected. Although the party members formally eligible to stand are from more diverse occupational backgrounds, it is mainly those with higher status who try to become candidates.

*Education*

The pattern for education is similar to that for class. In the Conservative Party MPs, candidates and applicants are highly qualified, but party members are significantly less so. Labour follows much the same pattern. The most plausible explanation seems to be supply – the better educated are more likely to come forward.

*Gender*

Here there are some differences by party. In the Conservative Party the proportion of women applicants and candidates is about the same. In the Labour Party more women come forward than are selected, although not in proportion to their membership of the party. So for the Conservatives the explanation is supply – selectors are not offered many women applicants – whilst in the Labour Party both supply and demand factors play a part.

*Race*

It is very difficult to generalise from the data on race because the numbers are so small. Our data and previous research suggest that in the Conservative Party few black candidates are chosen because few come forward, while in the Labour Party supply and demand interact (Norris et al., 1992; Norris and Lovenduski, 1993).

*Age*

Age affects both supply and demand: MPs are older than applicants or candidates, as we would expect. But candidates tend to be younger than applicants, reflecting perhaps preferences selectors have for more energetic, younger candidates. Party members are significantly older than applicants and candidates, which indicates that older people do not come forward to apply for selection.

To summarise, those least likely to come forward as Conservative applicants are the elderly, women, the lower middle class and the less educated. For Labour those least likely to seek office are the elderly, the less educated, manual workers and non-trade unionists. The influence of demand is apparent in selector preferences for younger candidates and, amongst Labour selectors, a disproportionate number of selections of white men. But the sharp social bias in favour of well-educated and middle-class candidates in both parties reflects not the prejudices of selectors, but the supply of those who come forward to be candidates.

Supply and demand in their effect on who comes forward to be a candidate. Potential candidates may be discouraged by their perceptions about the kind of individual selectors are looking for, by complex application procedures or anticipated failure. The concept of hidden unemployment ('Why apply, I won't get the job') provides a perfect analogy for the discouraged aspirant. Nevertheless, our research suggests that supply-side explanations may account for a substantial amount of the social bias of Parliament. Constraints on resources such as time, money and political experience, and motivational factors such as drive and ambition play a large part in determining who applies to go to Westminster. The narrow path leading to a political career is usually risky, gruelling and unglamorous. Nursing a hopeless seat for a couple of years – slogging up to the constituency every weekend, banging on unfriendly doors to drum up support – all of this requires stamina, optimism and dedication. The resources and motivations applicants bring to the job will vary according to their social background. Parliamentary careers are facilitated by the resources which certain middle-class occupations offer: flexible working hours, useful political skills, social status and political contacts are all enhanced by what Jacob (1962) has termed 'brokerage occupations'. The argument is simple, but the insight is important. To get into Parliament an individual must have financial security, public networks, social status, policy experience, technical and social skills. Those who have brokerage jobs – barristers, teachers, trade union officials, journalists, political researchers – work in fields which are complementary to politics. Their skills translate between public and private life.

The importance of brokerage jobs and sympathetic employers was stressed by many applicants:

> Certain employers are quite keen to encourage their employees to do things, and I have to say that unless you are lucky – the silver spoon touch – you've either got to be self employed or work for such a company. (Labour candidate)

> What I thought, rightly or wrongly, was that as a solicitor in London I could earn my living there and be an MP . . . (Conservative candidate)

Brokerage employment helps to illuminate class, ethnic and gender disparities between the composition of Parliament and that of the electorate. Women and members of ethnic minorities are often concentrated in low-paying skilled and semi-skilled occupations or in small family businesses. Such jobs are characterised by inflexible schedules and long hours which do not fit in with the demands of political activism. The concept of brokerage jobs is, therefore, a useful shorthand for understanding the interrelated effects of occupational class, gender and ethnicity on British political recruitment.

## Conclusion

Party selection mechanisms may be judged on the basis both of their outcomes and their procedures. Our account suggests that outcomes may be less amenable to change. The striking similarities between the supply of applicants seeking selection and those who are selected indicates that existing procedures do little to modify the profile of those who come forward. The concentration of resources among certain social groups makes it unlikely that the social composition of those who come forward will alter quickly. Although parties might, and should, do more to encourage more women and members of ethnic minorities, it is difficult to think of a procedural change that could modify the outcome and at the same time be politically acceptable. The 1993 Annual Conference decision to require all-women shortlists in at least half of all vacant Labour and marginal seats was referred by the Equal Opportunities Commission immediately after it was taken. The opposition to such quotas is strong and it is far from clear that their implementation will be smooth. Arguably the practice of union sponsorship in the Labour Party does have such an effect on the social composition of the parliamentary party, as it increases the chances that working-class candidates will be selected. But this practice is proving unpopular, and the party and unions are under increasing pressure to change it.

Reform of selection procedures has been more successful in the Conservative than in the Labour Party, perhaps because Conservatives are in more agreement about the kind of candidate they seek. The Conservatives' procedures are functional to the party and are generally approved by members. They give selection committees a good choice of well-qualified applicants. Labour selectors have less choice; the procedures are controversial and may not be finally agreed for some years to come. A political context set by four successive electoral defeats has generated a favourable climate for reform. It is tempting to recommend that Labour might draw on the Conservatives' experience of reform. For example, an approved list combined with national or regional selection boards might both facilitate a party consensus and give selection committees a wider choice of applicants. But reformers face a party context which includes widespread suspicion of the leadership, the entrenched powers of trade unions and a preference for highly formalised rules and procedures. In this setting it is likely that Labour's selection procedures will continue to develop in a piecemeal and *ad hoc* manner.

## Acknowledgement

The authors gratefully acknowledge the support of the ESRC, which has funded the British Candidate Study (Grant R 000-23-1991).

## Notes

1. For information on the minor and nationalist parties see P. Norris and J. Lovenduski, *Political Representation in Britain*, forthcoming.
2. **Appendix A: The research design of the British Candidate Study, 1992**
   (1) Party members: The survey of party members includes 1,634 Labour and Conservative activists who attended twenty-six selection meetings in constituencies throughout Britain. The constituencies to which we had access were chosen to be broadly representative in terms of party, major census region, and marginality. The seats were: Beckenham, Sutton and Cheam, Feltham and Heston, Croydon North East, Putney, Brentford and Isleworth, Eastleigh, Milton Keynes North East, Gloucester, Bristol West, Colne Valley, Ashfield, Dudley

West, Stoke on Trent South, Warley East, Monmouth, Manchester Withington, Glanford and Scunthorpe, Leeds South and Morley, Oldham Central and Royton, Littleborough and Saddleworth, Edinburgh Central, Tweeddale, Ettrick and Lauderdale, Caithness and Sutherland, and Dumfries. Fieldwork was conducted from January 1990 to October 1991. The main questionnaire was distributed in person to members at meetings, and collected there, producing a response rate of 74 per cent. A more detailed follow-up postal questionnaire was given out for self-completion (with a response rate of 43 per cent of all members at the meeting). Project staff observed meetings and interviewed officials and key participants in these selections.

(2) MPs and candidates: This survey includes 1,320 MPs and prospective Parliamentary candidates who were selected by constituencies for the April 1992 general election at the time of the fieldwork. We included MPs and PPCs for the Conservative, Labour, Liberal Democrat, Scottish National, Plaid Cymru and Green parties. We excluded incumbent MPs who were retiring and independents. Fieldwork was conducted in two main waves, from April 1990 to October 1991. Respondents were sent a postal questionnaire with covering letter, a postcard reminder, and a full reminder a month later. Out of 1,913 names, we received completed replies from 1,320, which represents a response rate of 69 per cent.

(3) Applicants: This survey includes 361 applicants who failed to be selected to become candidates. Respondents were selected using a random sample of one in three applicants on the Labour Party 'A' and 'B' lists, and one in two names on the Conservative Party Approved List, who had not been adopted by parliamentary constituencies. Respondents were sent the same questionnaire as above, following the same procedure. Out of 656 names we received replies from 361, which represents a response rate of 55 per cent.

(4) Personal interviews: To pursue questions about their experiences and motivation in greater depth the study includes thirty-nine hour-long personal interviews with MPs, PPCs and applicants. The list of respondents who agreed to a further interview was stratified by party, type (MP, PPC or applicant) and gender. Using a stratified random sample we selected 39 names for further interview after the election, from April to October 1992.

3. Notes on procedure for the adoption of Conservative parliamentary candidates in England and Wales. Issued under the authority of the National Union's Standing Advisory Committee on Candidates, Revised 1981.

4. The SACC is a sub-committee of the Executive Committee of the National Union of Conservatives.

5. The twelve-member SACC is chaired by the Chairman of the National Union. The committee draws on the three parts of the Conservative Party. Its membership includes leaders of the National Union, the parliamentary party and the Vice-Chairman of the Party Organisation responsible for Candidates (normally an MP) attends

the SACC in an advisory capacity and the Secretary of the National Union acts as honorary secretary of the Committee.
6. Conservative interview 26.
7. Conservative interview 30.
8. Conservative interview 24.
9. Interview with member of Conservative selection committee.
10. Interview with member of Conservative selection committee.
11. Interview with Labour applicant.

## References

Back, L. and Solomos, J. (1992), 'Who Represents Us? Racialised Politics and Candidate Selection', London, Birkbeck College, Department of Politics and Sociology: Research Papers, No. 3.

Bochel, J. and Denver, D. (1983), 'Candidate Selection in the Labour Party: What the Selectors Seek' British Journal of Political Science, 13.

Burch, Martin, and Michael Moran (1985), 'The Changing Political Elite', Parliamentary Affairs, 45.

Castles, F.G. (1981), 'Female Representation and the Electoral System', Politics, 1(2).

Criddle, Byron (1992), 'MPs and Candidates' in David Butler and Dennis Kavanagh (eds), The British General Election of 1992, London, Macmillan.

Guttsman, W.L. (1968), The British Political Elite, London, MacGibbon and Kee.

Hills, J. (1981), 'Candidates, The Impact of Gender', Parliamentary Affairs, 34.

Jacob, H. (1962), 'The Initial Recruitment of Elected Officials in the US–A Model', Journal of Politics, 24.

Lovenduski, J. and Norris, P. (1989), 'Selecting women candidates: obstacles to the feminisation of the House of Commons', European Journal of Political Research, 17.

Mellors, Colin (1978), The British MP: a Socio-economic Study of the House of Commons, Alton, Hants, Saxon House.

Minkin, L. (1991), The Contentious Alliance: Trade Unions and the Labour Party, Edinburgh, Edinburgh University Press.

Rasmussen, J. (1983), 'The electoral cost of being a woman in the 1979 British General Election' Journal of Comparative Politics, 15.

Seyd, P. (1987), The Rise and Fall of the Labour Left, London, Macmillan.

Vallance, E. (1981), 'Women Candidates and Elector Preference', Politics, 1(2).

# 8
# Nationalist parties in Scotland and Wales

*Roger Levy*

From 1945 until 1966, political nationalism in Scotland and Wales excited little interest among either voters or academics. In so far as it was visible at all, it was as a historical rather than a current phenomenon. The behavioural models predominant in the analysis of British politics at the time reinforced this view. It was argued that culturally based non-economic social and political cleavages had been substantially replaced by the homogenising forces of urban-industrial society. Thus, occupational or class-based cleavages were now the principal determinants of political behaviour (Butler and Stokes, 1976; Pulzer, 1972). This left little room for nationalist parties to prosper.

As usual, reality proved to be extremely fickle in sustaining such theories. In the first place, political uniformity across the UK was always more apparent than real. There is a sense in which all parties in Scotland and Wales can be considered to be 'nationalist', irrespective of their label. All the British parties maintain separate Scottish and Welsh incarnations and pander more or less to national sentiment. Even the Conservatives have made a virtue of their Unionism by cloaking it in the 'true' attributes of Scottishness or Welshness as they see it. The Welsh and Scottish arms of the other two British parties have been far more overt in their espousal of the cause of self-government and in their promotion of the scope of the existing regional bureaucracies, although their claims would be hotly denied by the nationalist parties themselves.

Second, there has now been nationalist representation in Parliament since 1966. In that year, the Plaid Cymru candidate, Gwynfor Evans, was elected MP for Carmarthen in a by-election. This was followed by Winnie Ewing's celebrated victory for the Scottish National Party (SNP) at the Hamilton by-election in 1967. With the exception of 1970–74 when there was no Plaid Cymru MP at Westminster, both parties have been continuously represented in the House of Commons. It has not been a picture of uninterrupted expansion, however. Compared to the heady period of the two Labour governments of 1974–79, support for Plaid

Cymru and the SNP declined throughout the 1980s, only recovering towards the end of the decade, and reaching its present levels in the 1992 general election. Current representation in the Commons, at a combined total of seven MPs, is half the level of the 1974–79 Parliament. The 1979 devolution referenda and the general election which followed them marked a watershed for the two parties, and they are still grappling with the consequences.

Nor has it been the case that the two parties' fortunes have run exactly in tandem ever since. There has been much less overall fluctuation in Plaid support compared to that of the SNP, and this betrays the very different nature of the two parties and the electorates they relate to. This is one of the issues we will seek to explore in this chapter, in order better to understand the prospects for and direction of the two parties' development in the future. In addition, we will compare their organisational structures to see what kind of parties they are, and review their policy goals and orientations over the past ten years or so as we enter the second half of the 1990s and beyond.

## Electoral performance, 1979–92

Discounting the exceptional circumstances of by-elections, the late 1960s and early 1970s were the period of sustained growth in support for the two nationalist parties. The best electoral performance by the SNP was achieved at the October 1974 election, when it obtained 30.4 per cent of the Scottish vote and won eleven parliamentary seats. Plaid's performance has been slightly different. It achieved its highest share of the vote (11.5 per cent) in 1970 when it won no seats, but won four seats (the highest total ever) in 1992 when it gained only 8.8 per cent of the vote.

As we can see from Table 8.1, whilst the electoral performance of the two parties between 1979 and 1992 confirm that support has weakened since the 1970s, it has remained significantly above the levels typical (around 5 per cent) in the mid-1960s. In broad terms, theories explaining the rise and fall in nationalist support can be grouped into two main categories, which are nevertheless sometimes interlinked by their proponents. In the first are those which focus on UK-wide factors such as the decline in partisanship, the rise of issue and protest voting and/or the development of post-material values among voters, and in the second are those which concentrate on the importance of indigenous cultural and issue factors.

In this debate, there is far less disagreement about the nature of Plaid support compared to the voting base of the SNP. Studies carried out since the 1970s (Balsom, 1979a; Balsom et al., 1983; Balsom, 1985 and Johnston et al., 1988) have shown that support for Plaid Cymru is strongly correlated with language variables, and is geographically

**Table 8.1** Support for the SNP and PC at general elections 1979–92 (percentate of vote in Scotland and Wales)

|      | 1979 | 1983 | 1987 | 1992 |
|------|------|------|------|------|
| SNP  | 17.3 | 11.8 | 14.0 | 21.5 |
| PC   | 8.1  | 8.0  | 7.3  | 8.8  |

**Table 8.2** Change in support for Plaid Cymru, 1979–92, % average swing (+/−)

|               | 1979–92 | 1983–92 | 1987–92 | 1979–83 | 1979–87 | 1983–87 |
|---------------|---------|---------|---------|---------|---------|---------|
| Wales         | 0.7     | 0.8     | 1.5     | −0.1    | −0.8    | −0.7    |
| Welsh Wales   | 0.0     | 1.0     | 2.2     | −1.0    | −2.2    | −1.2    |
| Y Fro Gymraeg | 7.4     | 5.8     | 3.8     | 1.6     | 3.6     | 2.0     |
| British Wales | −1.1    | 0.0     | 0.4     | −1.1    | −1.5    | −0.4    |

*Sources*: Linton (ed.), 1992; *The Times* 13.6.87; Balsom, 1985.

concentrated in the most Welsh-speaking counties. Thus, whatever the origin of the initial surge in the 1960s, continued Plaid voting is primarily interpreted as a culturally-based phenomenon.

Following his earlier work, Balsom (1985) has suggested a 'three Wales' model of voting behaviour, classified geographically by the dominant characteristics of national self-identification and first language. These three areas are 'Welsh Wales' (fifteen of the most heavily populated south Wales constituencies), 'Y Fro Gymraeg' (the six constituencies in the west and north-west which have the highest proportion of Welsh speakers), and 'British Wales' (seventeen constituencies in the east and south west of Wales). Only in Y Fro Gymraeg, where it holds all four of its parliamentary seats currently, is Plaid a serious challenger for office. Elsewhere, it has generally trailed in third or fourth place.

Since 1979, this pattern has been reinforced. In Welsh Wales, the party managed to save eight deposits in 1992 (but would have saved only one under the old 12.5 per cent threshold), while in British Wales it has averaged less than one saved deposit per election since 1979. Aggregate data for the change in Plaid support over the four general elections between 1979 and 1992 show three instances where there was a swing to Plaid (1979–92, 1983–92 and 1987–92), and three instances where there was a swing against (1979–83, 1979–87 and 1983–87). Table 8.2 shows the regional aggregation of the data.

While there were some significant changes in constituency boundaries in 1983, the trends are clear. In Y Fro Gymraeg, all swings to Plaid have been well above average and there have been no swings against in the aggregate. In British Wales, on the other hand, there has only been one swing to Plaid (well below average), with all the swings against, bar one, being above average. Welsh Wales presents a more mixed picture, but is neutral over the whole 1979–92 period. These figures raise interesting questions about the party's strategy, which we will review later. However, if Plaid has been trying to diversify its support base, then it has singularly failed to do so. Its strength has become increasingly concentrated in the Welsh-speaking areas.

There is more ambiguity about both the nature and the origin of SNP voting. Early studies (MacLean, 1970; Kellas, 1973) tended to focus on the heterogeneous social base of SNP support (very similar to that of the Liberals), arguing that nationalist supporters were either voters with no pre-existing party loyalties ('non-partisans'), previous abstainers, or disaffected weak partisans of the major parties. Voting for the SNP was thus essentially a protest phenomenon.

As the nationalist vote persisted and then strengthened, later studies challenged this view. One interpretation (Jaensch, 1976; Hanby, 1976; Brand, 1978) was that SNP voting represented the development of a national or ethnically-based partisanship, which had either replaced or added a new dimension to political allegiances based on social class. Thus, the SNP, or any other party proclaiming its 'Scottishness', might be able to mobilise these voters irrespective of whether they supported party policy on specific issues. The purely issue-driven model (Miller et al., 1980; Miller, 1981) of SNP voting has focused principally on attitudes to self-government and North Sea ('Scottish') oil during the formative period of the 1970s. Its conclusion that voting decisions were determined by issue attitudes, at least as far as the SNP was concerned, is debatable to say the least, but no more so, arguably, than any of the other explanations. In this context, studies suggesting a combination of explanations (Brand et al., 1983; Baxter-Moore, 1979) have much to recommend them.

Latterly, the debate has been incorporated into the wider discussion concerning the development of post-industrial values among electors, with some studies claiming to show that nationalist voters are more likely than others to adhere to a post-industrial issue agenda (Studley and McAllister, 1988). In the context of the changing strategy of the party, there has also been a re-examination of the social base of SNP support. Newman's recent (Newman, 1992) study lends weight to the view that the nationalist electorate is becoming more like that of the Labour Party in Scotland, a finding which does not sit particularly easily with the apparently greater disposition towards post-industrial values, however.

If similar techniques as were used to analyse the Plaid Cymru vote are applied to the performance of the SNP over the period 1979–92, then

**Table 8.3** Change in support for the SNP, 1979–92, % average swing (+/−)

|  | 1979–92 | 1983–87 | 1983–92 | 1987–92 | 1979–83 | 1979–87 |
|---|---|---|---|---|---|---|
| Scotland | 4.2 | 2.2 | 9.7 | 7.5 | −5.5 | −3.3 |
| Strathclyde | 7.1 | 2.8 | 11.5 | 8.6 | −4.3 | −1.7 |
| E. Cent. Scot. | 3.5 | 2.9 | 10.9 | 8.0 | −7.4 | −4.5 |
| Rural Scot. | −0.2 | 0.5 | 5.2 | 5.1 | −5.0 | −5.8 |
| Clydeside | 7.8 | 2.3 | 11.4 | 9.1 | −3.3 | −1.4 |
| Scott. Indt. Constits. | 5.3 | 3.5 | 11.9 | 8.4 | −6.8 | −3.3 |
| Scott. Rural Areas Modest. Affl. | 0.5 | 2.4 | 6.8 | 5.1 | −5.8 | −5.0 |
| Urban Scot. | 1.1 | 1.2 | 7.0 | 5.8 | −5.9 | −4.8 |

*Sources*: Linton (ed.), 1992; Parry, 1988; Johnston et al., 1988.

some interesting patterns result. Grouping the seventy-two Scottish constituencies into coherent sub-units is by no means easy, but Johnston et al. (1988) suggest two models: a rough geographical schema dividing Scotland between Strathclyde (thirty-two of the thirty-three constituencies in that region), East Central Scotland (nineteen constituencies), and Rural Scotland (twenty-one constituencies, including one in Strathclyde); and a more sophisticated functional model based on common socio-economic characteristics, giving Clydeside (seventeen constituencies), Scottish Industrial Constituencies (twenty-five constituencies), Scottish Rural Areas (seventeen constituencies), and Modestly Affluent Urban Scotland (six constituencies).

In comparison with the Plaid vote, SNP support is quite diffuse both geographically and demographically. This is best illustrated by the fact that the party did not lose a single deposit at the last election (indeed, its vote fell below 10 per cent in only two constituencies). In very broad terms, the SNP has performed best in rural constituencies where the Liberal vote is low, and all of the three seats the party holds currently fall into the 'Rural Scotland' or 'Scottish Rural Areas' categories. It performs worst in affluent urban Scotland and moderately elsewhere, with Edinburgh and Glasgow showing below average support. Between 1979 and 1992, there were four occasions (1979–92, 1983–87, 1983–92 and 1987–92) when there was a swing to the SNP and two occasions (1979–83 and 1979–87) when there was a swing against. Aggregating the data into the geographical and functional regions suggested gives the picture shown in Table 8.3.

Taking the 1983 changes in constituency boundaries into account, two trends stand out whichever classification is used. First, the party has been performing better than average in the urbanised West of Scotland and 'Clydeside'-style constituencies generally. Swings to the party are all above average, and swings against are all below average. On the other side, the nationalists have been losing ground either relatively or absolutely in rural Scotland, their 'traditional' area of strength, with swings there showing an opposite trend to those in Strathclyde/ Clydeside. The party's performance is also well below average in affluent urban areas.

These developments are in striking contrast to the further concentration of the Plaid vote in the 1980s. In the case of the SNP, the party has been experiencing a gradual repositioning in the electoral marketplace towards the western and industrial (and therefore Labour-held) areas, a strategy advocated by many activists over the years. One consequence of the party moving in this direction is that support becomes more rather than less geographically diffuse, a development which brings its own problems. The process is nowhere near complete, and the party still has a long way to go before it represents a really serious challenge to Labour hegemony. But while progress may be slow, it is unmistakable, and adds weight to Newman's observations on the changing composition of the nationalist electorate in Scotland.

## Party organisation and membership

The organisation of Plaid and the SNP is conditioned by two main factors. The first is their status as 'party-movements', or 'movement-parties'. Nationalism has generally been portrayed as a broad socio-political movement, or even a state of mind, rather than a phenomenon which is coterminous with a political party. In this case, are Plaid Cymru and the SNP really movements as opposed to parties? And if so, do they display the looser structures, vaguer objectives and diverse support (rather than membership), typical of political movements? On the other hand, are they indeed a hybrid, retaining some of the characteristics of a movement, while acquiring others typical of electorally-oriented political parties?

Assuming that the answer to this question is positive, the second conditioning variable relates to the position of Plaid and the SNP as 'third' parties operating within a first-past-the-post electoral environment. This affects both the type of party structures and the nature of membership which can sustain its effort, and by that token the internal dynamics of the party itself. As we will see, the formal organisational structures of Plaid and the SNP are typical of mass, branch-type parties as described by Duverger in his classic typology (Duverger, 1954: 17 and 35). In addition to the desirability of this type of organisation *per se*, our earlier studies (Levy, 1988; 1990) have argued that there are compelling reasons why 'third' parties choose to adopt it. Given their relatively late entry into the party system and the lack of major sponsors (such as employers' organisations or the trades unions), to provide the necessary resources, such parties are disadvantaged in comparison with their electoral competitors. They must of necessity rely on party members for finance, logistics and candidates. Expanding the membership is a prerequisite to expanding the electoral base. 'Third' parties must not only offer attractive policy alternatives, therefore, but must also facilitate opportunities for participation so as to entice people to join.

Since both parties entered the electoral arena as full, zealous and indeed effective participants, their movement status has been played down by most analysts (Balsom, 1979b; Webb, 1977; McAllister, 1979). Thus, while they may have been parties in name only up until the 1960s, Plaid and the SNP have now become fully-fledged parties in reality too as their membership bases have expanded, detailed electoral pro- grammes been devised and elections fought, and systems developed for maintaining both organisations locally and nationally. It is indisputable that both parties are now relatively well-organised electoral machines which can stand comparison with their competitors.

That does not mean, however, that they no longer possess any movement characteristics. Brand points out that movements and parties are best seen as points on a continuum 'where there is no strict separation of characteristics' (Brand, 1992: 81). At the doctrinal level, both parties retain movement features, with singular, broad aims and a wide variety of opinion across the ideological spectrum. Indeed, many party members have no interest in the ideological spectrum and make a virtue of this disinterest. The debate between fundamentalist 'move- ment' nationalists and party modernisers is one which has not been definitely concluded in either party.

The debate about party organisation has focused on issues relating to size, participation and accountability, and as we will see, these are interlinked matters as regards party growth and development. Given that the recruitment of party members is of necessity carried out at a local level, it is difficult to get accurate overall figures. Indeed, both parties use local systems for keeping records of party membership, although there are some differences between them. Traditionally, local SNP branches have obtained membership cards from headquarters, and have then sold them on to existing or new recruits. Thus, any calculations of membership based on the issue of membership cards was always subject to inaccuracy. From a simple accuracy point of view, the party's official policy of not publicly disclosing membership figures is thus understandable, as Edinburgh could not possibly know exactly how many members there are at any one time. However, this policy only serves to fuel speculation, based on local figures, as to what total membership might be.

The Plaid system differs in crucial respects. Official figures for total membership are available from party headquarters, and these are based on the registration of Plaid members nationally through the return of a membership counterfoil to Cardiff from local branches. McAllister (1979) notes that the introduction of this system in 1964 produced more accurate figures for the number of active Plaid members, but it nevertheless remains the case that Cardiff must rely on the localities for its information. Thus, the party's official history estimated membership at 12,000 in the late 1980s (Williams, 1990), while Plaid sources indicate a total membership of around 8,500 organised in 200 or so branches currently. It seems likely that there has been an overall decline in Plaid membership since 1979, as the number of branches is down from Balsom's (1979b) estimate of 350 in that year.

Figures for SNP membership have traditionally ranged at much higher levels, with greater fluctuations in comparison to those for Plaid. Whichever figures are chosen, SNP membership and organisation experienced some very significant changes during the course of the 1980s. It is generally agreed that the low point was reached around 1982–83, although there is disagreement about the actual size of the party at that time. While Kellas put membership at 20,000 in 1983 (Kellas, 1984: 142), Brand estimated it at 5,000 (Brand, 1992: 90). Since then, the party has increased it membership, with semi-official sources estimating the total at around 16,000 organised in about 200 branches in 1993. Brand's estimate of 8,000 for 1992 is considerably at variance with these figures, and if correct, would make the SNP only the same size as Plaid at present.

There are no data on the background characteristics of Plaid members, beyond impressionistic accounts of the party's supposed 'worker-intellectual' base. Brand's recent study of SNP members does furnish some interesting information in this regard, however, with the average member being in their late forties, male, subjectively (but not objectively) working-class, and likely to hold similar political opinions to those of the party leadership (Brand, 1992: 84–89).

As already indicated, the primary 'unit' of the two parties is the individual member. Unlike the Labour Party, there is no system of corporate membership, although there are elements of corporate representation in both parties. As Figure 8.1 shows, in terms of their formal organisational structures, the two parties show many similarities. The most significant of these include the emphasis on membership and recruitment, and the base level of organisation – the party branch – in the localities. The evident diversity of organisation at the local level in the SNP is more apparent than real, as 'groups' and 'sub-branches' are simply small branches. Between the branch level and the central decision-making mechanisms (in both cases, the national executive and the annual conference), there is a comprehensive range of interlinked local and national structures in which members may participate, provided they can get elected to them. Officially, both parties are

| Level | SNP | Plaid Cymru |
|---|---|---|
| Local | Group<br>Sub-branch<br>Branch | Branch (*Cangen*) |
| Intermediate | Constituency Association<br>Regional Council | District Committee<br>Constituency Committee |
| National | National Assembly<br>National Council<br>National Executive<br>Annual Conference | National Sections<br>National Council<br>National Executive Committee<br>Annual Conference |

**Figure 8.1**  Summary structures of the SNP and Plaid Cymru

committed to systems of internal democracy, with the annual conference being constitutionally supreme in all matters.

Within this framework, there are differences. For example, the constituency level has far more formal control over the branch level in the SNP than is the case in Plaid. SNP constituency associations are given wide authority by the party constitution, and decisions taken by them are binding on the branches making up the association. In Plaid, constituency committees are responsible only for coordinating the work of the branches, and it is the latter which must draw up a 'local annual programme comprising, political, educational, cultural and social activity' (Plaid, 1991: 2) in line with the decisions taken by the annual conference.

Both parties have consultative mechanisms for general and specific interests at national level. The SNP's National Assembly is purely a consultative forum without formal powers, but the 'Affiliated Organis-ations' (e.g. Young Scottish Nationalists), are entitled to representation at, and to send resolutions to, the annual conference. The National Sections (e.g. the women's section), in Plaid perform a similar role, but are only entitled to send resolutions to the annual conference, although they can send delegates to the party's National Council.

The two National Councils have a more substantive role in so far as they provide an interim policy making/ratification mechanism between annual conferences. On the other hand, the SNP variant has more responsibility in terms of drawing up annual conference agendas, the setting of fees and the investment and disposal of party assets than appears to be the case in Plaid. At the national executive level there appears to be very little difference, however, as both executives are invested with wide strategic and organisational powers.

Party constitutions are a useful but imperfect guide to reality. The empirical evidence points in contradictory directions, however, suggesting considerable local autonomy on the one hand, and *de facto* centralisation of power on the other. Early studies of the SNP and Plaid following their initial growth periods suggested a picture of decentralisation which bordered on anarchy (Butt-Philip, 1975; Mansbach, 1972; Brand, 1978), with the centre having little knowledge of or control over local branches. In the context of a rapid expansion of the membership base, such findings were not altogether surprising. Indeed, a rather similar picture of ambiguity emerged in the relationships between the national leadership in Scotland and the party in Parliament when the SNP suddenly acquired a parliamentary group of eleven in October 1974.

Later studies (Balsom, 1979b; Crawford, 1982; Levy, 1990) have taken different perspectives on the organisation of the two parties and suggest a far greater degree of centralisation. The thrust of the arguments made by Balsom and Crawford in particular is that both parties were always more centralised than they appeared to be; first, because there really was no mass membership until the 1960s and thus little local organisation, and secondly because efficient central organisation was a prerequisite for expansion. Balsom argues that Plaid has 'a centralised party structure where real influence is in the hands of relatively few people', which enables it to maintain a high public profile out of all proportion to its actual size (Balsom 1979b: 148), and Crawford's study of the SNP concludes that the expansion of the party's membership actually required less participation, rather than more.

While there may be either an imperative or a desire by party leaders to keep the membership in their place (Bayne, 1991), it may simply boil down to apathy and opportunity. In the case of the SNP, the majority of ordinary members seem to be content with a fairly minimal degree of activity, leaving decision making to an activist elite, comprising the party leadership and those who are willing to involve themselves at the national level (as National Council or annual conference delegates, for example) (Levy, 1990). Even Brand's recent study, which characterised the SNP as a 'lively organisation', found that the average attendance at branch meetings in his sample was only nine (Brand 1992: 83).

It is clear that debate and dissent within this stratum is vigorous if not vicious on occasions, and can lead to internal factionalism characterised by prolonged periods of disruption. It is interesting therefore, that both parties experienced such turmoil in the early 1980s following the trauma of the devolution referenda results and the subsequent outcome of the general election in 1979. In both cases, left- and right-wing factions emerged as the two parties turned inwards and contracted, although the process seems to have been more sudden and severe in the SNP, probably due to the relatively greater scale of its electoral and organisational collapse compared to Plaid. Such factionalism has been characterised by an accelerated turnover of elected national office holders and the loss of coherence in policy making as the balance of influence changed between the factions and their supporters.

In the case of the SNP, the left in the form of the '79 Group', was at first triumphant, and then apparently routed by its alter-ego, the Campaign for Nationalism in Scotland, when factions were proscribed at the 1982 annual party conference. Yet, by 1985, the party was firmly left of centre, and well to the left of the Labour Party on some issues. It has broadly remained there since. Within Plaid, the Welsh Socialist Republican Movement formed and splintered off in early 1980, followed by the creation of National Left within the party in 1981. As in the case of the SNP, this produced an alter-ego in the form of the Hydro Group in 1982. The latter's attempt to reverse Plaid's commitment to socialism in 1981 lasted until 1986, when the group disbanded. Thus, both parties emerged from the process with a more socialist hue, and we shall explore the impact of these developments on party policy in the following section.

## Policy development, 1979–93

Despite their many similarities, the underlying approach to policy is fundamentally different within the two parties. This may explain why the SNP is broadening its support, while Plaid remains narrowly based in the Welsh-speaking areas despite its efforts to the contrary. Plaid's *raison d'être* is the defence of the Welsh language and Welsh culture against homogenising and corrosive forces spilling over from its neighbour. Self-government or independence is a means to this end. The SNP, on the other hand, believes in independence as an end in itself. There are some references to the defence and promotion of indigenous cultural icons (e.g. Gaelic and Lallans Scots), at party conferences and particularly in the semi-official *Scots Independent* newspaper, but these are not central to the party's overriding goal.

In spite of this difference, the same three themes have nevertheless dominated the policy agendas of the nationalist parties since 1979. These include opposition to Thatcherism, the place of Scotland and Wales in the European Community and the strategy for constitutional change.

Of the three, opposition to Thatcherism has, unsurprisingly, been one of the principal battlegrounds of left-right factionalism. It necessarily takes in a multitude of issues, too. The radical agenda of the early Thatcher years served to widen existing ideological divisions in the nationalist parties between those who advocated an equally radical, if not militant response from an overtly socialist perspective, and those who supported a continuance of the single-issue approach. In general, it is clear that the left has been victorious in each party, but not without a prolonged and debilitating period of factionalism which still erupts from time to time.

In addition to a socialist policy agenda, the left within both parties has promoted the use of civil disobedience tactics. With the exception of Gwynfor Evans' hunger strike in 1980 over the government's decision (later reversed) to abandon the Welsh-language TV channel, all these activities have been associated with left-wing issues and activism. Some forms of nationalist militancy have fallen outside the bounds of acceptability – the burning of holiday homes in Wales being the most obvious example – and have not been officially sanctioned. Plaid has had a special problem in this regard which is compounded by its own oft-stated opposition to incomers (i.e. English people) buying property in Welsh rural communities. It has not been able to escape guilt by association, in the minds of many voters, for the fire raising campaign. For the most part however, civil disobedience has comprised token occupations, demonstrations, and non-payment campaigns.

Within the SNP, the left's progress has been rather more arduous than is the case in Plaid, and the waxing and waning of civil disobedience tactics has been one measure of this. In the early 1980s, the left in the SNP advocated and participated in 'industrial' campaigns, where activity ranged from occupying job centres to supporting worker occupations. Backed by conference for a while, this strategy of 'direct action' was abandoned in 1982 with the temporary defeat of the left in the party. However, it continued in a rather low-key way in local protests at nuclear waste sites, and indirectly through the involvement of party activists in Scottish CND. The civil disobedience strategy was to re-emerge in full in 1987, when it was decided to support a community charge (poll tax) non-payment campaign over the introduction of the tax in Scotland.

In the meantime, the party adopted a variety of socialist policies including the adoption of a 'worker's charter', withdrawal from NATO, nuclear disarmament, repeal of 'anti-trade union' legislation and the re-nationalisation of the Scottish steel industry (Levy, 1990: Chapters 4 and 5). The 1992 election manifesto consolidated these commitments, adding extra ones in the areas of public housing and increased spending on pensions and health, and the decisions taken at the 1992 annual conference reaffirmed the party's socialist orientation. Nevertheless, tension continues over this agenda. Areas of strong SNP support showed above average levels of poll tax payment, and the non-payment campaign was wound down in 1991. Attempts have also been made to reverse the commitment to steel nationalisation. However, the consternation caused within the SNP by the decision of the party leader Alex Salmond (himself elected on a left-wing platform in 1991) to support the government during the passage of the Maastricht legislation in 1993, and his subsequent hasty back-tracking on the issue, shows the strength the left now musters.

Plaid has involved itself in types of direct action similar to those of the SNP. This included a water non-payment campaign in the early 1980s as a protest against rising water charges, which was eventually called off after a court case in 1983. The party gave material support to miners and their families during the miners' strike of 1984–85, and afforded similar backing to slate-quarry workers. Plaid also mounted an anti-poll tax campaign in 1989, but this did not advocate mass non-payment – rather, it invited people 'to use all lawful measures to obstruct collection of the poll tax' (*Welsh Nation*, 6, 3 1990: 1). The campaign did, however, pledge support to those who did not pay the tax, and established a 'Committee of 100' 'can-pay-won't-pay' non-payers.

Unlike the SNP, Plaid's commitment to (community) socialism is embodied in its constitution. Plaid is formally affiliated with CND Cymru, and has affiliated trade union and women's sections within its own structure. The formal commitment to socialism was made as early as 1981, and stems from the majority report of the five-member party Commission of Inquiry established in the wake of the 1979 debacle. The report suggested a distinctive Welsh concept of community socialism, and advocated less involvement with Westminster politics and other parties generally (such isolationism was also evident in the SNP after the referendum experience). Sections of the party, most readily epitomised by the leadership of Dafydd Elis Thomas (elected in 1984), embraced such fashionable totems as feminism, ecology, anti-nuclearism and anti-racism. According to Davies, this 'bewildered the more traditional of the party members' (Davies, 1985: 157). Since its confirmation at the 1985 conference, and the subsequent winding up of the Hydro group, there has been little serious opposition to the party's socialist goal, despite the retirement of Elis Thomas in 1990 and the resumption by Dafydd Wigley of the party leadership.

The question of how to achieve self-government is central for both parties and has been a continual source of difficulty, particularly for the SNP. The controversy over the Labour government's devolution proposals between 1974 and 1979 was the principal cause of internal friction within the SNP and seriously damaged the party. While devolution has hardly been at the top of the policy agenda during the era of Conservative government, it has not gone away; moreover, the issue of cooperation within those opposition parties seeking consti-tutional change has been very much to the fore.

In many ways, the two parties drew similar conclusions about the referendum experience, although their immediate reactions were rather different. Disagreement over whether and how to support the Labour government's proposals had been building up steadily within the SNP since 1976, so that the referendum 'defeat' (i.e. a slight majority of those who voted were in favour, but the total failed to reach the 40 per cent minimum required by the legislation) came almost as a relief. In an atmosphere bordering more on triumph than dismay, the party's National Council meeting two days after the 1 March referendum instructed the parliamentary group to follow an uncompromising strategy and bring down the government (Levy, 1990). Thus, when it came to the vote of confidence in Parliament later in the month, the SNP MPs voted with the opposition and the government was defeated. Plaid's first reaction was one of utter despondency at the scale of the defeat of devolution for Wales. Given the support of large numbers of Labour activists and MPs in Wales for the 'No' campaign, Plaid had good reason to withdraw support from the government. Yet it did not do so. Plaid MPs voted with the government in the motion of confidence, having in the meantime extracted promises on industrial compensation in the slate quarrying industry.

The post-mortems in both parties took different forms, but arrived at rather similar conclusions. In the SNP, the 'debate' consisted of a fundamentalist backlash and an accompanying rearguard action by left-leaning pragmatists which tore the party asunder for three years. In Plaid, a Commission of Inquiry was established in June 1979 which reported back to the party in 1981. In both cases, the upshot was a withdrawal from cross-party cooperation on the constitutional issue, a greater focus on local politics and a hardening of attitudes, particularly in the SNP, against support for devolution.

Throughout the 1980s, there were calls from within the SNP for cross-party collaboration in achieving self-government, an assembly or staging a multi-option referendum on the constitutional issue. It never actually materialised, however, despite the 'tartanising' of parts of the Labour Party in Scotland (Geekie and Levy, 1989), and the movement of the SNP towards a socialist agenda. Relationships between the two parties are probably as bad now as they have ever been. The lack of trust between the SNP and Labour was most graphically illustrated by the SNP's decision not to participate in the cross-party (but Labour-dominated) Constitutional Convention established in 1989, even though SNP members thought that non-participation in the Convention would harm the party (*Glasgow Herald*, 30.3.89). While there are still those within the party who support devolution as a tactic and who continue to urge a united front with other opposition parties (Bayne, 1991), the 'Independence – Nothing Less' policy has predominated since 1979.

Historically, Plaid has been less concerned about sovereignty and more concerned about cultural preservation. 'Devolution' is therefore not so much of a bogeyword, although the 1979 referendum campaign has hardened the party's official policy. Plaid now calls for a parliament for Wales with full 'national status' and independent representation in the EC. However, in the mid-1980s, it supported the creation of a devolved assembly in the form of a hundred-member Senate (*Y Senedd*), and the party continues to use the term 'self-government' in preference to 'independence', so leaving some room for ambiguity. Since 1979, many anti-devolutionists in the Welsh Labour Party have been won over to the cause of devolution as a result of their prolonged experience of opposition and, as in Scotland, all-party groups such as the Campaign for a Welsh Assembly have sought to galvanise a cross-party campaign. At its 1992 conference, the Welsh TUC called for the establishment of a cross-party 'convention' and this was welcomed by Plaid. Such initiatives have not produced the desired result so far, and are unlikely to do so as long as Plaid seeks to broaden its electoral base into the Labour heartlands.

In the 1992 general election, Plaid and the SNP officially supported a policy of 'Independence in the EC'. In both cases, this represented a substantial turnaround from the 1970s when the two parties opposed EC membership. Baxter-Moore points out that it was Plaid rather than the SNP which led the change in strategy (Baxter-Moore, 1992: 11), although it only adopted the 'Independence in Europe' policy officially at its 1990 annual conference. The turning point for the SNP came in 1983, when the party conference dropped its outright opposition to EC membership in favour of a pragmatic but positive approach. The formal commitment to 'Independence in Europe' was made five years later at the 1988 conference, but that did not stop leading figures in the party proclaiming it as official policy in the period in between (Levy, 1990: 121).

The case against EC membership has rested on the issues of loss of sovereignty and the perceived threat to Scottish or Welsh national interests from Brussels. The 'Independence in Europe' strategy is particularly heinous for some nationalists because it accepts Scottish and Welsh membership of the Community as a *fait accompli* effected by a 'foreign' government (the UK). From this point of view, EC membership is something which can only be considered after independence from the UK has been achieved. Many opponents of EC membership in the SNP additionally see the Community as inimical to the interests of a resource-rich primary producer such as Scotland, and argue instead for the longstanding Norwegian style solution of keeping Scotland out of the EC but able to enter into agreements with it.

Supporters of the policy counter that sovereignty can only be lost if it is possessed in the first place, and that, in any case, Scotland or Wales would be legally bound to accept the agreements entered into by their predecessor state. Given the realities of the European economy and Scotland and Wales' close integration into it (in particular, into the remainder of the UK economy), 'Independence in Europe' would ostensibly guarantee stability and continued access to these markets. At the same time, independent Scottish and Welsh governments could defend national interests within the framework of constraints of

Community institutions and policies, and would have representation right up to the 'top table' of the Council of Ministers.

Whatever its other merits, the SNP's 'Independence in Europe' policy has been at least in part designed to overcome the gap between the aspirations of SNP members and the caution and conservatism of potential nationalist voters. In this sense, it is an equally neat solution for Plaid. In seeming to promise all benefits and no costs and minimal disruption in the meantime, 'Independence in Europe' has proved popular with voters, although it is clear that many of them like it much more as an idea than as a practical policy. If it were otherwise, the nationalists might be negotiating (or trying to negotiate) for independence now. Instead, the SNP's election slogan of 'Free in '93' has turned into the embarrassing reality of 'Three (MPs) in '93'.

## Conclusion

Plaid and the SNP have entered the 1990s enjoying a modest renaissance. Their vote has improved, party membership has recovered somewhat from the low levels of the 1980s and factional activity is relatively light. However, this may be no more than a peak in the cycle of organisational and electoral renewal which will just as surely be followed by decline, as it has been on previous occasions.

In common with other 'third' parties, the nationalists suffer from a huge credibility problem. To transform themselves into purely vote-winning machines would mean ditching cherished policies and principles, and jettisoning most of the committed members. Neither alternative is attractive or practicable, and might not produce the desired result anyway. Both parties are trying to broaden their appeal to Labour voters who, having seen their party out of office for almost a decade and a half and watched a large hole open up where Labours' beliefs used to be, might be tempted to vote for another party. As there are other options in the form of the Liberal Democrats and the Greens on offer, the nationalists have not got the field to themselves. The evidence suggests that the SNP has been more successful in this venture, but progress is much slower than expectation. So far, Plaid has failed to break out of the Welsh-speaking camp to any significant degree.

Another option is to try and attract disaffected Conservative voters. Given the already low Conservative vote in Scotland and Wales, such a strategy is unlikely to produce any significant rewards. In any case, a cornerstone of Conservative policy is the defence of the constitutional status quo, and thus Conservative supporters are hardly likely to be attracted to the nationalists as an alternative. An attempt could be made to squeeze the Liberal vote, which if successful, could produce one or two extra seats for the nationalists in the rural areas. This would not produce the big breakthrough in the populous urban areas, however.

Outside events are not working in the nationalists' favour either. The EC's disarray over its future direction, its pitiful failure to intervene effectively in the former Yugoslavia and the recession in the continental economies make the 'Independence in Europe' policy begin to look more like an albatross than an asset. On the wider stage, nationalism has resumed the ugly mask which has characterised it for much of the twentieth century. Like everywhere else, Scotland and Wales have not been immune from the effects of xenophobia. It is to be hoped that this unappetising meal will be left on the plate by the nationalist parties. It is neither a pretty sight nor a good prospect.

## References

Agnew, J. (1984), 'Place and political behaviour: the geography of Scottish nationalism', *Political Geography Quarterly*, 3 (3): 191–206.

Balsom, D. (1979a), *The Nature and Distribution of Support for Plaid Cymru*, Glasgow, Centre for the Study of Public Policy.

Balsom, D. (1979b), 'Plaid Cymru: The Welsh National Party', in H.M. Drucker (ed.), *Multi-party Britain*, London, Macmillan.

Balsom, D., Madgwick, P. and van Mechelen, D. (1983), 'The Red and the Green: Patterns of Partisan Choice', *British Journal of Political Science*, 13 (3): 299–325.

Balsom, D. (1985), 'The Three Wales Model', in J. Osmond (ed.), *The National Question Again: Welsh Political Identity in the 1980s*, Dyfed, Gomer.

Baxter-Moore, N. (1979), *The Rise and Fall of the S.N.P.: Revisited*, paper delivered to the European Politics Group Workshop, London, Ontario, 17–19 December.

Baxter-Moore, N. (1992), *Independence in Europe? Scottish Nationalism and European Integration*, paper delivered to the Annual Meeting of the Canadian Political Science Association, Charlottetown, 31 May–2 June.

Bayne, I.O. (1991), 'The Impact of 1979 on the S.N.P.', in T. Gallagher (ed.), *Nationalism in the Nineties*, Edinburgh, Polygon.

Brand, J. (1978), *The National Movement in Scotland*, London, Routledge.

Brand, J., McLean, I. and Miller, W. (1983), 'The Birth and Death of the Three Party System: Scotland in the Seventies', *British Journal of Political Science*, 13 (4): 463–88.

Brand, J., 'SNP members: the way of the faithful', in P. Norris, I. Crewe, D. Denver and D. Broughton, *British Elections and Parties Yearbook 1992*, Hertfordshire, Harvester Wheatsheaf.

Butler, D. and Stokes, D. (1976), *Political Change in Britain*, (2nd college edn), New York, St. Martin's Press.

Butt-Philip, A. (1975), *The Welsh Question*, Cardiff, University of Wales Press.

Crawford, R.M. (1982), *The S.N.P., 1960–74: An Investigation into its Organisation and Power Structure*, unpublished Ph.D. thesis, University of Glasgow.

Davies, C. Aull (1989), *Welsh Nationalism in the Twentieth Century: The Ethnic Option and the Modern State*, New York, Praeger.

Davies J. (1985), 'Plaid Cymru in Transition', in J. Osmond, *The National Question Again: Welsh Political Identity in the 1980s*, Dyfed, Gomer.

Duverger, M. (1954), *Political Parties*, New York, Wiley.

Hanby, V. (1976), 'The Renaissance of the S.N.P.: From Eccentric to Campaigning Crusader', in L. Maisel (ed.), *Changing Campaign Techniques: Elections and Values in Contemporary Democracies*, Beverly Hills, Sage, 217–41.

Hechter, M. (1975), *Internal Colonialism: The Celtic Fringe in British National Development 1536–1966*, London, Routledge.

Jaensch, D. (1976), 'The Scottish vote 1974: A Realigning Party System?', *Political Studies*, 24 (3): 306–19.

Johnston, R.J., Pattie, C.J., Allsop, J.G. (1988), *A Nation Dividing: The Electoral Map of Great Britain 1979–87*, London, Longman.

Kellas, J. (1973, 1984), *The Scottish Political System* (1st edn, 3rd edn), Cambridge, Cambridge University Press.

Levy, R. (1988), 'Third Party Decline in the U.K.: The S.N.P. and S.D.P. in Comparative Perspective', *West European Politics*, 11 (3): 57–74.

Levy, R. and Geekie, J. (1989), 'Devolution and the Tartanisation of the Labour Party', *Parliamentary Affairs*, 42 (3): 399–411.

Levy, R. (1990), *Scottish Nationalism at the Crossroads*, Edinburgh, Scottish Academic Press.

Linton, M. (ed.) (1992), *The Guide to the House of Commons: New Parliament*, London, Fourth Estate.

Lutz, J. (1990), 'Diffusion of nationalist voting in Scotland and Wales: emulation, contagion and retrenchment', *Political Geography Quarterly*, 9 (3): 249–66.

Mansbach, R.W. (1973), 'The S.N.P.: A revised Political Profile', *Comparative Politics*, 5 (2): 185–210.

McAllister, I. (1979), *Party organisation and minority nationalism: a comparative study in the United Kingdom*, Glasgow, Centre for the Study of Public Policy.

McLean, I. (1970), 'The Rise and Fall of the S.N.P.', *Political Studies*, 18 (3): 357–72.

Miller, W., Brand, J. and Jordan, M. (1980), *Oil and the Scottish Voter, 1974–79*, London, Social Science Research Council.

Miller, W. (1981), *The End of British Politics: Scots and English Political Behaviour in the Seventies*, Oxford, Oxford University Press.

Newman, S. (1992), 'The rise and decline of the Scottish National Party: ethnic politics in a post-industrial environment', *Ethnic and Racial Studies*, 15 (1): 1–35.

Parry, R. (1988), *Scottish Political Facts*, Edinburgh, T. & T. Clark.

Plaid Cymru, (1991), *Constitution of Plaid Cymru*, Cardiff, Plaid Cymru.

Plaid Cymru, (1992), *Towards 2000: Plaid Cymru's Programme for Wales in Europe*, Cardiff, Plaid Cymru.

Pulzer, P. (1972), *Political representation and Elections in Britain* (2nd edn), London, Allen and Unwin.
Rawkins, P. (1979), 'An Approach to the Sociology of the Welsh Nationalist Movement', *Political Studies*, 27 (3): 440–57.
*Scots Independent*, Stirling, Scots Independent (Newspapers) Ltd.
Scottish National Party (1992), *Independence In Europe, Make it Happen Now!*, Edinburgh, Scottish National Party.
Scottish National Party (1991), *Constitution and Rules of the S.N.P.*, Edinburgh, Scottish National Party.
Sillars, J. (1989), *Independence in Europe*, Glasgow.
Studlar, D. and McAllister, I. (1988), 'Nationalism in Scotland: A Post-Industrial Phenomenon?', *Ethnic and Racial Studies*, 11 (1): 48–62.
Watson, M. (ed.) (1990), *Contemporary Minority Nationalism*, London, Routledge.
Webb, K. (1978), *The Growth of Nationalism in Scotland*, Harmondsworth, Penguin.
*Welsh Nation*, Cardiff, Plaid Cymru.
Williams, D. (1990), *The Story of Plaid Cymru, the Party of Wales*, Aberystwyth, Plaid Cymru.

# 9
# The political parties of Northern Ireland

*Arthur Aughey*

It has been the traditional assumption of politics that there are two very different systems of party competition in Britain. These party systems are defined by the subject matter of policy debate and by the mobilisation strategies of party organisations. The first – and dominant – system is that which operates in Great Britain. The lines of party political division are social and economic. The policy discourse reveals argument about the intricacies of financial management, about collective provision versus self-reliance, about the distribution of wealth between citizens. The popular perceptions of the parties and the images which the parties desire to project are intimately bound up with that division and that discourse. The traditional ideological shorthand which has been used to describe this party system proposes a contest between varieties of socialism and varieties of conservatism appropriate to the history and sentiments of the British electorate. And class remains the major sociological factor in electoral mobilisation.

The second system is that which operates in Northern Ireland. Here the divisions between parties have to do with the constitution, with the fundamental issue of whether the state should exist at all. In short, the central question between the parties and the question which defines the imperatives of party organisation and image has been and continues to be: should Northern Ireland remain a full and integral part of the United Kingdom; or should that position be changed such that Northern Ireland becomes part of a united, federal or confederal Ireland or its governance shared equally between the British and Irish states? This party system is characterised by the competition between varieties of Ulster Unionism and varieties of Irish Nationalism. And the major sociological factor in electoral mobilisation is not social class but religion. Support for Unionist parties is overwhelmingly Protestant and support for Nationalist parties is overwhelmingly Catholic. Such has been the distinctiveness of this passionate and particular party system that it has been the custom of many texts on British politics to exclude it altogether or only to make passing reference to it (see, for example, Ingle, 1987; Leach, 1991).

Whatever the qualifications one might like to enter about the absolute distinctiveness of these two party systems – such as the growing importance of constitutional issues in Great Britain and the social and economic problems which Northern Ireland has in common with the rest of the United Kingdom – the traditional assumption of students is substantially accurate and the custom of the texts reasonably sound. Distinctiveness is also the foundation of British government policy for Northern Ireland. This has been an article of faith for successive Secretaries of State. In the mid-1970s Merlyn Rees explained to Prime Minister James Callaghan that Northern Ireland was distinguished from the rest of the Kingdom by the 'presence of two separate communities', Unionist and Nationalist. 'Its problems', he argued, 'are not those of Scotland and Wales and therefore do not necessarily require the same treatment' (Rees, 1985: 329). Nor has Northern Ireland always had – necessarily or not – the same treatment. For instance, except for elections to the seventeen Westminster seats which are conducted on the general system of 'first-past-the post', all other elections in Northern Ireland, local and European, operate according to the single transferable vote method of PR. This is designed to reflect as fairly as possible the proportionate balance of these 'two communities', Unionist and Nationalist. And until very recently none of the major British parties organised and campaigned in Northern Ireland, treating it as a place apart and its concerns a world apart from the normal civilised conventions of British political life (a prejudice to which we will return). Two points need to be made here. First, while the battle line between Unionism and Nationalism dominates political life, the divisions within Unionism and within Nationalism have often been deep and bitter and of great consequence. Secondly, although there is a distinctive and subordinate party system in Northern Ireland it is not autonomous. The substance of the debate between the parties, indeed the very framework within which that debate takes place, has been significantly influenced by the decisions taken by the British government. The history of party politics in Northern Ireland since 1979 illustrates the truth of both those propositions.

The history of the last fifteen years has been dominated by three major political events. The first was the hunger strike of Republican prisoners in 1980–81 which increased the bitterness of party politics and directly encouraged Sinn Fein, the political wing of the Provisional IRA, to contest elections. The consequences of the emergence of Sinn Fein as an electoral force have been profound. Without its rise it is arguable that the second major political event of recent years, the signing of the Anglo-Irish Agreement in November 1985, would not have taken place. The Anglo-Irish Agreement, which provided the government of the

Republic of Ireland with a consultative role in the affairs of Northern Ireland, outraged Ulster Unionists and drove their representatives into a condition of 'internal exile'. Unionist hostility to the provisions of the Agreement was matched by Nationalist expectation of its possibilities. The third event, the so-called 'Talks' process, represents an attempt by the British government (and the Irish) to encourage the constitutional parties to agree some workable and durable political settlement for the governance of Northern Ireland, to reconcile or at least balance the contesting forces of Ulster Unionism and Irish Nationalism. The three events are interrelated, politically if not logically. The hunger strike promoted Sinn Fein's electoral strategy, which generated the momentum for the Agreement, the failures of which have promoted the elaboration of the Talks. The rest of this chapter assesses the impact of these events upon the fortunes and policies of respectively the Unionist, Nationalist and non-communal parties in Northern Ireland.

## The Unionists

There was both fragmentation and cooperation within Unionist politics in the 1970s. Once the institution of a devolved legislature which had provided cohesion for the old Ulster Unionist party (effectively the party of government) was removed in 1972, and once the opportunities of PR were recognised, a new era of intra-Unionist competition opened up. This was mitigated by the traditional political wisdom that only Unionist unity could prevent the subversion by its enemies of Northern Ireland's constitutional position. By the end of the decade the smaller, sectional Unionist parties had either dissolved or been absorbed by the two main parties, the Ulster Unionist Party (often known colloquially as the Official Unionists) and the Democratic Unionist Party. The UUP and the DUP saw each other as rivals for the mantle of Unionist fidelity. As one commentator put it: 'the Democratic Unionists became the focus for a loyalist tendency and the Official Unionists for a unionist tendency' (Elliott, 1992: 86). The competition between these 'loyalist' and 'unionist' tendencies became quite acute in the first half of the 1980s. However, the course of the 1980s was to reveal a similar pattern to that of the 1970s. Competition transformed itself into cooperation as, after 1985, both parties attempted to shift the ominous bulk of the Anglo-Irish Agreement.

The Ulster Unionist Party is the oldest of the Northern Ireland parties and can trace its origins back to the Home Rule crises of the turn of the century. A key to its character lies in the fact that for most of its history the Ulster Unionist Party maintained a direct organisational link with the British Conservative (and Unionist) Party. It was the convention – of political sympathy as well as tactical convenience – that the representatives of the party at Westminster would take the Conservative whip. It was only after the Conservative government of Edward Heath prorogued the Unionist-controlled devolved legislature in Belfast in 1972 that the Ulster Unionists began to organise themselves as a distinct party in the House of Commons; and only after the signing of the Agreement in 1985 that the remaining links with the Conservative Party organis- ation at National Union and Executive levels were severed. In their leader since 1979, James Molyneaux MP, the Ulster Unionists have had the quintessential House of Commons man, a paragon of constitutional respectability as well as of tactical astuteness. And, of course, the Westminster party was educated in the possibilities of intelligent parliamentarianism by Enoch Powell, who joined the UUP after his break with the Conservatives in 1974. Powell was a major influence in Unionist ranks throughout the 1980s and continued to be even after he lost his South Down seat in 1987. The contemporary Unionist Party is conscious of its potential as a minority (though fourth largest) party in the House of Commons. And it intends to exert as much influence as possible over policy on Northern Ireland by exploiting the opportunities of what now appears to be a new era of small government majorities in the 1990s.

The electoral image of the UUP is conservative in two senses of that word. Firstly, it is conservative on the constitutional position of Northern Ireland's place within the United Kingdom. Secondly, it is conservative in the colloquial sense of being 'respectable'. It presents itself to the (Unionist) electorate as the party of traditional Unionism, as both representative of that tradition and the most responsible advocate of it. While the party does have a character, an image, analogous to that of the Conservative Party, that is not the whole of the matter. Organically linked to the UUP is the Orange Order, *the* major institution of popular Protestantism (albeit in a very different manner, the social, cultural and political influence of the Order within the UUP is similar to that of the association between the trade unions and the British Labour Party). The UUP is, then, not only a middle-class party of farmers, business people and professionals *but also* a party of cross-class Protestant interest. Therefore, in the 1980s and 1990s the UUP could not possibly be Conservative in the mould of the Thatcherites, for that would have alienated a large proportion of its electoral support, especially amongst the working class.

The Democratic Unionist Party is a product of the current Troubles. It was founded in 1971 as a radical Protestant opposition to the UUP. As its original formulation put it, the DUP was to be 'right wing in the sense of being strong on the Constitution, but to the left on social policies' (Flackes, 1983: 76). This curious formulation does capture something of the spirit of the DUP. What it leaves out is the influence of the Free Presbyterian Church in the party's organisation and finance and, of course, the dominant influence on its policy of the Reverend Ian Paisley, the leader of that Church. One student of the party has called it a 'politico-religious organisation' in which Paisley's 'twin commitments to Protestantism and loyalism are replicated throughout the DUP' and explain 'both the party's extraordinary cohesion and its ruthless electioneering zeal' (Smyth, 1986: 42). Unlike that of the UUP, the DUP's electoral image is populist first and foremost. It appeals to the robust communalism of the working class in areas like East Belfast as well as to the fundamental Protestantism of rural Northern Ireland. Nor is its image 'respectable' in the conservative sense of the UUP. The DUP expresses a tradition of indignant righteousness which ranges from political showmanship to public disorder and threats of disruption. The politics of the DUP are not only about defending the Union against Nationalist subversion or even Protestantism against Catholicism; they are also about protecting the righteous against the ungodly.

The relationship between the two Unionist parties has never been particularly harmonious, even though they share the same basic constitutional objective. If Unionists understand themselves to be a 'family', as the frequently used term has it, then it is not a very happy family. In the early 1980s the junior member of that family, the DUP, seemed set to supplant the senior member, the UUP. This electoral competition between the Unionist parties entered a new phase following the result of the first direct election to the European Parliament in June 1979. In the Westminster elections of May of that year, the DUP had taken two seats from the UUP in East and North Belfast. Though the actual percentage increase in DUP support was small (from 8.5 to 10.2 per cent), the possibility was intimated of a new radical loyalist alternative to the conservative alliance of the Ulster Unionists. That the old order was truly changing seemed confirmed by the result of the European election. Paisley came top of the poll in the Euro-constituency constituted by the whole province of Northern Ireland. This vote, confirmed in all subsequent European elections, allowed Paisley to claim that he had a mandate to speak for the (Protestant) people of Ulster and that his own party represented the will of the (Protestant) people in a way in which the UUP could not (Smyth, 1987: 171).

This, however, was to misinterpret the nature of the Unionist 'general will'. That will, in so far as it may be said to exist, expresses at one level *opposition* to the idea of a united Ireland. Because Paisley is understood to embody that opposition in an uncompromising way, the European elections have about them the character of a referendum conducted on the basis of personalities which the DUP leader wins hands down. But that negative statement – no to a united Ireland – does not constitute a positive statement in favour of the DUP either as a party or as a style of politics. For the other level of that general will expresses a *commitment* to the Union and the DUP is not necessarily seen as the best vehicle for that commitment. Nevertheless, the early 1980s seemed to suggest otherwise. The hunger strike; the rise of Sinn Fein; the beginnings of Anglo-Irish cooperation; divisions within the UUP over government policy; continuing sectarian violence – all helped to polarise public opinion and provided a perfect opportunity for the DUP to prosper. In the politically tense district council elections of 1981 the DUP overtook the UUP, polling 26.6 per cent to the UUP's 26.5 per cent. The DUP now appeared to be in the ascendant and more appropriate to Protestant interests in the embittered political scene produced by the IRA's intervention in electoral politics.

As it turned out there was to be no irresistible rise of the party. The 1981 result was the DUP's high water mark. In 1982 the UUP recovered its position in the elections to the new local assembly established by the Secretary of State, James Prior. Its vote rose to 29.7 per cent, while the DUP's fell back to 23 per cent. The DUP made no further advances in the Westminster election of 1983. By the end of the 1980s the UUP had pulled away even more, recording an average vote of 32 per cent against a DUP vote of 19 per cent. In some ways this might appear surprising. When the British government signed the Anglo-Irish Agreement in November 1985 the expectation of most commentators was that the crisis and alienation this promoted in Unionist politics would be conducive to a dramatic rise in support for the DUP. It was believed that the conditions of 1981 would reassert themselves. James Molyneaux, the parliamentarian, would be no match for Ian Paisley, the defender of the faith. This did not happen.

Instead, the two parties came together to cooperate for the purpose of removing the 'monstrous conspiracy' of the Anglo-Irish Agreement. They concluded an electoral pact in January 1986 which lasted until the general election of 1992. In terms of the tactics of opposition to the Agreement, it has been the Molyneaux style which has dominated (despite the media impression to the contrary). In terms of the benefits of electoral success, it has been the UUP which has drawn the advantage. This offended many DUP activists and was a source of division within that party. The feeling was that the pact had frustrated the DUP's advance and had compromised its position as the unmovable defender of British Ulster. Pressure to end the pact became irresistible in 1992. It was the expectation of younger DUP members such as Sammy Wilson, a former Lord Mayor of Belfast, that the party would significantly improve its position within the Unionist alliance. The result of the 1992 general election was a profound disappointment to them. Even with a larger number of candidates in the field the DUP vote rose to only 13.1 per cent (1.4 per cent over its 1987 vote). While the UUP vote did fall three percentage points to 34.5 per cent, this may be put down not to DUP competition but rather to the intervention of a new rival, the Conservative Party. The 1992 general election confirmed the

UUP's status as the dominant Unionist party and confirmed the appropriateness, for the bulk of the Protestants of Ulster, of its cautious 'constitutional' opposition to the Anglo-Irish Agreement. What is the character of that opposition, and what has been the position of the Unionist parties in the political Talks of the last few years?

The Agreement was a profound shock to both parties and promoted a joint effort to get Unionists off what the DUP deputy leader Peter Robinson MP called 'the window ledge of the Union' (Aughey, 1989: 80). The Agreement had changed the focus of the Ulster question. In the first years of the Thatcher government the main concern of the Unionist parties had been the relative merits of a strong devolved system of government for Northern Ireland (the DUP position) or a more limited form of administrative devolution within a reformed structure of direct rule from Westminster (the UUP position). These differing attitudes had influenced the parties' interest and participation in the Northern Ireland Assembly, established in 1982 to foster 'rolling devolution'. The DUP was enthusiastic, the UUP lukewarm. What both parties did have in common was an assumption that while Mrs Thatcher was Prime Minister there would be little concession to Irish Nationalism. In particular, it was felt that the so-called 'Irish dimension' to Northern Ireland's political affairs would remain strictly subordinate to an internal settlement. The Agreement, by giving the Irish government a role in the affairs of Northern Ireland, represented an outflanking of the Unionist position by that very Irish dimension.

The challenge facing the two Unionist parties after November 1985 was one of political recovery. They had been out-manoeuvred by their Nationalist opponents and by their own government. Their task was, firstly, to try to reaffirm the United Kingdom status of Northern Ireland which had been compromised by the Agreement. Secondly, they had to redress the perceived imbalance which the Agreement had created between Unionist and Nationalist within Northern Ireland. This meant working towards some structure of government which would acknowledge the right of the majority, if not to have *control* of policy in Northern Ireland at least to *define* the form of any policy-making arrangement. Thirdly, the UUP and DUP had to confront the possibility of an ever deepening process of Anglo-Irish cooperation by proposing a new relationship between the two states which would more satisfactorily guarantee their interests. In the words of their joint manifesto of 1987, Molyneaux and Paisley had to negotiate 'an alternative to and a replacement of the Anglo-Irish Agreement'. This has been no mean task. Differences between the two parties remain on what that alternative/replacement should involve. However, the common ground is more extensive than these differences.

In the course of the Talks initiated in 1991 by Secretary of State Peter Brooke and carried on by his successor Sir Patrick Mayhew, the UUP and the DUP have envisaged the establishment of a broader British–Irish Agreement which would conform to the well-defined parameters of inter-state cooperation. It would involve, amongst other things, a devolved legislature for Northern Ireland guaranteeing a proportionate role for the minority; an inter-Irish relations committee to promote the common interests of Northern Ireland and the Irish Republic; a Council of the British Isles to discuss the common problems of all the regions of the two islands; and a British–Irish parliamentary body along the lines of that set up by the two governments in 1988. What has been central to the negotiating strategy of both parties has been the demand that the Irish Republic should remove the territorial claim to Northern Ireland contained in articles two and three of its constitution. For this is part and parcel of the Unionist aim to compel the British government to reassert, in Paisley's words, the 'integrity of the state' by pressing the Irish to do what was not demanded under the Agreement; in short, to confirm clearly and absolutely Northern Ireland's present status as a part of the United Kingdom.

In the round of Talks which ended in the winter of 1992 the DUP and the UUP had made some headway in their objectives. For the first time in a decade they had recovered some of their self-confidence and political composure. The Anglo-Irish Agreement ignored the Unionist parties and was imposed upon their electorate. The Talks are about bringing the Unionist parties into a new political arrangement which they can sell to their voters. Of course, any satisfactory outcome does not depend upon the Unionists alone but involves Nationalists as well.

## The Nationalists

It was not until August 1970 that Nationalists in Northern Ireland constructed for themselves a recognisably modern party organisation. The Social Democratic and Labour Party (SDLP) was formed at that date and replaced the old and moribund Nationalist Party as the main opposition to Ulster Unionism. The SDLP was a coalition of political interests. It brought together the traditional elements of Catholic Nationalism, civil rights activists who had come to prominence in the late 1960s and the urban labour tradition represented by such figures as its first leader, Gerry Fitt MP (now Lord Fitt). Its original statements included much socialist rhetoric about democratic control of industry and the use of the state to promote equality. The practical politics of the SDLP, despite its name, fell within the category of 'constitutional Nationalism'. However, it did seek to participate in the government of Northern Ireland on a power-sharing basis so long as the Irish government were to play a role in the institutions agreed with Unionists and the British government. The SDLP did seem to have achieved most of its immediate policy objectives in the power-sharing Executive/ Council of Ireland structure which involved the party briefly in the government of Northern Ireland in 1973–74. In the elections for the Northern Ireland Assembly in 1973 it had achieved a vote of 22.1 per cent and confirmed its role as a key player in politics as the acknowledged representative of the Catholic minority. The collapse of the power-sharing arrangement – because of Protestant resistance to the Council of Ireland – and the frustrations of the political stalemate of the rest of the 1970s encouraged the SDLP to turn towards a more straightforward Nationalism in the 1980s and 1990s.

Gerry Fitt resigned as leader in 1979, claiming that the party had lost its social radicalism and had become too 'green'. He was replaced by John Hume, who promoted a new policy position from that of the 1970s. The Hume policy was not to stress the priority of an 'internal settlement' with Unionists but to work for an agreement between the British and Irish governments which would compel the Unionists to accede to SDLP demands. The SDLP has pursued this policy consistently and with some success. This success was not due to the merits of the argument alone. It had more to do with the emergence of a rival to the SDLP within the Catholic community, a new party which transformed the politics of Northern Ireland. That party was Sinn Fein, the political wing of the Provisional IRA, which began contesting elections during the hunger strike. Sinn Fein provoked a response on the part of the British and Irish governments which led to the Agreement of 1985. And one of the purposes of that Agreement was to aid the constitutional Nationalism of the SDLP in its engagement with the political Republicanism of Sinn Fein.

The emotional impact on Ulster Catholic opinion of the hunger strike campaign by Republican prisoners provided an opportunity for Sinn Fein to seek popular legitimation for the 'armed struggle' of the IRA. Originally there was a good deal of reluctance to engage in electoral politics. The IRA's command feared that party politics might divert attention from military activity and hijack Republican energies into unnecessary electoralism. However, the propaganda success of the hunger strike could not be denied and the lesson seemed to be that the art of political mobilisation could be an effective complement to, though not a substitute for, the IRA's military campaign. When the leader of the hunger strikers, Bobby Sands, was elected as MP in a by-election in Fermanagh-South Tyrone in April 1981 the die was cast.

There were two immediate reasons for Sinn Fein developing an electoral strategy. Firstly, there was the opportunity to gain not only local but worldwide legitimacy for the IRA's campaign. Secondly, there was the possibility of overcoming the SDLP in the popular vote, thereby undermining 'constitutional' (by which Sinn Fein understands 'collaborationist') Nationalism within the Catholic community. That would change everything. Not only Northern Ireland but the whole of Anglo-Irish relations would be destabilised. As the Sinn Fein director of publicity Danny Morrison was to put it to the party conference in Dublin in November 1981: 'Will any one here object if with ballot paper in this hand and an Armalite in this hand, we take power in Ireland?' (Aughey, 1988: 106). Very few did. Only the previous year the same conference had voted resoundingly against participation in Northern Ireland elections. Sinn Fein's impact on party politics was to have dramatic consequences.

In local elections in October 1982 Sinn Fein polled 10.1 per cent of the vote against 18.8 per cent for the SDLP. In the Westminster elections of June 1983 the figures were 13.4 per cent and 17.9 per cent respectively. The president of Sinn Fein, Gerry Adams, had won the West Belfast seat from the incumbent Gerry Fitt. This was a victory of enormous symbolic importance. What is more, the vote for Sinn Fein revealed that 40 per cent of the Catholic electorate were prepared to vote for a party which supported the IRA's murder of security force members. The majority of local security force members happen to be Northern Ireland Protestants. Only a moment's reflection reveals the enormity of that statistic. Even though there may be many *individual* reasons for someone to vote Sinn Fein (which may not include support or sympathy for the IRA) the *collective* impact of these results was shocking (see Patterson, 1989). Of course, the IRA does not need an electoral mandate for the 'armed struggle'. As Adams has argued: 'It derives its mandate from the presence of the British in the six counties' (Aughey, 1988: 106). Nevertheless, the prospect of political Republicanism displacing constitutional nationalism as the organised expression of the Catholic community sent messages of panic throughout the corridors of power in London, Dublin and Belfast.

Confronting the Sinn Fein threat and bolstering support for the SDLP involved two parallel strategies. The first involved the attempted reformulation of Irish Nationalism by the SDLP and the political parties of the Republic of Ireland. The stated purpose of this Forum for a New Ireland, which held its first session on 30 May 1983, was to consult on the manner in which 'lasting peace and stability could be achieved in a new Ireland through the democratic process and to report on possible new structures and processes through which this objective might be achieved' (New Ireland Forum, 1984: 1). What was important about the Forum was that it presented the SDLP as the party which was acknowledged by the Irish state as the voice of Northern Nationalism. It also allowed the SDLP to play the role of mover and shaker on an Irish and international stage. This was designed to take the limelight away from Sinn Fein and to refocus the attention of Northern Catholics once more on the political possibilities of constitutional Nationalism. The report of the New Ireland Forum, which was published on 2 May 1984, also refocused attention upon the Irish dimension to the Northern Ireland crisis. One of the models it proposed for the achievement of a new Ireland – joint sovereignty – became a lever to press for wider concessions from the British government to the SDLP.

The second strategy involved secret negotiations between the British and Irish governments for a joint political initiative which would help to undermine Sinn Fein and the IRA, stabilise Catholic politics and sponsor a settlement between Unionists and Nationalists. The fullest record of these negotiations to date has been provided by Garret FitzGerald in his autobiography. What FitzGerald makes plain is the initial concern of the Irish and British governments to stop the apparent rot of SDLP support. The Irish, in discussions with the British, even talked in a histrionic manner about their fear for the very survival of the SDLP. But some years into these secret negotiations the purpose had changed. As FitzGerald explained the situation as it appeared in early 1985:

> the Provisionals were not now expected to threaten the SDLP's position as had been feared in 1983 and 1984. But the negotiations had now gained a momentum of their own, and the joint fear of Sinn Fein electoral success had been replaced on both sides by a positive hope of seriously undermining its existing minority support within the nationalist community (FitzGerald, 1992: 532).

This was something which FitzGerald did not want Mrs Thatcher to know. He advised Hume not to let slip in his conversations with the British Prime Minister the fact that the Sinn Fein threat had already been headed off by the SDLP.

The consequence of both these parallel strategies was the Anglo-Irish Agreement. Since the signing of that Agreement the position of the SDLP within Catholic politics has improved considerably. As Elliott (1992: 89) has noted in summary, elections after 1985 'have seen the Sinn Fein vote level out at around 11 per cent while the SDLP progressed to 21 per cent'. Yet as we have seen, this improvement cannot be attributed to the Agreement. Sinn Fein's vote had already peaked in 1983. The immediate threat was receding before the Agreement was signed and has receded even further since then. Indeed, it is the case that the SDLP and Sinn Fein were not competing for the same vote. What Sinn Fein had mobilised, in the main, was the support of those who had formerly abstained from voting. And it had articulated the grievances of those, especially in Belfast, who felt socially and economically marginalised by the 'bourgeois' Nationalism of the SDLP. In the general election of 1992 the SDLP continued to increase its vote to 23.5 per cent, the second best performance in its history. Sinn Fein's vote dropped back slightly to 9.7 per cent, though this was the sort of vote which in 1981 had set the cat amongst the political pigeons. More importantly, Adams lost his

Westminster seat of West Belfast to the SDLP candidate Dr Joe Hendron. This was a severe blow to the morale of Sinn Fein but a sweet victory for the SDLP, which increased its House of Commons representation to four. One might argue, therefore, that the Agreement was of importance in confirming the representative status of the SDLP's constitutional Nationalism. There is undoubtedly something in this argument, at least at the level of political atmospherics. However, the opinion poll data appear to show that the Agreement is not viewed with any great affection within the Catholic community.

However one assesses the impact of the Agreement, there can be little doubt that the period since 1985 has witnessed increasing confidence on the part of the SDLP that things are going its way. The Agreement was a major political achievement for the strategy of Hume to redefine the relationships not only between Unionist and Nationalist within Northern Ireland but between the British and Irish states. But it was not to be an end in itself, only the beginning of a process leading to a 'new Ireland' based on the SDLP's analysis of the problem. In the meantime, the SDLP has established for itself a privileged role *vis-à-vis* the Unionist parties in the administration of Northern Ireland. For what the Agreement put in place was a modified form of direct rule which provides for British consultation with the Irish government within the framework of the intergovernmental Conference; and which, through the Anglo-Irish Secretariat, provides for the monitoring of existing policy within Northern Ireland. In the words of the Agreement it is the obligation of the British government to 'make determined efforts' to accede to the points raised by the Irish government.

The present structure provides for a privileged empowerment of the SDLP in at least two ways, one positive and the other negative. Positively, the SDLP has the ear of the Irish government. Whatever proposals are brought forward in the Conference for discussion and resolution are likely to be suggested by the SDLP. Whatever problems are monitored by the Secretariat are likely to be those identified by the leaders of Catholic opinion in the North. Negatively, the Unionist parties have no such access to the good offices of the British government, for the British government is the sovereign authority in Northern Ireland and cannot be partisan. The Agreement was designed not only to be immune to Unionist opposition but also to be immune to Unionist influence. In such circumstances the logic of the Unionist position could only be to say No. And of course this is what the Unionist parties did do, much to the satisfaction of the SDLP, which hoped that this would further alienate the majority from the British state.

But if the Agreement was a political success for the SDLP it did not achieve the stated objectives of 'peace, stability and reconciliation'. And it has been this failure of its broader policy that has encouraged the British government to propose the possibility of a new agreement which addresses the profound Unionist objections to the present one. However, the SDLP is not particularly interested in conciliating the Unionists. It wants to beat them. It understands the Talks process to be about 'transcending' the Agreement. This means making no concessions on devolved government for Northern Ireland, which would give the Unionist parties a significant degree of control over potential constitutional developments. It does mean trying to expand the scope of the present Agreement towards joint sovereignty/joint authority as a precondition for eventual Irish unity. The papers which the SDLP submitted to the Talks in 1992 clearly illustrate this strategy. And this is a strategy which the SDLP hopes it can sell not only to the British government but also to the IRA/Sinn Fein. If the SDLP could convince the IRA to declare a cessation of violence as part of that common Nationalist agenda, then a political momentum might be built up that would further isolate and marginalise Unionists.

## The non-communal parties

A number of parties have competed for the non-communal or non-sectarian vote (in the normative and non-normative senses of the term) which may be said to constitute the narrow middle ground of Northern Ireland politics. Some of these, like the Northern Ireland Labour Party, have been dissolved; others, like the Workers' Party, have failed to make any significant electoral impact. The party which has carried the banner of self-conscious non-sectarianism throughout the period of the present Northern Ireland crisis has been the Alliance Party. In 1989 the Alliance Party was faced with a new, though very different, competitor for the non-sectarian vote. At that time the Conservative Party entered Northern Ireland politics as a fully-fledged electoral organisation. This section of the chapter examines the fortunes of both these parties.

The Alliance Party was formed in April 1970 to promote the reform of Northern Ireland's political system. Its objective was to support those institutions of government which would be as inclusive as possible. In practice, this meant supporting power-sharing between the parties of Ulster Unionism and Irish Nationalism. Given the divisions of political life in Northern Ireland, this position had both its possibilities and its dangers. On the one hand, the Alliance Party could be the essential non-sectarian fulcrum in any power-sharing arrangement, the balancing point between the political blocks but vital to their institutional stability. On the other hand, the Alliance Party could be squeezed by the extremism of non-negotiable and irreconcilable constitutional arguments advanced by the Unionist and Nationalist parties. Its self-conscious moderation and ecumenism was therefore an ambivalent quality.

The collapse of the power-sharing Executive in 1974 was a tremendous blow to the Alliance Party, since that arrangement had provided it with a definite and attractive role in the politics of the province. Its demise, and the failure of policy to resurrect something like it, has left the Alliance Party for the last twenty years in a barren no-man's land. It has maintained a presence in the district councils but has never won a Westminster seat. Unfairly, the party has the electoral image of middle-class do-gooding – which in Northern Ireland terms means that it is seen as too Unionist for working-class Catholics and as not Unionist enough for working-class Protestants. In the 1980s the party witnessed a slow attrition of its support. That is not surprising, since the 1980s were years of polarisation and sectarian bitterness. There has been some consolidation of its position in the 1990s. For instance, in 1977 the Alliance Party polled 14.5 per cent in the local government elections and 12 per cent in the Westminster election of 1979. In 1981 its local government vote fell to 8.7 per cent, in 1985 to 7 per cent and in 1989 to 6.8 per cent. In the general election of 1987 it got 10 per cent of the vote, though this had dropped back to 8.7 per cent in 1992 (Wilford, 1992: 106).

Because some durable and practical form of devolved government has always been crucial to the fortunes of the Alliance Party, it has been an enthusiastic supporter of and participant in the Talks process since 1991. The party gave only very reluctant and provisional acceptance to the Anglo-Irish Agreement, for it was realistic enough to recognise the impossibility of reconciling Unionists to it. Within the structure of the Talks, Alliance has promoted the concept of 'partnership' government, which is another way of advocating power-sharing, and a limited form of cross-border political cooperation. This has aligned it more closely with the two Unionist parties simply because the SDLP no longer has any great interest in devolution (certainly not at the expense of a watering down of the Agreement).

We observed above that it was only in 1985 that the UUP broke its remaining bonds with the British Conservative Party. Hence that latter party could no longer substantiate its claim to be represented in every constituency, to be, in effect, the 'national party'. It was partly because of these circumstances that there emerged in Northern Ireland a movement strongly committed to achieving full Conservative organisation and representation. The political purpose of this movement was to distinguish Conservative politics from its association with the practice of Unionism as a form of exclusively Protestant interest. It was the intention of Conservative activists to present the electorate with an opportunity to join or to vote for a 'party of government' as an alternative to the existing Northern Ireland parties. In sum, it represented a new concern to mobilise support for the Union on a non-sectarian basis and to democratise direct rule from Westminster. In November 1989 the Northern Ireland Conservatives won their battle over membership with the party leadership in England and their 'model' constituency associations were recognised as legitimate by the National Union.

Since its formation the impact of the Conservative Party in Northern Ireland elections has been modest, though it can claim some successes. It has won seats at district council level and it has encouraged a number of conversions to the Conservative cause of elected members of the UUP. The party was hoping to make an important breakthrough in the general election of 1992. It had two key objectives. There appeared, first, to be a possibility of its area chairman, Dr Laurence Kennedy, winning the seat in the heartland of Conservative support, North Down. The second possibility was to overtake the Alliance Party in the popular vote. As it turned out neither of these objectives was achieved. Kennedy secured a very respectable vote of 14,371 (32 per cent of the poll) but failed to wrest the seat from the incumbent, Popular Unionist James (now Sir James) Kilfedder. North Down excepted, the Alliance Party succeeded in out-polling the Conservatives in the constituencies where they were competing. The Alliance vote had fallen to 8.7 per cent but they had stayed well ahead of the Conservatives, who had achieved an overall percentage of 5.7. To some extent the Conservatives had been upstaged in this battle with the Alliance Party because of the prominence the latter had gained as an equal participant in the Talks. The Conservative Party has not been represented because the Secretary of State (a Conservative, of course) claims to speak on the party's behalf. Nevertheless, the party's performance in the general election should be put into some perspective. In its first major contest the Conservative Party's vote in Northern Ireland was two-thirds that of the long-established Alliance. Its vote was three-fifths that of Sinn Fein. If, as some commentators have done, one takes the combined Alliance and Conservative vote to represent an index of liberal tolerance (15 per cent); and if one compares this with the index of militant intolerance, Sinn Fein's 10 per cent; and with the index of Protestant fundamentalism, the DUP's 13 per cent; then one gets another interesting, and less well-publicised, perspective on the character of public opinion in Northern Ireland.

## Conclusion

The years since 1979 have witnessed some interesting patterns of party competition in Northern Ireland. The great division is still between those who support the Union of Great Britain and Northern Ireland and those who want to end that Union. As I have tried to show, the politics of Unionism and Nationalism have also their internal distinctions. Between 1979 and 1986 the UUP and the DUP had battled it out for the leadership of Ulster Unionism only to come together in the common defence of the Union after the signing of the Anglo-Irish Agreement.

Since the mid-1980s the UUP has reasserted its traditional position as the dominant voice of organised Unionist opinion. The DUP has experienced a marked decline in its support. The electoral pact with the UUP which operated between 1986 and 1992 did not bring it any advantages. The DUP has been a victim of the survival principle of Unionist unity. Some voices have been heard recently advocating a merger of the two parties. In practice, that would mean the absorption of the DUP by the UUP and is not likely to be an attractive prospect for DUP activists. Both Unionist parties continue to advance a replacement of and an alternative to the Agreement. Both of them (along with the Alliance Party) are in general accord about what that replacement should be. But they are not the masters of their own fate.

It was the electoral impact of Sinn Fein in Nationalist politics which provided the reason (excuse?) for the Anglo-Irish Agreement. And one of the central purposes of that Agreement was to underpin the fortunes of the SDLP. Since 1985 the SDLP vote has been on an upward trend and that of Sinn Fein on a downward trend. However, this was a trend which pre-dated the Agreement, and there is little evidence to show that it was accelerated by the Agreement. What the Agreement did do was to give the SDLP a distinct party advantage in the strategic arguments about the future of Northern Ireland. It encouraged the SDLP to believe that the British government is neutral on the Union, and that the ambitious SDLP goal of joint sovereignty is the next logical step in Anglo-Irish relations. Hume, the SDLP leader, has been trying to convince the leadership of Sinn Fein that joint sovereignty is an attainable objective; that it is worth the cessation of the IRA's campaign; that it is a necessary stage on the way to Irish unity; above all, that by subscribing to it Sinn Fein can be brought in from the political wilderness to be a participant in the Talks.

Party politics is not the only sort of politics in Northern Ireland. It is played out against the politics of violence conducted by Loyalist and Republican paramilitaries. There has been as yet no diminution of that political violence in the 1990s. Constitutional parties face not only a public sceptical of their promises, but also a public sometimes sceptical of their value. The task of public policy in Northern Ireland is to ensure that party political engagement dries up support for political violence. That was not achieved in the 1980s. It remains to be seen if it can be done in the 1990s. The prospects are not promising.

# References

Aughey, A. (1988), 'Political violence in Northern Ireland', in H.H. Tucker (ed.), *Combating the Terrorists*, Oxford, Centre for Security Studies.

Aughey, A. (1989), *Under Siege: Ulster Unionism and the Anglo-Irish Agreement*, London, Hurst; Belfast, Blackstaff Press; New York, St. Martin's Press.

Elliott, S. (1992), 'Voting systems and party politics in Northern Ireland', in B. Hadfield (ed.), *Northern Ireland: Politics and the Constitution*, Buckingham, Open University Press.

FitzGerald, G. (1992), *All in a Life*, Dublin, Gill and Macmillan.

Flackes, W.D. (1983), *Northern Ireland: A Political Directory*, London, BBC.

Ingle, S. (1987), *The British Party System*, Oxford, Blackwell.

Leach, R. (1991), *British Political Ideologies*, London, Philip Allen.

New Ireland Forum (1984), *Report*, Dublin, Government Stationery Office.

Rees, M. (1985), *Northern Ireland: A Personal Memoir*, London, Macmillan.

Smyth, C. (1986), 'The DUP as a politico-religious organisation', *Irish Political Studies*, 1: 33–45.

Smyth, C. (1987), *Ian Paisley: Voice of Protestant Ulster*, Edinburgh, Scottish Academic Press.

Patterson, H. (1989), *The Politics of Illusion*, London, Hutchinson.

Wilford, R. (1992), 'The 1992 Westminster election in Northern Ireland', *Irish Political Studies*, 7, 105–11.

# 10
## The 'fringe' parties

*Stephen Hunt*

'Fringe' parties, by definition, operate on the margins of the political arena and have limited impact on the decision-making process. They command the minimum of popular support in electoral terms and, therefore, play an insignificant role in the party-political system.

In Britain many parties on the periphery of this system have tended to be associated with fanaticism, irrespective of their stated policies and ideological stance. Collectively then, such parties are frequently subject to the stigmatising label of the 'lunatic fringe' and equated with 'extremism'. To some extent this reputation was earned during the 1970s, when some fringe parties of an overtly revolutionary and anti liberal-democratic persuasion seemed to have earned a more heightened public profile in Britain. Indeed, they appeared so active that they could scarcely be dismissed as a mere irrelevance and threatened to under-mine Britain's alleged cultural attributes of moderation and consensus which, traditionally, are perceived as underpinning the country's fundamental political institutions.

On the electoral level there was some evidence to suggest that the fascist National Front, by exploiting issues related to race, was beginning to play a part in the creation of a widened multi-party system, at least at the constituency level. Yet political influence could not be measured by electoral success alone. Many political writers also pointed to the way in which smaller left-wing parties directly, or indirectly, effected the lives of thousands of people by influencing the course of industrial disputes and through their involvement in campaigns such as Nuclear Disarmament, the Anti-Nazi League and the Right-to-Work marches.

In many respects the 1970s, at least by British standards, were an exceptionally violent period and for this the parties of the far left and right were often blamed. The events in Southall weeks before the 1979 general election, in which 300 people were injured when left-wing demonstrators attempted to break up a National Front meeting, seemed to epitomise the decade. For some commentators these scenes not only questioned assumptions about national political stability but reflected a wider economic and moral malaise (Clutter-buck, 1982).

At the beginning of the 1980s several experienced politicians warned that extremist groups were 'becoming endemic' and that, as a result, Britain's democratic institutions were under threat (Grimond, 1981). While it was true that extreme right- and left-wing groups continued to proliferate numerically, this was a sign of their inherent weakness rather than of increasing strength and popularity. In retrospect the 1979 election was a watershed. For the National Front the result was a disaster. Despite offering 301 candidates (the largest number ever fielded by so small a party) only 191,719 votes or 0.6 per cent of the poll was achieved. In the same election the Marxist parties forwarded 106 candidates in the most concerted effort ever undertaken to gain parliamentary seats. In the event they could muster little more than 32,000 votes between them.

This does not mean that there have not been any 'achievements'. Perhaps the most influential fringe group has been Militant Tendency on the far left, which had based its policies on the ideas of the Russian revolutionary and Bolshevik leader Leon Trotsky. Even if Militant was attributed greater influence than really warranted by the British media, it was able to conduct a successful long-term campaign of infiltration (commonly referred to as 'entryism') into the Labour Party for several years.

For the most part, however, the extremist parties have been resigned to the political wilderness and internal conflicts have led to groups adopting fresh strategies, disbanding, forming, and re-forming. The cause of this instability was the key problem of how to boost public support. One direction was to dilute the ideology and moderate policies, but this courted the risk of losing supporters who might refuse to compromise and therefore create a breakaway faction. Another tactic was to infiltrate or merge with other parties, although this was not to the taste of those members who preferred to remain independent and loyal to fundamental principles.

While the extremist parties struggled to survive, environmentalism emerged as a new radical phenomenon. The Green Party, with its commitment to democratic ideals, during a short period in the 1980s seemed poised for an electoral breakthrough. For those, particularly among the young, who found the established Westminster parties uninspiring, 'green' politics had the attraction of raising new issues and appeared to provide many of the answers for the problems that beset the modern world; not least of all, the prospect of environmental disaster. While many traditional ideas of the far left appeared redundant, the ecological lobby offered an innovating channel of protest against a multitude of social and political ills. Conceivably the Green Party also represented a profound change in wider social values and aspirations. Environmental issues, it was argued, were flourishing in post-industrial affluent societies less concerned with unrestrained economic growth and more inspired by non-materialistic, ethical issues and a pursuit of alternative lifestyles (Inglehart, 1977).

## The far right

The difficulties which plagued the extreme parties were evident in the demise of the National Front (NF). Created in 1967 from an amalgamation of anti-immigration lobbies and several small fascist groups, the party became the major vehicle for the far right (Troyna, 1986). The 1970s saw a monumental effort by the NF in electoral intervention by significantly increasing its candidature and by attracting public attention to any controversy connected with race (Hunt, 1992). In doing so the party stood in good tradition with British fascism ever since Oswald Mosley, at the 1959 general election, contested North Kensington, which included Notting Hill – the setting (along with Nottingham) of Britain's first racial disturbances.

The NF purported to reflect the white majority's desire to end black Commonwealth immigration and to instigate 'humane repatriation'. While clearly making political capital out of Enoch Powell's prediction of future racial conflict in his 'Rivers of Blood' speech in 1968, the NF went further and overtly articulated its Nazi inclinations. Central to the ideology was the alleged superiority of the white race and the need to protect the 'authentic British community' believed to be under threat by 'non-whites'.

The 1979 general election was awaited with some anticipation, since it was possible that the NF was about to become Britain's 'fourth' or even 'third' party. However, the evidence had already indicated that the NF was faced with severe limitations. This was obvious with the differences between national and local levels of support (Edgar, 1977). In general elections the NF carefully selected the constituencies which it contested. The great majority of them were in London and Birmingham, and these cities duly delivered 50 per cent of the party's support. In its earliest electoral effort in 1970 the NF polled 3.6 per cent of the total vote. At the elections of February and October 1974, 3.3 per cent and 3.1 per cent of the vote respectively was achieved. These results were hardly impressive and there is good reason to believe that the Front had done little more than monopolise the percentage of votes which had always gone to the far-right parties (Fielding, 1981: 28).

Within the context of parliamentary by-elections, as well as municipal local elections, the NF fared better. Throughout the 1970s there were some spectacular by-election results including 16 per cent of the vote in West Bromwich and 8.2 per cent in Stechford (Birmingham) in 1977, when the Liberals were beaten into third place. The party also performed well in Greater London Council elections in 1974 and 1977, and local elections elsewhere in 1975–76. Most of the votes however, were 'one-off' and could not be sustained into general elections when voters returned to their usual allegiances (Steed, 1977).

When the facts were scrutinised it was clear that support depended upon certain crucial variables. Firstly, the proximity of sizeable non-white immigrant populations. This proved to be so much the case that debate simply focused on whether the NF vote was greater *in*, or *adjacent* to, black communities (Husband, 1977). Secondly, in terms of voters and members the NF was attractive to only certain social categories, especially economically insecure skilled manual and lower middle-class workers (Nugent, 1977).

Thirdly, there was every indication that a vote for the National Front had nothing to do with fascist sentiment but constituted a protest vote indicative of an increasingly volatile electorate weary of the ineptitude of the two major parties of government. Voting for the NF was, therefore, part of a wider phenomenon where a disgruntled public was prepared to vote for smaller parties including the Liberals and the Scottish and Welsh Nationalists.

A more sophisticated interpretation suggested that as the Conservative Party had moved to the centre ground of consensus politics the NF had replaced it on the political right. For this reason the NF had found backing for a number of contentious issues including law and order and capital punishment, as well as immigration and race-relations, which the major parties had long deemed too sensitive to put on the political agenda (Walker, 1977: 217). As it transpired the 1979 general election gave this viewpoint considerable credence.

Although the election was a huge disappointment for the NF, the writing had been on the wall ever since the local elections in the previous year had pointed to a decline in support. Certainly, the party had suffered damage as a consequence of ideological rifts and personal rivalries amongst the leaders which culminated in a breakaway faction establishing the (short-lived) National Party in 1975. However, the principal reason for the NF's demise lay elsewhere, and was essentially connected with the Conservative Party's drift towards the right following Mrs Thatcher's ascendancy to the leadership.

Thatcherism brought its own distinct popular appeal, which built electoral success on promises to take concerted action on unemployment, law and order and industrial relations – all major planks in the NF's policy. The Conservative manifesto also emphasised one-nation Toryism, which claimed to 'speak for the country as a whole' and argued for an uncompromising stance on the European Community. Then there was the matter of 'race'. This was given attention by Mrs Thatcher in her speech in 1978 in which she expressed her fear that

Britain's population would be 'swamped by people of a different culture'. Further legislation for immigration control was envisaged and eventually instigated in the 1981 Nationality Act. The National Front vote was thereby captured. The evidence was apparent in the fact that the swing to the Conservatives was often highest in those areas which had given the NF some of its highest support (Butler and Kavanagh, 1984).

Electoral defeat led the increasingly beleaguered fascist movement to concentrate on alternative tactics to further its cause. Direct attacks upon ethnic communities intensified to such an extent that they became the subject of a report by a Parliamentary All-Party Joint Committee, which informed the Home Secretary in 1981 that in the previous eighteen months there had been 250 known attacks upon Caribbeans, Asians and Jews. The blame was apportioned not only to the National Front but to the British National Party and the British Movement.

A second ploy involved entryism into the Conservative Party. To the dismay of the Conservative leadership, a number of individuals attempted to stand as official candidates who were later found to have connections with fascist organisations. The most embarrassing episode involved Thomas Finnegan, prospective candidate for Stockton, who damaged what had hitherto been a smooth electoral campaign for the Conservatives in 1983. In May of that year there were revelations that he had twice stood for the National Front nine years previously. To make matters worse, the incident coincided with a report of fascist infiltration into the Young Conservatives which was presented to the party's chairman. The details were never published.

Ever since the 1979 election the NF has been racked by a series of internal conflicts and schisms. The cause of the divisions was not the leadership and personality struggles to which most fascist parties are invariably prone, but primarily a result of attempting to foster a more respectable image to widen the party's appeal. The model to emulate was held to be that of Le Pen's National Front in France, which had spectacularly increased its electoral support by courting the vote of all social strata.

In order to bring about what was scornfully described by the Front's political enemies as 'designer fascism', it was necessary to oust those leaders with infamous fascist histories. This meant the departure of some personalities long connected with the NF. As a result of an aborted attempt to usurp the party's chairmanship from John Tyndall in the autumn of 1979, Fountaine and Kavanagh were removed from the party's Executive. They were soon followed by the party's solicitor, Anthony Reed Herbert, who founded the British Democratic Party. In the early 1980s Tyndall relinquished the chairmanship and created the New National Front which became, with some other groupings, the British National Party (BNP).

Compared with the National Front, the BNP is a more extreme expression of Nazism. While the NF claims to stand for voluntary and 'phased' repatriation for immigrants, the BNP advocates instant and forced repatriation and displays an unashamedly violent racist stance. The NF and BNP lost all their deposits in the fifty-three constituencies in which they stood in the 1983 general election. The electoral support for the NF (27,065 votes, a mean average of 1.1 per cent) was not only lower than in 1979 but the party's worst ever general election performance. The best results were once more in the East End of London, yet the highest vote, in Tower Hamlets and Newham, was still only 2.4 per cent compared with 5.1 per cent in 1979. The BNP could do no better, winning just 14,621 votes (average vote per candidate 0.6 per cent) (Butler and Kavanagh, 1984: 354).

By 1986 the National Front had once more divided and for a period two groups operated under the NF banner. One faction, known as the Flag Group, retained the familiar trappings of the old National Front. The other faction, calling itself the Political Soldiers, became increasingly maverick as the decade progressed. Principal tactics involved setting up front organisations and infiltrating other movements, including those concerned with animal rights. In January 1990 the Political Soldiers split again with the establishment of the Third Way, which has proved to be one of the fastest growing and more menacing far-right groups.

Neither the National Front nor the BNP forwarded candidates for the 1987 election on the basis that the increased cost of electoral deposit was too high. In 1992 both parties entered the fray again, but with pitiful results. The NF could only accumulate an average of 343 votes in the fourteen seats in which it stood, and the BNP 532 votes in its twelve selected constituencies. The fact that the BNP had performed better was an indication that the mantle of the nation's number one fascist party was passing to them.

The attempt to present an image of respectability had decreased rather than increased the Front's appeal. In the mid-1970s the membership had stood at 20,000. By 1983 it had dwindled to a little over 6,000 and at the end of the decade the numbers could be counted in hundreds rather than thousands. By 1992 the NF's political impact was so limited, and the ideology had been so diluted, that even the Anti-Nazi League contemptuously described the party as 'no more than a right-wing pressure group on immigration' (*Searchlight*, January 1992). The BNP refuses to disclose the size of its membership and estimates have ranged from 1,000 to 3,000. Although smaller than the NF at its height, the party is potentially a more serious force. Increasingly the BNP has become overtly neo-Nazi and it has forged strong links with the British National Socialist Movement (originally the British Movement), which regards itself as an elite hardline Nazi party. The BNP is also known to have connections with the violent 'Blood and Honour' – an umbrella organisation for a number of factions centred around fifteen or so 'skinhead' rock groups who openly call for 'race war'. Some of the BNP's senior activists, including Tyndall himself, have been convicted for offences ranging from the possession of explosives, to criminal damage and inciting racial hatred. Activities in the early 1990s have included marching through areas of Asian populations, and targeting schools with racist material.

The BNP, along with other far-right groups, have taken advantage of the increasing racism and xenophobia in Europe to make propaganda by forging links with foreign fascists, especially through the Belgium-based Odal Ring. If it is any measure of success, the BNP stood in a number of local elections in 1991 on a straightforward 'rights for whites' platform, gaining 12.8 per cent of the vote in parts of East London and 7–8 per cent elsewhere.

The 1992 general election results appeared to show that Britain remained largely immune from the fascist undercurrents to be found in some continental countries. However, the election of a BNP councillor in Tower Hamlets in 1993 was a timely reminder that the racist vote could be exploited against a background of economic deprivation and important local issues. The ensuing street battles in the East End of London between the BNP and left-wing protesters also proved that racism could still be the basis of violent protest in Britain.

## The far left

*The Communist Party of Great Britain*

The far left in Britain had for many years been divided between the Stalinist Communist Party of Great Britain (CPGB) on one hand, and a variety of Trotskyite groups on the other, which had come and gone from the political scene. Since the 1920s the CPGB had supported the doctrines of the Russian dictator Joseph Stalin who, through his doctrine of 'Socialism in One Country', espoused his own variety of Marxism. The Trotskyite factions, taking Leon Trotsky as their mentor, insisted on the policy of 'permanent' and international revolution.

By 1991 the CPGB had undergone substantial changes which were to ultimately lead to the party being relaunched and renamed the Democratic Left. This was a culmination of severe difficulties which had beset the party since the Second World War. A rapid erosion of Britain's industrial base undermined its few areas of working-class support, especially in South Wales and 'Red' Clydeside. In 1950 the CPGB could boast two parliamentary seats and an electoral support of 100,000 votes nationwide. By comparison only 16,858 votes were gained in the 1979 general election and the February 1974 election was the only time a single candidate deposit was saved.

In 1942 the CP membership of 56,000 was the largest of any far-left party. Thereafter, a slow decline was hastened with mass membership resignation following the Soviet invasion of Hungary in 1956 and Czechoslovakia in 1968. By 1984 the membership had diminished to 13,500, and the party's once vibrant youth wing had collapsed. The CPGB could also once claim to have considerable industrial muscle through the leadership of some trade unions such as the National Union of Miners, and enjoyed significant backing at TUC congresses. However, the CP influence had declined to such an extent that it no longer performed its function of providing the focus point for those on the Marxist or extreme left of the Labour Party against the moderate or 'reformist' tendencies of many of the larger unions who were prepared to work within the framework of capitalism rather than against it.

At the root of the CP's dilemma was whether to adapt its ideology and policies in order to enhance its waning public appeal or to stay loyal to basic principles and face probable extinction. One possible way forward was to imitate the Communist Parties in countries like France, Italy and Spain, which had embraced Eurocommunism in the 1970s. These parties had accepted that the societies of Western Europe had changed out of all recognition since the time Marx wrote the Communist Manifesto, and that the manual classes were enjoying a far greater standard of living and political liberty than he had predicted. The consequence was that a working-class revolution was unlikely and that if a socialist society was to be created it must be through liberal-democratic means. Secondly, they had realised that the teachings of Lenin, the principal leader of the 1917 Russian Revolution, including his designation of the Communist Party as the 'vanguard' of the workers' movement, was totally inappropriate to western-style democracies. Eurocommunism, disenchanted as it was with the Soviet model of socialism, sought the wider consensus of the majority of the population and attempted to establish a broader democratic alliance to oppose capitalism.

Throughout the 1970s pragmatists within the CPGP began to stress a more parliamentary strategy and sought to disassociate themselves from the Soviet Union. They maintained that it was necessary to adapt to what were perceived to be the unique conditions of Western capitalist democracy. Those who believed that this revisionist line was a betrayal of Marxist principles formed a breakaway party in 1977 – The New Communist Party (NCP) – which was everything but 'new', but which, remarkably, has continued to survive into the 1990s.

In 1980 the hardline Soviet supporters remaining in the CPGB argued that the party had travelled too far down the Eurocommunist road. A number of them were expelled, including Ken Gill, the secretary-general of the engineers' union TASS.

The middle of 1982 saw the traditionalists, centred around the *Morning Star* newspaper, go on the offensive and argue that to abandon Leninism was one thing but breaking with many of the fundamental tenets of Marxism was quite another. Bitter dissension broke out at the 1983 party congress, with the leadership once again heavily criticised by the Stalinist old-guard led by a prominent journalist of the *Morning Star*, Mick Costello. The pro-Soviet faction was heavily defeated and seven critics were expelled from the executive committee (Cook, 1985).

What had brought matters to a head was the 1983 general election. For one thing the party's own long-term electoral decline continued, with only 11,606 votes collected by its thirty-five candidates (Butler and Kavanagh, 1984). More importantly, the CP had also become involved in a wider debate that concerned all those broadly on the political left. In the 1983 election the Labour Party had crashed to its worst defeat in fifty years. For academics and intellectuals on the left the key question was 'must Labour lose?'. The debate was sounded out in the prestigious Eurocommunist Journal *Marxism Today*, which answered 'yes' unless there was a major policy change. Going further, the publication argued that the success of the new right and Thatcherism could not merely be interpreted as the capitalist ruling class duping the working class into voting Conservative by a sophisticated system of propaganda. Rather, the main thrust was that the left generally needed to reconsider its socialist policies in the light of social and political developments, and that to defeat the Conservatives an alliance might be necessary with the parties of the centre. This stance was not acceptable to the traditionalists of the *Morning Star*, represented by the 'Leninist' faction, who still clung to their loyalties and accused the Eurocommunists of abandoning the class struggle (Pitcairn, 1985).

By 1985 the revisionists gained control of the party's vital institutions and proceeded to purge the opposition. After a prolonged struggle to regain the party those outside (some 1,500 individuals) reorganised as the Communist Campaign Group in April 1988 and brought the number of parties claiming to be the 'real' Communist Party to three. In August 1988 the CP began to articulate its new programme by publishing the document *Facing Up to the Future*, which included a 'realistic' analysis of the working class under modern capitalism and challenged the fundamental assumptions of orthodox Marxism of the nature of class conflict. All this led to a reconsideration of revolutionary socialist ideas for the ownership of the economy, and it was argued that policies in general should be geared to winning public support.

The collapse of the Soviet regime and the wave of democratic revolutions in Eastern Europe at the end of the 1980s ensured that further changes for the CP were a matter of urgency. In April 1991 the

Communist Party, as represented by the Eurocommunists, was relaunched and in 1992 changed its name to the Democratic Left. Essentially, there has been an attempt to create a more democratic, pluralistic and 'radical' party structure as well as undergoing a change of image. The revamped constitution makes no reference to Marxism-Leninism, nor does it insist that the party line should be unquestionably followed by its members. Nina Temple, the general secretary, has claimed that in order to widen the party's appeal it was necessary to throw off 'the irrelevant trappings of Bolshevism'. Yet with a membership of only 6,300 the party has emerged as a severely depleted force.

## Militant Tendency

Militant Tendency (which began as the Revolutionary Socialist League in 1957 and has now been relaunched as Militant Labour) has, with little doubt, been the most successful of the far-left factions. As with other Trotskyite groups, Militant came to sustain greater support in the 1960s against the background of student radicalism and new-left politics which itself was derived from the disenchantment with the Labour government at home and the oppressive Soviet regime, as well as opposition to American foreign policy in Vietnam. In 1981 there were about fourteen significant Trotskyist organisations (Shipley, 1981) and the great majority were convinced that the way forward was the building of alternative political parties rather than infiltrating the Labour Party and seeking control of the Labour movement as a whole.

These factions felt sufficiently confident to stand in direct competition with one another and the CPGB as the revolutionary vanguard of the working class. Each group advanced its own interpretation of the thoughts of Trotsky and the correct strategies to adopt for the destruction of capitalism. Beyond this, however, there was a general agreement on the evils of capitalism and the state socialism of the Soviet Union. The remedy was to be workers' control of the economy and the 'permanent revolution'.

Until 1978 Militant was practically the only group prepared to take the entryist path. It had long been one of the least successful of the Trotskyist movements and it was probably for this reason that it had infiltrated the Labour Party and, for a short period, the CPGB. This was ideologically compatible with Trotskyism since Trotsky himself argued that it was legitimate to enter the wider Labour movement, which could eventually be captured and used for revolutionary purposes.

The 1970s had presented good opportunities for Militant to increase its influence. Labour constituency parties became increasingly radical as a result of the sentiment that socialism had been betrayed by the Wilson administration (1964–70). At the same time, the party's traditional working-class base became increasingly inactive. As early as 1970 Militant was able to dominate the Labour Party's Young Socialists. In 1973 the party's list of proscribed organisations was abandoned, allowing Militant to infiltrate the constituencies in earnest claiming that 'Many wards and branches can become citadels of the ideas of Marxism' (*British Perspectives and Tasks*, 1974).

For many on the left of the Labour Party the Wilson/Callaghan government of 1974–79 was a bitter disappointment, especially since it was defeated after the so-called 'Winter of Discontent' in which conflict between trade unions and the government resulted in widespread industrial disputes. Numerous activists in the constituencies abandoned the party, while those who remained undertook a discernible left-wing shift (Williams, 1983). They found common cause with disgruntled hard-left Labour MPs who articulated their grievances through the Labour Coordinating Committee (Shaw, 1988). The aim was to change the party into a mass extra-parliamentary organisation for 'real' socialism, with policies calculated to attract all those on the far left. Militant regarded this as an open invitation.

As early as 1977 Labour's National Executive Committee had resisted investigation of alleged Trotskyite infiltration of the party, but Militant's growing strength was beginning to prove an electoral liability. In 1979 seven Labour parliamentary candidates were Militant supporters and three eventually became MPs. In 1980 sixty-four out of 523 constituency delegates to party conference were Militant members.

Labour's response to the growing threat of Militant came in several stages; first, the NEC voted for an inquiry into Militant's activities in 1981 which resulted in the Hayward-Hughes report in June the following year and which was accepted by party conference largely through the trade union block vote. The outcome was that a register of all non-affiliated organisations within the party was established; moreover, they would only be allowed to operate as long as they displayed an 'open democratic structure'. On these grounds Militant could be expelled since it operated as a 'party within a party' and consequently violated Clause 11(3) of Labour's Constitution. After fifteen months and a complicated court action five members of Militant's editorial board, including long-serving Trotskyist Ted Grant, were ostracised.

In early 1983 the NEC accepted recommendations by the party's general secretary to take further measures and in December approved a motion to further proscribe Militant. However, the actual identification and removal of Militant's members proved difficult since the implementation was largely left to the constituency parties, many of whom were against what they perceived as a 'witch-hunt', reminiscent of the 1950s, by the party's leadership. The policy towards Militant also appeared to be inconsistent. None of the nine Militants who were Labour candidates in the 1983 general election were refused nomination, although Pat Wall in Bradford North had first been denied approval by the NEC on a technicality.

The decision by the Labour Party to take further action was largely due to Militant's strength on Merseyside, where there had been infiltration into the constituency parties since the late 1950s. Sixteen of Labour's fifty-one councillors in 1983 were Militant supporters, including the deputy chairman of Merseyside Council, Derek Hatton. By effectively controlling the council Militant refused to comply with the Conservative government's 'rate-capping' policy and failed to set a legal rate in 1985. Ultimately forced to capitulate, the Militant leadership implemented its expensive flagship programme known as the 'Urban Regeneration Strategy' at the cost of 3,000 redundancies which, ironically, had the consequence of the Militant-dominated council facing the opposition of trade unionists (Ridley, 1986). In 1985 the Labour Party leadership instigated the Whitty Report into the District Party in Liverpool, which found evidence of entryism and intimidation. The findings were accepted by Conference and by the NEC in February 1986 leading, eventually, to forty-two Militants being expelled on Merseyside.

The process of expulsions were speeded up in the following year with the establishment of the National Constitutional Committee. From that time membership of Militant, if proven, has been sufficient ground for expulsion. Thirteen individuals were expelled in 1987, and approximately another hundred in 1988. A further investigation was called by the NEC in December 1989, when Militant was largely deemed responsible for the deselection of Frank Field as Labour MP for Birkenhead. Finally, in September 1991 two Labour MPs with Militant connections, Dave Nellist and Terry Fields, were suspended from holding office and barred from Conference.

At the height of its success Militant could claim over 4,000 subscribers to its newspaper with a regional and district organisational structure having a permanent staff almost as large as that of the Labour Party itself. But there is the danger of overstating the case (Crick, 1984); although it infiltrated many local constituency parties it probably only dominated between fifty and sixty. In some trade unions it had considerable influence; for example, one estimate published in the *Sunday Times* (31.1.88) claimed that thirty leading officials of the NUM were Militant supporters. However, traditional trade unionism was also a barrier against Militant and this is why, in some parts of the country, its power was negligible.

The Labour Party's policy of identifying and expelling members of Militant eventually had the intended effect. In May 1992 Militant stood *independently* in local elections in Glasgow; by exploiting local issues two candidates were able to secure council seats at the expense of Labour, joining two other Militant council members who had been disowned by the Labour Party. When these were added to the one seat won on the Aberdeen council in 1990 and the two in the Provan district council in September 1992, Militant could claim a total of seven local government representatives in Scotland. Encouraged by this initial success and renamed Militant Labour, the great majority of supporters (a small number fought to retain the entryist position) reorganised as a separate political party in the autumn of 1992. However, despite standing in a number of local elections and local by-elections in 1993, Militant has failed to make an impact of any further significance.

*Other Trotskyist groups*

Militant had not been the only group attracted by the prospect of working within the parameters of the Labour Party since the 1970s (Forrester, 1980). Of these probably the best known was the International Marxist Group (IMG). Since 1977 the IMG believed that its task was to establish a wider revolutionary front by uniting as many Trotskyist groups as possible. To this end it designated itself the official British division of the (Trotskyist) 4th International, but this proved to be to little avail since other factions refuse to cooperate.

The IMG also expressed solidarity for, and established links with, Third World liberation organisations in an attempt to fulfil Trotsky's doctrine of a global revolution. For much the same reasons the IMG had played a prominent part in both the anti-Vietnam demonstrations and the 'Troops Out' (of Northern Ireland) movement, since these were perceived to be areas of the world oppressed by capitalist colonialism. In 1979, it had also gained a measure of publicity for contributing towards the violence which accompanied the Anti-Nazi League's demonstration in Southall in 1979.

A change in direction came in 1980, when the IMG reformed as the Socialist League (SL) with its newspaper *Socialist Action*. In December 1981 Tariq Ali, the most well-known member of the IMG, announced his intention to join the Labour Party while refusing to abandon his revolutionary posture. Before being denied membership he argued that it was possible to exploit the polarisation taking place in the party and support the Labour Coordinating Committee's call for rank-and-file democracy and an attack on the leadership. Eventually, the opportunity would arise, he surmised, for the left of the Labour Party to be united with the Marxists outside (Ali and Hoare, 1982).

Another 'front' organisation was the Socialist Campaign for a Labour

Victory (SCLV) formed from the Chartist Group and Workers' Action (a splinter group from the Workers' Revolutionary Party). The Chartist Group itself had been established in 1970 by supporters of the Workers' Revolutionary Party, the International Marxist Group and Militant Tendency, with the aim of imposing a 'revolutionary programme' on the Labour Party. In 1981 the SCLV was renamed the Socialist Organizer Alliance when the Community League and the Workers' Socialist League also joined. Lastly, in 1980 there was the formation of the London Labour Briefing (LLB) which was another attempt to represent the interests of various Trotskyist factions and other left-wing organisations in London under one umbrella. The LLB was influential in the Labour Party in the GLC until the latter's abolition by the Conservative government in 1986.

The apparent unity amongst these different factions was ultimately short-lived. Proscription by the Labour Party and failure in principal aims led to internal conflict, and splits occurred when members sought to return to the greater independence afforded by belonging to separate and smaller groups. The Socialist League was divided in 1985 when members of the editorial board of *Socialist Action* seceded in order to create the Socialist League of Great Britain. The Socialist Organizer broke down in 1984 after a wave of expulsions, but continued to endure into the 1990s as the Alliance for Workers' Liberty (AWL) dedicated to working 'in the trade unions and the Labour Party to win the existing labour movement to socialism'. The ultimate aim of the AWL was to end the 'wage slavery' of capitalism and establish a 'workers' democracy' in which the elected representatives could be recalled by the electorate at any time should they fail to reflect the wishes and interests of the 'people' (*Socialist Organizer*, No. 519, April 1992).

Other Trotskyist groups have consistently preferred to put themselves up for election and the most enduring of these has probably been the Workers' Revolutionary Party (WRP). It has derived much of its strength from its secrecy and internal discipline. It has rejected entryism and has refused to compromise its ideals. Despite its willingness to stand in general elections, the party has not been afraid to claim that Parliament is no more than 'a facade to hide the [capitalist] conspiracies taking place outside it' (Vanessa Redgrave, quoted in Tomlinson, 1981).

The WRP could claim a membership of 2,500 and an active youth wing in the 1970s, but in the 1979 general election a mere 2,834 votes or 0.5 per cent of the vote was won in the sixty seats contested. The policy platform expressed in the 1983 election manifesto called for a battle against the Thatcher government which, it was suggested, was preparing the army, police, judiciary and the rest of the 'capitalist state bureaucracy' for a pre-emptive strike on the working class and its trade unions. Also instigated in the plot was the Labour Party which, allegedly, had long distracted working people from the revolutionary path. These sentiments gained little support and the WRP achieved only 3,643 votes in the 1983 general election (Butler and Kavanagh, 1984).

In October 1985 the WRP appeared to be disintegrating; its founder and charismatic leader, Gerry Healy, was expelled for alleged sexual indiscretion. Supported by Corin and Vanessa Redgrave, Healy launched the Marxist Party in August 1987 and by 1988 nine groups had emerged from the original WRP including the International Socialist League, the International Communist Party and the Communist Forum which, for a short period, was close to the 'Leninist' faction of the CPGB. In part these divisions arose because of clashes of leadership personalities, but they were mainly due to different interpretations of Marxism and Trotskyism, and the strategies which should be adopted to fight capitalism. In the 1992 general election the WRP, along with the CPGB, the Communist League, the International Communist Party, the Revolutionary Communist Party, the Workers' Party, and Workers Against Racism put forward twenty-eight candidates. Just under 6,500 votes were gained.

The Socialist Workers' Party (before 1977 the International Socialists) has, like the WRP, continued to maintain that the Labour Party offered little to the cause of socialism and that it has therefore been necessary to build a strong revolutionary movement elsewhere. With an estimated membership of 8,000–9,000 in 1993, and operating as an extremely efficient party, the SWP has recruited well from students and has attempted to win support from unemployed youth. At times it has been prominent in up to 150 trade union organisations as diverse as those representing civil servants, teachers, journalists and hospital workers. The party has managed to grow, building upon the many grievances against successive Conservative governments including the anti-poll tax campaign in the early 1990s. In the 1980s the SWP was the main force behind the formation of the Anti-Nazi League. In 1991 it revived the Anti-Nazi League, just after a more widely-based moderate Anti-Racist Alliance had been established, to combat rising levels of racism in Europe in the 1990s (*Searchlight*, 1992).

The SWP has also been uncompromising in its Trotskyist doctrines and advocates a workers' state based upon councils of workers' delegates and workers' militia (*Socialist Worker*, February 1993). It also calls for a struggle against 'capitalist imperialism' and has long been opposed to the 'state capitalist' imperialism of the governments of the former Soviet bloc and China, as well as to their internal regimes.

The SWP has itself been subject to several splits, including that of the Revolutionary Communist Group (strong in the anti-Apartheid movement) in 1974, from which a further division occurred in the form of the

Revolutionary Communist Tendency (RCT) – infamous for its full support of the IRA and organised attacks upon the far right. In 1981 the RCT became the Revolutionary Communist Party and has been responsible for setting up 'Workers Against Racism' cells, which have sought not only to protect black communities but to intimidate their would-be racist attackers.

### *'Class War'*

There are those factions which have continued to offer a radical alternative to Marxism. Although the aversion to political prescriptions makes it difficult to place anarchism on the far-left of the ideological spectrum, and while the amorphous and transitory nature of the key anarchist movements prevents them being called 'parties', no survey of 'fringe' politics would be complete without a mention.

Throughout the 1980s, as in previous decades, anarchism had appeared in various forms but perhaps the most well known is Class War. During the 'Thatcherite' 1980s Class War verbally, and sometimes physically, attacked the 'establishment', with its own distinct moral outrage principally aimed at what was perceived to be a materialistic and increasingly authoritarian society marked by the polarisation of wealth. The enemy identified was a 'ruling class' supported by a 'parasitic' middle class which collectively 'wages war' on the workers through capitalism and the state. It is the class-based society, argued Class War, which manufactures other forms of oppression including discrimination against the disabled, homosexuals, and ethnic groups, as well as cruelty against animals (*Class War*, No. 52).

The appeal of Class War is often to the frustrations of some sections of youth in deprived urban areas. Typical are the events in July 1992, when rioting broke out on the Hartcliffe housing estate in Bristol and lasted for two nights. Residents claimed that initially trouble had been stirred up by a 'small minority' of youths who were locally based and who had distributed leaflets proclaiming 'No cops, no politicians, no bailiffs! You are entering Free Hartcliffe' and declaring to be supporters of Class War (*Guardian*, 17.7.92).

The *Class War* journal has continued to call for direct action, and the dislike of the parliamentary process was highlighted in its 1992 anti-general election rally at Trafalgar Square. At the same venue, according to the British press, the anarchists were to blame for starting the rioting during the poll tax demonstration in London in 1990. Class War has also instigated such events as the 'Stop the City' demonstration in March and September 1985 and disruptions of the Henley regatta under the slogan of 'kill the rich'.

## The Green Party

Supporters of the Green Party would undoubtedly argue that although the party is on the 'fringe' of British politics the issues which it addresses are of central, not peripheral, political interests. On the other hand it can be argued that environmental issues have always been part of a wider radical agenda and, while the party may plead that its politics are beyond partisan politics, there is a discernible left-wing orientation (Parry et al., 1992). Some ecological concerns – reducing pollution, preventing rural development and encouraging organic farming – may well be politically neutral, but other policy areas such as the call for withdrawal from Nato, unilateral nuclear disarmament, and the phasing out of nuclear power have long been associated with the more left-wing orientated groups. Similarly, a manifesto advocating the redistribution of wealth, job-sharing and gay rights, community politics and the democratisation of commerce and industry has been interpreted as not being entirely 'neutral' (Frankland, 1989).

Throughout the 1970s 'green' parties had been so successful in Western Europe that many commentators envisaged environmental politics as the new political force in the late twentieth century. The evidence was that some countries, including Belgium and Germany, had green representatives in their own legislatures while others had Euro MPs of the ecological persuasion. The Ecology Party in Britain was the first in Europe and had roots going back to 1973. However, despite the fact that it was established to give a greater voice to lobbies expressing their concern over the dangers of pollution since the 1960s (Lowe and Goyder, 1983), public concern over environmental issues emerged rather late in the day.

The earliest general election contested by the Ecology Party was that of October 1974, when the party put up five candidates who gained only 0.8 per cent of the mean vote. In 1979 fifty-three candidates achieved only 39,918 votes (an average of 1.5 per cent of the vote in seats contested). However, the party had performed better than any party of the far left and beat the National Front in two-thirds of the constituencies in which they were in competition (Butler and Kavanagh, 1980).

In the 1983 general election 108 candidates were fielded, but the 54,000 plus votes amounted to only 1 per cent of the total. At the time of its relaunch as the Green Party (1985) the membership had risen to over 5,000 and shortly afterwards sixty seats were gained on parish and community councils. During the May local elections three weeks before the 1987 general election, the Greens promised much by polling 8.6 per cent of the vote and as much as 30 per cent in some areas. The total vote in the general election did increase to 89,753, but since this was shared between 133 candidates the mean vote was only 1.4 per cent. It was also apparent that as a general rule the safer a constituency was for one of the two major parties, the greater the success of the Green Party, and that considerable support came from former SDP/Liberal Alliance voters – suggesting that a vote for the Greens amounted to a protest, rather than a vote of conviction (Butler and Kavanagh, 1988: 344).

As late as June 1989 an impressive 15 per cent of the vote was gained by the Greens in the European parliamentary elections and in many constituencies the Liberal Democrats were edged into fourth place. However, by the end of the year support in opinion polls began to decline and the worse fears were realised in the 1992 general election, when 256 candidates achieved only 1.3 per cent of the vote (Butler and Kavanagh, 1993: 343).

Despite favourable media coverage and public interest the Greens have remained on the wings of the political stage. Some fundamental difficulties were always evident. First, there was nothing to suggest that the party would overcome the problems facing other minor parties. This included the all too familiar disadvantages of the first-past-the-past electoral system and the shortage of funds necessary to field candidates. For this reason three Green Party candidates in 1992 stood jointly with Plaid Cymru, who strongly emphasised environmental issues in their manifesto. Secondly, the public perceived the Green Party as promoting only a single platform which scarcely presented a coherent remedy for the nation's acute economic problems. In turn this suggested that the 'post-material values' theory was a little premature and that economic concerns remain a priority for most British people. Thirdly, the Green Party, paradoxically, was the victim of its own radicalism. The party had prided itself on being a grass-roots democratic movement but the rather amateurish approach to party organisation was fraught with difficulties. In the early 1990s a party which at one time boasted 18,000 members began to lose support after complaints about mismanagement at the top of the party. At the same time the party's insistence on 'spokespersons' rather than a single leader proved a disadvantage since, to some extent at least, highly visible and credible leaders can win votes through media coverage.

More seriously, long before the troubled 1989 conference, differences had emerged between the 'Light Greens' and the 'Dark Greens'. The latter, whose extreme wing was almost anarchic, preferred to cling to their true principles rather than sacrifice them for electoral expediency. The former realised that some of the party's policies would be labelled as 'extreme' and therefore unpopular with the voter. In other words, internal conflict resulted from the familiar dichotomy of pragmatism versus idealism.

The apparent failure of the Greens also emphasised important and enduring characteristics of the British political system. The 'fringe' parties do not necessarily play an 'insignificant' role but often operate rather like pressure groups. From this 'pluralist' viewpoint the competition for votes forces the major parties to adopt ideas espoused by the smaller ones if it is politically expedient to do so. This has been confirmed since the late 1970s, not least of all in the way the major parties jumped onto the 'environmental band-wagon' in the search for votes. The Westminster parties have undoubtedly displayed their ecological credentials, but in doing so have diluted the principal tenets of green politics as to effectively render them harmless and therefore secure the traditional party system and, for that matter, the political establishment. Indeed, the success of fringe groups perhaps should be seen not in terms of the votes they gather at election time or in by-elections, but in their contribution to mobilising and crystallising public opinion around certain issues in-between elections.

# References

Ali, T. and Hoare, Q. (1982), 'Socialists and the Crisis of Labourism', *New Left Review*, 132, April–March.

'British Perspectives' (1974), quoted in Seyd, P. (1987), *The Rise and Fall of the Labour Left*, Basingstoke, Macmillan.

Butler, D. and Kavanagh, D. (1980), *The British General Election of 1979*, London, Macmillan.

Butler, D. and Kavanagh, D. (1984), *The British General Election of 1983*, London, Macmillan.

Butler, D. and Kavanagh, D. (1988), *The British General Election of 1987*, London, Macmillan.

Butler, D. and Kavanagh, D. (1993), *The British General Election of 1992*, London, Macmillan.

Clutterbuck, P. (1982), *Britain in Agony. The Growth of Political Violence*, London, Faber & Faber.

Cochrane, R. & Billig, M. (1984), 'I'm not National Front myself, but . . .', *New Society*, 68.

Cook, D. (1985), 'No Private Drama', *Marxism today*, 29 (2).

Crick, M. (1984), *Militant*, London, Faber & Faber.

Edgar, D. (1977), 'Racism and the Politics of the National Front', *Race and Class*, 4.

Fielding, N. (1981), *The National Front*, Routledge & Kegan Paul.

Forrester, T. (1980), 'The Labour Party Moles', *New Society*, 51.

Frankland, E. (1989), '*Does Green Politics have a Future in Britain?*', Paper delivered at the Annual Meeting of the American Political Science Association, Atlantic, Gad.

Grimond, J. (1981), in the foreword to Tomlinson, J. *Left–Right: The March of Political Extremism in Britain*, London, John Calder.

Hunt, S.J. (1992), 'Fascism and the "Race Issue" in Britain' *Talking Politics*, 5 (1), Autumn: 23–8.

Husband, C.T. (1977), *Racial Exclusion and the City: The Urban Support of the National Front*, Allen & Unwin.

Inglehart, R. (1977), *The Silent Revolution: Changing Values and Political Styles Among Western Parties*, Princeton, Princeton University Press.

Lowe, P. and Goyder, J. (1983), *Environmental Groups in Politics*, London, Allen & Unwin.

Nugent, N. (1977), 'The Political Parties of the Extreme Right' in King, R. and Nugent, N. (eds), *The British Right: Conservative and Right Wing Politics in Britain*, Farnborough, Saxon House.

Parry, G., Moyser, G. and Day, N. (1992), *Political Participation in Britain*, Cambridge, Cambridge University Press.

Pitcairn, L. (1985), 'Crisis in British Communism: An Insider's View', *New Left Review*, 153, September/October: 113–166. See also Samuel, R. (1985) 'The Lost World of British Communism', *New Left Review*, 154, November/December: 16–25.

Ridley, F. (1986), 'Liverpool is Different', *Political Quarterly*, 57 (2), April–June: 26.

Scott, D. (1975), 'The National Front in Local Politics', in Crewe, I. (ed.), *British Political Sociology*: 2.

*Searchlight*, the official magazine of the Anti-Nazi League, (1992), 199, January: 11.

Shaw, E. (1988), *Discipline and Discord in the Labour Party, 1951–87*, Manchester, Manchester University Press.

Shipley, P. (1981), 'Extremism and the Left', *Politics Today*, July, 13: 299.

Steed, M. (1977), 'The National Front Vote', *Parliamentary Affairs*, 31 (3): 282–93.

Tomlinson, J. (1981), *Left–Right. The March of Political Extremism in Britain*, John Calder, London.

Troyna, B. (1986), 'Reporting the National Front: British Values Observed' in Husband, D. (ed.), *Race in Britain Continuity and Change*, Hutchinson University Press.

Walker, M. (1977), *The National Front*, London, Fontana.

Williams, P. (1983), 'The Labour Party and the Rise of the Left', *Western European Politics*, 6 (4): 229.

# 11

# A concluding thought: should parties be funded by the state?

*Allan McConnell*

One could be forgiven for seeing the findings of many of the chapters in this book as a damning indictment of the British party system in the post-1979 period. For example, it has seen four consecutive Conservative victories on less than 50 per cent of the vote (Chapter 1); the electoral system has helped mitigate the rise of a powerful 'third' party (Chapter 5), and individuals seeking to enter Parliament are effectively debarred unless they possess a host of 'non-typical' characteristics such as financial security, public networks and social status (Chapter 7).

Amidst all this, however, it is easy to forget that political parties perform much more wide-ranging and pervasive roles in society. Indeed, the Houghton Committee (Cmnd. 6601, 1976: 53) on Financial Aid to Political Parties suggested that 'effective political parties are the crux of democratic government. Without them democracy withers and decays.' Certainly, much is expected of political parties in a modern industrialised liberal democracy such as Britain. In *general* terms, they:

1. aggregate and articulate interests;
2. 'simplify' issues for voters;
3. instruct and help 'educate' voters on a wide range of issues;
4. allow voters to choose between rival policies and programmes;
5. provide a means of forming a government and opposition;
6. provide channels for communication between the parties and the 'people'; and
7. provide opportunities for political participation.

In more *concrete* terms, however, such roles need to be translated into specific activities, and this does not come without financial outlay. As Johnston (1986: 466) suggests, there is *long-term* spending on the maintenance of a central office, a research organisation, support for local activities and the employment of agents. Equally, there is *short-term* spending on election campaigns and such matters as press advertising, commissioning of private opinion polls, administration, staffing and party publications.

In the light of all this, a very important matter is raised; namely who pays for all these activities? Should it be a 'private' matter for the parties? Should it be a duty of the state? Or, should it be some combination of the two? Such matters are of particular relevance because of the way that the issue of party financing leapt to the forefront of the political stage in the summer of 1993, when an investigation by the Select Committee on Home Affairs coincided with the 'Asil Nadir affair' and an outcry over the funding of the Conservative Party.

In order to explore the issue of state financing in greater depth, this chapter takes the following form. First, it provides a historical background to the issue of party financing in Britain – focusing on the origins of the existing minimalist system of state funding in Britain, and a subsequent investigation by the 1976 Houghton Committee into the financing of political parties. Second, it identifies the sources of funding for the major political parties in Britain in the post-1979 period. Third, it builds on these and identifies ways in which they combine to create serious problems for the contemporary British party system – many of which have come to the surface in 1993. Fourth, it identifies a range of possible state-funded alternatives, and outlines the arguments both for and against state funding. Finally, it pulls these together by looking at what the previous chapters of this book have identified as the main issues intrinsic to the British party system in the post-1979 period, and asking to what extent these would change if the state was to embark on a system of major funding for political parties.

## The 'minimalist' system of state financing in Britain

The Representation of the People Act 1918 was the first (albeit small and indirect) step in the direction of state assistance for political parties in Britain. The main impetus for this lay in the gradual extension of the franchise, which put continual upwards pressure on election expenses. Hence, the Act reduced the level of permitted campaign expenditure, but introduced three 'compensatory' measures in the form of indirect state assistance. These were (i) that the cost of registering electors be borne by local authorities, (ii) that parliamentary candidates be entitled to free postal facilities and that both parliamentary and local election candidates be allowed the right to hold public meetings in a suitable room within public elementary schools, and (iii) that the costs of returning officers be borne by the Treasury (Ewing, 1987: 104–8). These measures were amended slightly in 1948 (and then latterly in 1983), whilst the principle of free broadcasting time for party political broadcasts (the costs actually being borne by the broadcasters – not the government) has been in existence since 1947. Apart from this minimalist system of state assistance, however, by the time we arrive at the mid-1970s, the substance of the funding issue was clear – the parties could raise finances from any legal source that they wished. Figures calculated from evidence given to the Houghton Committee (Cmnd. 6601, 1976: 96–109) reveal that in terms of the central party machines for the years 1974–75 (more recent and detailed figures will be given later in the chapter), roughly 76 per cent of Conservative Party income came from company and 'private' donations, roughly 80–90 per cent of Labour Party income came from the trades unions, and roughly 91 per cent of Liberal Party income came from individual donations.

By the mid-1970s, however, this substantial reliance on organised interests seemed to be providing incompatible with the multiplicitous demands made on parties in a modern-liberal democracy. As Bogdanor (1982: 367) suggests, in summarising the arguments that were beginning to emerge:

> Inflation had made it impossible for them [i.e. parties] to fulfil the manifold requirements imposed by local government reorganisation, direct elections to the European Assembly, referendums and elections to the House of Commons. After the two general elections of 1974 and the EEC referendum of 1975, the parties seemed to be in such a parlous state that democracy itself, according to this view would be threatened if there was not a rapid injection of state aid.

It was principally these factors which resulted in two further but nevertheless tentative steps towards state financing of political parties. First, on 29 July 1974, Edward Short, the Leader of the House, announced the setting up of a system of subsidies to finance the parliamentary activities of opposition parties in the House of Commons. Parties would qualify for this if they had at least two Members elected, or one Member and a minimum of 150,000 votes. By 1988, this subsidy would total £1,203,322.97, with the opposition parties receiving £2,250 for each seat won, and £5.10 for every 200 votes at the last general election (European Parliament, 1991: 35). Second, there was the setting up of the Houghton Committee in May 1975, which reported in August the following year. Based on its remit to investigate the possibility of public funds being used to assist political parties, it recommended (subject to qualifying conditions) annual grants to party central organisations and limited reimbursement of elections expenses at a local level for both parliamentary and local elections (Cmnd. 6601, 1976, xv).

In the event, however, the report was accorded 'a somewhat frosty reception on its publication' (Seidle, 1980: 83). It was rejected wholeheartedly by the media and opposed by large sections of the

Labour Party left wing and some trades union leaders on the grounds that it would break the traditional Labour Party–trades union link. Furthermore, Labour's small majority within the Commons had been eroded and it was in the precarious position of requiring the support of the opposition for any reforms. The Conservative Party, however, was in no mood for such accommodation. Its finances had actually improved after 1976 under the charge of new treasurer Alistair (later Lord) McAlpine, and the party (fitting in with the ideological shift to the right under Mrs Thatcher) did not want to disrupt the 'voluntary' nature of funding by introducing a major role for the state. Thus political realities prevailed, and the Houghton Report was 'quietly shelved by the government' (Ewing, 1987: 129).

## Sources of party financing in the post-1979 period

Despite a brief resurgence of interest in state financing of political parties with the publication of a report by the Hansard Society for Parliamentary Government (1981), the issue was effectively 'dead' until the matter was chosen in March 1993 as a subject of inquiry by the Select Committee on Home Affairs. By coincidence, shortly afterwards, the businessman and ex-Tory Party donor Asil Nadir (facing thirteen charges of theft totalling some £30m), broke bail and fled to Cyprus. This combined with several other factors to produce a high-profile public debate on the matter of party funding. The main focus of this, however, was on the need (or otherwise) for parties to disclose the source of their donations. This is largely a separate issue from the matter of state financing of parties, although a by-product of the debate has been that many issues regarding the financing of political parties have been brought to the surface. An understanding of these issues requires that we explore the vagaries of the existing minimalist system of direct and indirect state subsidies in Britain, because it is this *system* which creates the potential for a series of problems to emerge. Such matters can be considered, however, only after we identify contemporary sources of funding for the major political parties in Britain.

### The Conservative Party

Political parties in Britain are constituted legally as 'unincorporated associations', and hence are not required by law to publish accounts or details of contributors to party funds. This has enabled the Conservative Party to ensure the anonymity of donors, and in effect ensure that sources of funding for the party are shrouded in secrecy. Certainly, legislation in 1967, 1980 and then subsequently the Companies Act 1985

**Table 11.1** Conservative central income 1979/80–1991/92 (£m)

| Year | Donations | Constituency quotas | Interest | Affiliation fees | Total |
|------|-----------|--------------------|----------|------------------|-------|
| 1979/80* | 4.5 | 0.9 | 0.2 | – | 5.6 |
| 1980/81 | 2.2 | 0.9 | – | – | 3.1 |
| 1981/82 | 2.9 | 1.0 | – | – | 3.0 |
| 1982/83 | 3.7 | 1.0 | – | – | 3.8 |
| 1983/84* | 8.2 | 1.1 | 0.1 | – | 9.4 |
| 1984/85 | 3.0 | 1.0 | – | 0.3 | 4.3 |
| 1985/86 | 4.0 | 1.0 | – | – | 5.0 |
| 1986/87 | 7.6 | 1.2 | – | – | 8.8 |
| 1987/88* | 13.6 | 1.2 | – | – | 14.8 |
| 1988/89 | 6.7 | 1.2 | – | 0.2 | 8.1 |
| 1989/90 | 7.1 | 1.2 | – | 0.8 | 9.1 |
| 1990/91 | 10.6 | 1.3 | – | 0.8 | 12.7 |
| 1991/92* | 19.1 | 1.3 | – | 1.7 | 23.1 |

*Note*: Asterisk denotes financial years where general election income is accounted for. Figures have been rounded to the nearest £0.1m, and – denotes figures which were too small to be rounded up to this.

*Source*: Pinto-Duschinsky, (1985); *Parliamentary Affairs*, 38: 330; Pinto-Duschinsky, (1989); *Parliamentary Affairs*, 42: 198; and Conservative Central Office Annual Income and Expenditure Accounts for the years 1988/89 to 1991/92.

began to unravel some of the threads, with a requirement that companies disclose donations (in excess of £200) to political parties. As a result, this has allowed investigators (particularly the Labour Research Department – a body independent of the Labour Party) to trawl through individual company records at Companies House. Apart from information obtained in this way, however, or the highly minimal accounts published by Conservative Central Office, investigators of Conservative Party funding are at a distinct disadvantage.

In spite of all this, however, it is possible to pull together some loose strands (although recognising the necessity of concentrating, as with all parties, on the central party machine because of the near impossibility of calculating 'local' incomes). Table 11.1 illustrates that in recent years, Conservative Central Office has been provided with a fairly steady stream of income in excess of £1 million annually from the constituency associations – these being allocated 'voluntary' quotas which they can attempt to meet through subscriptions, fund-raising events, donations, etc. The most striking feature, however, is that party income is dominated by the 'catch-all' category of 'Donations'. A small proportion of this undoubtedly comes from legacies, direct-mail fund-raising and individual donations (the total is difficult to estimate and will vary depending on whether or not it is a general election year, but is probably in the region of 20 per cent). The bulk of income, however (over 82 per cent in 1991–92), comes from largely undisclosed corporate donations and wealthy supporters of the Conservative Party. Businessmen abroad who work in the UK for six months of the year can claim non-domicile status, allowing them to register UK assets abroad and so avoid 40 per cent capital gains tax and recover dividend-withholding tax at a rate of 25 per cent. In effect, what Cahill et al.(1993: 48) describe as this 'tax loophole, scrupulously maintained by British governments for the past 14 years', offers an incentive for those sympathetic to the Conservative cause to contribute to party funds. The party has set up what former Treasurer Lord McAlpine described as 'tons of off-shore accounts', precisely for the purpose of channelling such donations into its funds and (legally) avoiding the inquiries of the Inland Revenue (*Guardian*, 18.6.93). Companies operating in the UK can also make donations direct to the Conservative Party, or more discretely through such organisations as British United Industrialists (BUI), which then transfer the donations to party funds. In 1986–87, for example, thirty-five companies made donations to BUI (eleven of these not declaring this in company accounts) (*Guardian*, 13.3.93). Investigations by the Labour Research Department also reveal that between 1979 and 1993, the top ten corporate donors gave the party almost £7 billion, comprising donations from P&O (£727,500), Taylor Woodrow (£837,362), Hanson Trust (£852,000) and United Biscuits (£1,004,500) (*Daily Telegraph*, 16.6.93).

## The Labour Party

As almost a mirror image of the links between the Conservative Party and 'business', financial matters epitomise the symbiotic relationship between the Labour Party and the trades unions, and the fact that 'the Labour Party would be devastated without union finance' (Minkin, 1992: 509). As Minkin (1992: 508) identifies, the financial involvement of trades unions in the Labour Party occurs through five main channels. These are:

1.  to constituency and district Labour Parties through affiliation fees, grants and donations;
2.  to constituency parties through the sponsorship of candidates;
3.  to regional parties through affiliation fees, grants and donations;
4.  to the Parliamentary Labour Party through grants to the Leader's Office and members of the Front Bench; and
5.  to the National Party organisation via affiliation fees, grants and donations to particular funds – including the General Election Fund.

**Table 11.2** Labour Party central income 1979–1991 (£m)

| Year | Trade union affiliation fees | Constituency affiliation fees | State aid | Other | Total |
|---|---|---|---|---|---|
| 1979* | 1.8m | 0.2m | 0.1m | 1.0m | 3.1m |
| 1980 | 2.0m | 0.4m | 0.2m | 0.2m | 2.8m |
| 1981 | 2.5m | 0.6m | 0.3m | 0.3m | 3.7m |
| 1982 | 2.8m | 0.6m | 0.3m | 0.3m | 3.9m |
| 1983* | 3.0m | 0.6m | 0.3m | 2.4m[a] | 6.2m |
| 1984 | 2.9m | 0.7m | 0.3m | 0.2m | 4.2m |
| 1985 | 3.5m | 0.7m | 0.4m | 0.2m | 4.9m |
| 1986 | 4.0m | 0.8m | 0.4m | 0.8m | 6.1m |
| 1987* | 4.2m | 0.9m | 0.5m | 4.5m | 10.0m |
| 1988 | 4.1m | 0.8m | 0.8m | 0.7m | 6.4m |
| 1989 | 4.3m | 0.8m | 0.8m | 2.1m | 8.0m |
| 1990 | 4.2m | 0.7m | 0.8m | 4.0m | 9.7m |
| 1991 | 4.3m | 0.6m | 0.8m | 6.9m | 12.7m |

*Note*: Asterisk denotes general election years. Figures have been rounded to the nearest £0.1m. Totals until 1988 include special funds as well as the general fund. Totals thereafter, as a result of financial management reforms, include income from the business plan fund and the general election fund as well as that from the general fund. Separately collected regional funds are not included.
[a] Includes repayment of tax paid in previous years. Figures for state aid ('Short Money') constitute income for both the PLP and the NEC.

*Source*: Pinto-Duschinsky, M. (1985); *Parliamentary Affairs*, 38: 330; Pinto-Duschinsky, M. (1989); *Parliamentary Affairs*, 42: 198; Labour Party accounts 1988–1991, and House of Commons Information Office for 'Short Money' figures.

These relationships are complex, however, and any incursion into specific financial matters relies on estimates which 'need to be treated with caution' (Pinto-Duschinsky, 1981: 225–6). In terms of overall party income, the norm has been for trades unions to provide roughly 50–55 per cent of this (Pinto-Duschinsky, 1990: 95), with the bulk of the remainder coming from constituency parties. In terms of the National Executive Committee of the Labour Party, however (in effect, the equivalent of Conservative Central Office), there is a much greater reliance on union funding. This can be seen from the figures in Table 11.2, which reveal three main sources of funding.

The first, and generally the smallest source, is constituency affiliation fees. These are set by the NEC, and a 1979–80 crisis in party finance led to a series of increases, with CLPs paying 32p per member in 1980, and this increasing to £5.50 per member in 1987 (Minkin, 1992). Table 11.2 reveals that outwith general election years, they have tended to provide roughly 4–9 per cent of income, with recent figures being at the bottom end of this scale as a result of declining membership.

The second source is trades union affiliation fees. These have their roots in the Trade Union Act 1913, although the Conservatives' Trade Union Act 1984 deemed that political levies could be paid only after a positive declaration in a ballot of members at least every ten years. The results of the first series of ballots in 1985 and 1986, however, were what Taylor (1987: 427–8) describes as 'a triumphal affirmation of the role of the trades unions in British politics'. In total, the 'Yes' votes amounted to some 83 per cent of votes cast – thus resulting in *all* the balloted unions voting to continue with their political funds (Blackwell and Terry, 1987). The basis of this funding is a direct relationship between a union's affiliation fees and its block vote at the party conference. This potentially allows a union to increase its affiliation fee in order to increase its voting powers, although as Minkin (1993) observes, the overwhelming practice has actually been for unions to affiliate *at* or *under* the level which their levy-paying membership entitles them to. Table 11.2 reveals that between 1979 and 1988, trades union affiliation fees tended to provide roughly 65–72 per cent of party income outwith general election years, with this figure declining to roughly 40–60 per cent when party fund-raising takes on a much greater role around election time.

Third, and related to this, the category of 'Other' can help to explain figures after 1988. This category had traditionally been fairly small (just over 7 per cent in 1980), and comprised various sundry incomes – particularly fund-raising and donations. Yet a post-1987 reappraisal of the weakness of party income, compared with spending (particularly general election) demands, has resulted in a new Business Plan which is 'fast becoming one of the success stories of Labour Party management and trade union co-operation' (Minkin, 1992: 534). There has been a greater emphasis on financial services, development fund-raising and donations (much of this coming from the trades unions via incremental trade union contributions to a General Election Fund). By 1991, the party had raised over £1 million from development fund-raising and over £3 million from donations. Inevitably, this makes it more difficult than ever to assess the overall level of trade union contributions to the Labour Party.

## The 'centre' parties

Not only have the parties of the 'middle ground' in British politics had a chequered history in recent years, but there have been substantial differences in their financing activities. The SDP, from its formation in 1981 through to its effective demise in 1988, adopted a highly centralist and aggressive approach to fund-raising. Modern technology and direct-mailing techniques were used to attract 78,000 members and £760,000 in subscriptions in its first year (see Table 11.3), although income from this source fell rapidly and levelled out at around £400,000 per annum. On

Table 11.3   SDP head office income 1981/82–1986/87 (£s)

| Year | Members' subscriptions | Other | Total |
|------|------------------------|-------|-------|
| 1981/2 | 760,000 | 145,000 | 905,000 |
| 1982/3 | 584,000 | 928,000 | 1,512,000 |
| 1983/4* | 424,000 | 1,178,000 | 1,602,000 |
| 1984/5 | 381,000 | 398,000 | 779,000 |
| 1985/6 | 486,000 | 402,000 | 888,000 |
| 1986/7 | 469,000 | 522,000 | 991,000 |

*Note*: Asterisk denotes financial year when general election income is accounted for. Figures have been rounded to the nearest £1,000. Figures include by-election insurance funds, but exclude state aid ('Short Money') to opposition parties.

*Source*: Pinto-Duschinsky, M. (1985); *Parliamentary Affairs*, 38: 330; Pinto-Duschinsky, M. (1989); *Parliamentary Affairs*, 42: 198.

average, income from subscriptions tended to be matched by individual donations – notably David Sainsbury of the supermarket chain, who was reported to have donated several hundred thousand pounds to the SDP (Pinto-Duschinsky, 1985).

In contrast to the SDP's centralisation, the philosophy of the Liberals in both party political and financial terms has very much been one of decentralisation. For the investigator into party financing, however, autonomy from the central party organisation raises two particularly important matters. First, there is the need to recognise that the history of 'Liberal' financing has been characterised by secrecy and scandal. For example, a series of scandals emerged in Lloyd George's 1916–22 premiership, over the matter of his Political Fund seemingly being collected in return for dispensing honours. More generally, as Pinto-Duschinsky (1981: 186) notes: 'for many years during the postwar period, leading Liberals have collected funds, usually secret, earmarked for particular purposes. The accounts of some of these funds have been concealed even from the LPO [Liberal Party Organisation] treasurer.' Second, the decentralisation of party finances has meant a plethora of party divisions and bodies being responsible for receiving income from numerous sources, resulting in it being virtually impossible to present a picture of income for the party as a whole.

For the purposes of clarity in this present chapter, figures given in Table 11.4 are only for the present Liberal Democrats – formed in 1988 (initially as the Social and Liberal Democrats) out of the bowels of the Liberals and the SDP. Even the figures given, however, must be treated with some caution. The party's federalist financing structure means that they include only the income of the federal executive, and exclude that of the English, Scottish and Welsh parties (hence largely excluding donations from the Joseph Rowntree Social Services Trust Ltd, which

**Table 11.4**  Liberal Democrats, federal income 1988–91

FEDERAL INCOME FOR PARTY ACTIVITIES (£s)

| Year | Direct mail | Sundry income | Regional levies to federal party | Other | Total |
|------|-------------|---------------|----------------------------------|-------|-------|
| 1988 | 337,000 | 122,000 | 128,000 | 29,000 | 616,000 |
| 1989 | 399,000 | 18,000 | 34,000 | 185,000 | 636,000 |
| 1990 | 259,000 | 226,000 | – | 41,000 | 526,000 |
| 1991 | 317,000 | 106,000 | 157,000 | 118,000 | 698,000 |

FEDERAL INCOME FOR GENERAL ELECTION FUND (£s)

| Year | Direct mail | Donations | Interest | Other | Total |
|------|-------------|-----------|----------|-------|-------|
| 1988 | – | – | – | – | – |
| 1989 | – | – | – | – | – |
| 1990 | 97,000 | 60,000 | 22,000 | 3,000 | 182,000 |
| 1991 | 148,000 | 251,000 | 36,000 | 10,000 | 445,000 |

*Note*: Figures for 1988 cover only a ten-month period, because the party was not formed until March 1988. Figures have been rounded to the nearest £1,000. Direct mail figure is 'net' – only for the General Election Fund. All bank interest is gross. There was no specific General Election Fund in the years 1988/89. Figures do not take into account the income for regional parties (England, Scotland and Wales), regional parties within England, Constituency Parties, and the By-Election Guarantee Fund.

*Source*: Annual Accounts 1988–91 of the Federal Executive of the Liberal Democrats.

has made regular donations for local Liberal activities). Nevertheless, the main point which can be taken from Table 11.4, which gives figures both for general party activities and a separate general election fund, is that unlike the heavy reliance of Labour and the Conservatives on institutional sponsors, the Liberal Democrats rely much more on direct mailing and donations. On average, just over 75 per cent of the income shown in Table 11.4 comes from these sources.

## Impact of the 'minimalist' system of state funding in Britain

In effect, the foregoing sources of funding for political parties in Britain illustrate that the system, as a whole, operates loosely on market principles, tempered only by minimal state intervention. Thus, there is a 'market', in the sense that political parties are free to enter into agreements with a range of individuals and groups in order to obtain the finances to support their political activities. Alongside this, there is 'state intervention' at the margins to ensure (i) that all parties are relieved of such expenses as electoral registration, returning officers and broadcasting time, and (ii) that opposition parties in the House of Commons receive some monetary 'compensation' to finance their activities in a Chamber which is usually dominated by the government and its inbuilt majority. Just like any market, however, there may be both 'winners and losers' and 'shortages of supply'. In more political terms, the result may be accusations of political bias and an inability of parties to attract the levels of funding which they need to perform their roles. Each of these can be considered in turn – illustrating to us not only the vagaries (actual and alleged) of the British system, but also the wider matter, as stated by Heard (1960: 11) that 'deeper understanding of political money means deeper understanding of representative government'.

*Political bias?*

A number of accusations have been levelled that the British system of minimalist state funding leads to a distortion of representative democracy. These accusations tend to devolve into two main categories.

First, there is the accusation that 'he who pays the piper calls the tune'. More specifically, as Leonard (1975: 5) suggests it is plausible that:

> . . . though individual firms and unions do not expect a specific *quid pro quo* in return for their contributions, Labour governments shape their policies in order to please the trades unions, and Conservative governments further the interests of private business.

In attempting to assess whether this is an accurate portrayal of 'wealth buying power', we can approach this complex and difficult matter on two levels. In the first instance, we need to ascertain whether there is indeed evidence of governments pursuing policies which *favour* their financial backers. The simple answer to this is both 'Yes' and 'No'. On the one hand, for example, the 1974–79 Labour government could be seen (in part) as evidence of an explicit linkage, since Labour's Social Contract with the unions involved attempts at 'pro-union' policies such as a repeal of Heath's Industrial Relations Act, social security reforms, and planning agreements with the private sector. Similarly, the post-1979 Conservative government can be seen as explicitly 'pro-business', for the way that it has generally attempted to curtail the powers of the trades unions through a series of legislation to restrict their activities. On the other hand, however, there is a multitude of evidence which points in the opposite direction. The 1974–79 Labour government was unable to fulfil its promises to the trades unions, largely because its strategy became dominated by supporting the value of sterling – resulting in near Exchequer bankruptcy and an IMF loan which imposed stringent deflationary measures. Similarly, there have been numerous occasions when the post-1979 Conservative government has refused to heed the advice of 'business' – particularly over accusations of excessively high interest rate levels, and particularly in the early 1980s when CBI Director-General Terence Beckett promised a 'bare knuckle fight' with the government.

Looking at this ambivalent evidence on a second level, however, we must recognise that such policies (either 'for' or 'against' party financial backers), may have nothing to do with financial leverage. There are a series of analytical perspectives which would tend to suggest that party policies are shaped not by financial backers, but are constrained and shaped by wider interests. Such arguments may take completely different forms. For example, there is the neo-pluralism of Richardson and Jordan (1979: 74) who downgrade the role of parliamentary and party political influences, and suggest instead that Britain is a 'post-parliamentary democracy' which is dominated by the 'policy community of departments and groups, the practice of co-option and the consensual style'. At the other end of the spectrum, there are a variety of Marxist arguments which focus on British governments being dominated by a ruling class. This can occur through a complex range of influences from the common 'upper-class' social and educational origins of MPs and senior civil servants (Miliband, 1973), to more structural factors such as (for example) interest rates and exchange rates which have given the City of London the power to 'effectively write . . . the rules of the game for British governments' (Costello et al., 1989: 122).

Amidst all the ambivalence of this 'yes'/'no' evidence and influence of 'wider' factors, however, we must be wary of completely abandoning the view that financial leverage *may* have an influence over party policies. As the Institute for Public Policy Research (1993: 4) suggested in its submission to the Home Affairs Committee: 'a party that has received one donation from a businessman may be tempted to treat him differently in order not to jeopardise the chances of another donation'. For example, one of the many allegations of impropriety levelled at the Conservatives in 1993 was that the government's uncritical stance on the takeover of the Midland Bank by the Hong Kong and Shanghai Bank may have been influenced by the fact that billionaire Li Ka Shing, who held a 2.7 per cent shareholding, also contributed in excess of £1 million to Conservative Party funds (Cahill et al., 1993: 43–5).[1] Whatever the case, it seems reasonable to conclude that no party can continually and completely ignore the wishes of those who finance it. Thus, in overall terms, it is possible to suggest (whilst recognising the complexity and difficulty of this issue) that sources of party funding both may and may not be important, and that they can *interact* with the impact of 'wider interests' on policy, rather than negate them.

Second, a further accusation of bias is that the existing system disadvantages the 'centre' parties. With specific regard to the Liberals (now incarnated as the Liberal Democrats), the fragmented and often secret nature of party finances has meant, as Pinto-Duschinsky (1991: 179–80) puts it, that:

> the Liberals have, in matters of party finance . . . [not been] . . . as poor . . . as they have suggested. The party's income has in many years probably been double the amount shown in its published accounts . . . Nevertheless, it would be wrong to understate the financial difficulties with which the Liberals have been confronted.

In the 1992 general election, for example, estimates from the parties themselves were that the campaign cost the Conservatives £10.1 million, Labour £7.1 million, and the Liberal Democrats £2.1 million, with the average spending per candidate being £5,840, £5,090 and £3,169 respectively (Butler and Kavanagh, 1992: 245, 260). The matter of whether more spending actually 'buys' more votes is a problematic one, since the relative weakness of the centre parties is bound up with other factors – particularly the first-past-the-post electoral system and the 'class-based' electoral support (albeit declining in recent years) for the two main parties. Nevertheless, we should be wary of suggesting that the amount of expenditure makes *no* difference at all. As Johnston (1986: 472) concludes in his study of the 1983 general election: 'some seats were vulnerable to the amount of money each party spent and . . . the poorest of the parties – the Liberal Party – *may* have won substantially more seats *if* it had the same resources as its opponents.'

*A 'fiscal crisis' in the parties?*

If the first major feature of the existing system is that it helps distort representative democracy by holding the potential for allowing 'wealth to buy power' and facilitating the squeezing-out of the centre parties, then a second major feature refers more generally to 'fiscal' matters. The term 'fiscal' traditionally refers to the relationship between government spending and its derivation from taxation, whilst 'fiscal crisis' pertains to the situation described by Rose and Page (1982: 1) where 'there are more claims upon the public purse for services than there is money to meet these claims'. This provides a useful analogy for party financing, however, because it indicates that there is the potential for the spending demands on parties to outstrip their ability to raise the necessary finances. There is substantial evidence that this is indeed the case, and that the potential exists for associated problems.

First, the main parties have experienced severe financial difficulties in recent years. The Labour Party experienced a crisis of party financing in the period 1979–82, when it became clear that party spending was substantially outstripping income (see Minkin, 1992: chapter 16), and such problems now seem to be a perennial feature of party finances. By 1988, party debts were in excess of £2 million, and this forced major redundancies at party headquarters and closure of the party newspaper, *Labour Weekly* (Butler and Kavanagh, 1992). The following year (as Stephen Ingle reveals in Chapter 5), the Liberal Democrats were in financial crisis at the prospect of a projected £600,000 year-end deficit, although this was subsequently turned around after an intensive fund-raising campaign by the membership. More recently, the Conservative Party has suffered because of the expense of the 1989 Euro-elections, the refurbishing of Central Office, the installation of a new computer system, and a dip in corporate donations because of the recession and the stock market slump in 1990. As a result, it has run up an average deficit of £5 million per annum in the years 1988–92, and embarked (after the 1992 general election) on a major cost-cutting exercise to reduce costs by about 40 per cent (*Guardian*, 6.2.93).

Second, and linked to this, there is the expense of election campaigns, where skilful and costly use of the media is becoming increasingly important. For example, the 1992 general election saw, for the first time, a widespread use of large posters. The parties spent a combined total of £2.17 million on this, with the Conservative Party alone spending £1.5 million (Butler and Kavanagh, 1992).

Third, while the vagaries of the first-past-the-post tend to produce governments with an overall majority in the Commons, this is by no means certain. If John Major's slim majority of twenty-one in 1992 had given way to a hung parliament (as many polls suggested), then it is highly likely that party finances would *not* have been in a fit state to fight another campaign shortly afterwards, in the event that no party was able to govern with agreement from the others. Two elections in 1974, and the impetus that this gave to the setting up of the Houghton Committee, seems evidence enough that there is a potential for the minimalist system of state funding to 'crack' under such circumstances.

Fourth and finally, there is always the danger that financial linkage between powerful groups and political parties could result in corruption and scandal – particularly when party finances are under pressure. Press allegations amidst the 1993 'crisis' in Conservative finances suggested that the party had accepted a host of donations from disgraced businessmen such as Gerald Ronson, who was convicted for fraudulent conspiracy in the Guinness Affair, and notably Polly Peck's Asil Nadir, who was charged with thirteen cases of theft totalling some £30 million before breaking bail and fleeing to Cyprus. As one former Tory cabinet minister said ominously on the 'questionable' nature of Mr Nadir's funds – 'It's none of our business, we can get some money out of him' (*Guardian*, 6.5.93).

In overall terms, therefore, if the existing system in Britain helps create (i) problems of bias within a representative democracy and (ii) a general situation where parties are (or may not) be able to meet all the EU demands on them, it seems sensible to look to alternative systems – involving much-enhanced roles for state financing of political parties.

## Alternative methods of state financing: pros and cons

No major political parties in western liberal democracies are financed wholly by membership subscriptions. Thus, as Bogdanor (1982: 369) suggests, state aid to political parties falls into three main patterns. It should be recognised that states do not always fit neatly into any single category. Nevertheless, broad patterns can be identified.

First, there is a 'minimalist' system whereby state aid in any form is highly marginal. Table 11.5 summarises state aid to parties in EU member states, and it can be seen that only the UK and Ireland fall easily into this category. In the UK, for example (as we have seen), there is no direct state aid given to the parties outside Parliament, and there exist only subsidies in kind (free broadcasting, registration of electors, etc.). In Ireland, party leaders in the Dail receive grants for their parliamentary activities – provided that the party has at least seven members in the legislature.

Second, the system of state assistance has a much higher profile and is based on the principle, as identified by the Hansard Society for Parliamentary Government (1981: 36), that 'state aid for political parties should not be unconditional, but should require "triggering" by the decisions of individuals'. Reforms in the 1970s in both the USA and Canada exemplify these principles. In the USA, individuals can utilise a tax check-off box on their income tax declarations in order to allocate (at no additional cost to themselves) small portions of their tax liability to provide funds for candidates in presidential elections and presidential primaries. In Canada, individual donations (below a specified amount) to a registered agent allow the donor to receive a reduction in his/her income tax payable. An alternative scheme put forward by the Hansard Society for Parliamentary Government (1981) proposed that (subject to some restrictions which ensured that parties had a 'reasonable' level of support), every £2 donated to a party would be matched by £2 of state aid. A further alternative to this can be found in some EU member

**Table 11.5** State funding of political parties in EU member states

| Country | State funding of parties/groups | | State funding of electoral campaigns | |
|---|---|---|---|---|
| | Direct | Indirect | Direct | Indirect |
| Belgium | Minimal funding of political groups in (i) the European Parliament, where they receive subsidies for administrative expenses proportional to the number of representatives, and (ii) the Chamber of Deputies and Senate, where they receive an additional amount for secretarial staff. | Parties are funded by donations to political foundations. Donations by individuals and corporations are tax deductible up to BF 2,000,000. | None | Provided through a number of facilities, such as exemption from stamp duty on election posters, and free access to the state-owned television network. |
| Denmark | Under Law no. 940 (1986), political groups receive a flat rate amount per month of DKR 17545.20 per month for each member of the Folketing. In addition, all groups (irrespective of size) receive an additional sum of DKR 70180.79 for administrative expenses. | None | Under Law no. 940 (1986), parties or individual candidates receive annual grants. At national level, DKR 5 per vote is paid – provided that they obtained at least 1,000 votes in the previous general election. At local and regional elections, the amount is DKR 2 and DKR 3 per vote. | None |

| | | | |
|---|---|---|---|
| Germany | State subsidies are paid to political groups in the Bundestag. In contrast to parties, these have the status of organs of the state. | (i) free broadcasting in the media, in accordance with party strength in the Bundestag, (ii) granting of special subsidies for conferences, youth organisations, etc., (iii) tax deductibility on contributions and membership fees up to a specified amount. | Article 18 of the Law on Parties allows for a lump sum of DM 5 per registered voter, plus an 'extra amount to the lowest paid' of some 6% of total election expenditure. Allocation of these is by a complex procedure (linked to the % of First and Second votes) which ensures that only the very smallest parties do not qualify. | Free broadcasting in the media, in accordance with the strength of the parties in the Bundestag. |
| Greece | Law no. 1443 (1984) allows for 0.001% of the national income to be distributed to parties represented in Parliament. To qualify, parties must obtain 3% of total votes cast and present lists in at least 2/3 of the constituencies during the previous legislative elections. 10% of the total is distributed equally among the qualifying parties, whilst the remainder is allocated according to votes received. Subject to some conditions, party coalitions may also qualify. | State subsidies are exempt from tax. | State funding as detailed (left) also covers election campaigns. | Tax exemption for state subsidies also applies. |

| | | | |
|---|---|---|---|
| Spain | (i) Organic Law no. 3 (1987) allows for annual grants to each party, based on the number of seats and votes obtained in the last general election.<br>(ii) Parliamentary groups receive financial assistance, comprising a fixed amount for all groups and an amount varying with the number of members.<br>(iii) Parliamentary groups in regional assemblies receive grants, calculated on a combination of seats and votes obtained for each party. | None | Organic Law 5/1985 allows for state subsidies to political parties during election campaigns. Distribution is based on a combination of votes and votes and seats in the Chamber of Deputies and the Senate. | Premises, media advertising space and other benefits are paid to parties during election campaigns. |
| France | Since 1988, Parties and groups have been funded by grants proportional to the number of MPs declaring to their Assembly's Bureau that they are members of or affiliated to a political group. | None | Through an electoral finance association or a financial agent, a system of reimbursement is provided for the election expenses of candidates who receive 5% of the First Round votes. Reimbursement is equivalent to one tenth of a specified ceiling on election expenses. For Presidential elections, reimbursement is one twentieth of the ceiling. | Free media access during election campaigns. |

| | | | | |
|---|---|---|---|---|
| Ireland | Leaders of political parties in the Dail (with at least 7 members) receive grants for their Parliamentary activities. | None | None | None |
| Italy(*) | Organisational expenses are paid to parties in the Senate and the Chamber of Deputies. 2% is allocated equally to groups in Parliament, 23% is divided equally to parties presenting lists in at least two-thirds of the constituencies (or presenting their own list in a region where special status is given to linguistic minorities) and 73% is allocated in proportion to seats in Parliament. | None | Parties standing for election in at least two-thirds of the constituencies and obtaining at least 300,000 votes (or 2% of the votes cast) can qualify for an electoral fund. This applies to General, Regional and European Elections. 20% of the fund is shared equally, whilst the remainder is distributed in accordance with the number of votes polled. | None |
| Luxembourg | Groups represented in the Chamber of Deputies receive subsidies for their Parliamentary activities. Assistance varies in accordance with the number of members in a group (with the first five members receiving roughly 12 times that for each subsequent member). | None | None | Free postal services are provided for each candidate. |

221

| | | | | |
|---|---|---|---|---|
| Netherlands | Parliamentary groups receive small subsidies depending on the size of the group. | (i) Since 1972, grants have been paid to foundations (research institutes, educational institutes and youth movements) which are affiliated to political parties. (ii) Donations and subscriptions from individuals are tax deductible, provided that they constitute 1–10% of his/her gross annual income. (iii) Donations by private corporations are tax deductible, provided that they are in excess of HFL 500 and less than 6% of total profits. (iv) Parties have regular free access to TV and radio. N.B. in the Netherlands, this is actually considered direct state aid. | None | (i) free access to TV and radio, (ii) state finances the organisation of the election and the counting of votes. |
| Portugal | (i) Law No. 77 (1988) allows for an annual subsidy to parties in the Assembly | None | None | None |

| | | | | |
|---|---|---|---|---|
| | of the Republic. The subsidy is equivalent to 1/225th of the minimum national salary, allocated for every vote at the previous general election. (ii) A subsidy is also paid for the deputies' secretarial costs of parliamentary groups. | | | |
| United Kingdom | Since 1975, opposition parties in the House of Commons receive state subsidies to finance their Parliamentary activities. To qualify, parties must have two members elected or one member and a minimum of 150,000 votes. Subsides are £2250 for each seat won, plus £5.10 for every 200 votes at the last general election. | Parties receive regular and free radio and TV broadcasts, with allocations being based on the number of votes obtained at the previous general election. | None | The state ensures that the cost of registering electors is borne by local authorities; that parliamentary candidates are entitled to free postal facilities; that parliamentary and local candidates are allowed the right to hold meetings in suitable schools; that it bears the cost of returning officers; and that parties have free access to radio and TV broadcasts – provided that they have 50 or more candidates. Allocations are decided by the Committee of Party Political Broadcasting. |

*Note:* (*) As part of a backlash against bribery and corruption, a recent referendum in Italy saw a 90.3% vote in favour of abolishing state aid to political parties.

223

states, where there is a system of tax deductibility on donations to parties. As Table 11.5 indicates, this operates in both the Netherlands and Belgium – the latter allowing for parties to be funded through donations to political foundations, with individual and corporate donations being tax deductible up to BF 2,000,000.

Third, there is a system which is based essentially on direct state aid to political parties. As Ware (1987: 100) notes, this has 'been especially popular in those regimes in western Europe where democracy collapsed in the inter-war years, and where the reconstructed democratic regimes have accorded a major role to strong parties in the workings of the new state'. Systems of state aid, either for general party activities and/or to help finance electoral campaigns, operate in Denmark, Germany, Greece, Spain, France, Italy, Luxembourg and Portugal (see Table 11.5). In Spain, for example, Article 6 of the 1978 Constitution recognises the role of the parties in expressing the 'will of the people' (European Parliament, 1991: 17). The system of party funding, however, has evolved with the underpinning assumption that a healthy democracy requires a few strong parties, rather than what Ware (1987: 101) describes as 'extreme multipartism'. Thus, state financing in post-Franco Spain has developed in such a way that by being contingent on the seats/votes obtained in general elections and the existence of parliamentary groups, the smaller parties have been driven to near bankruptcy.

Each of the three broad patterns outlined above is underpinned by some form of rationale for state subsidies. Certainly, this is most evident in the latter two, and it is based on these that the main arguments both for and against state subsidies can be summarised.

*Arguments in favour of state financing of political parties*

The Hansard Society for Parliamentary Government (1981: 33) focuses on the general idea that state funding of political parties is in the 'public interest'. Thus, its criticisms of the existing system in Britain can be looked at from another angle in order to derive a number of arguments in favour of state funding. The general principles of these (although not necessarily each and every point) are accepted by the Labour Party and the Liberal Democrats, who both favour state aid to parties.

1. It helps prevent a class polarisation in electoral choice – something which may not be desired by voters.
2. It prevents unnecessary privileges being given to certain interests in the representative process, and equally prevents other interests being 'organised' out of this.
3. It helps parties to develop facilities for political research, hence encouraging coherent and practical policies.

4. It may be possible to find a system of financing which will increase the membership of parties by encouraging them to draw on a wider social base.
5. It will prevent parties such as the Liberals (now the Liberal Democrats) from being handicapped because they cannot command institutional finances.
6. It will prevent the situation where some trade unionists and some company shareholders are contributing to causes of which they do not approve.

*Arguments against state financing of political parties*

A counter perspective to the above is laid out in the Minority Report to the Houghton Committee (Cmnd. 6601, 1976: 78–81), which puts forward the case against state aid for political parties. These general principles (although again, not necessarily each and every point) are accepted by the Conservatives, SNP and Plaid Cymru, which are all opposed to state aid for parties.

1. Direct state aid would breach the principle whereby organisations with political ends exist in a strictly 'voluntary' capacity. Furthermore, taxpayers may have little sympathy with financing parties with whom they disagree – particularly 'extremist' parties.
2. There is no guarantee that public funding would actually 'improve' the performance of parties. Indeed, fund-raising acts as a cohesive force within parties.
3. Existing party alignments reflect real areas of conflict within society, and state funding would weaken the link between the parties and their traditional support. Hence, this would threaten to push both the 'left' and the 'right' into extra-parliamentary activities.
4. Rather than distorting the political direction of Labour and the Conservatives, the continued willingness of the 'trades unions' and 'business' to give their financial support indicates that legitimate interests are being represented.
5. Any subsidies that were given to the national party organisations would strengthen these central organisations at the expense of the party grass roots.
6. Public cynicism of politicians would be likely to increase at the sight of politicians voting to allow public money to be channelled to their parties.
7. The actual practice of funding takes place in different countries, in different political and economic contexts, and for different reasons. Hence, the arguments in favour of state funding cannot simply be transplanted into each and every country.

8. There is a danger in providing 'smaller' parties with artificial stimuli, after they have passed the qualifying threshold for state aid.


## Concluding thoughts: party financing from 1979 and onwards to the year 2000

The acceptability (or otherwise) of the foregoing arguments for and against state financing of political parties will depend on our views on the role of the state in society and the perceived pros and cons that would be brought about through a major role for state funding. Our thoughts on this matter can perhaps be assisted, however, by asking the question: would state funding help change the key features of the party system in the post-1979 period? In this regard, when we consider the findings of the previous chapters in this book, we find that they can be grouped with relative ease into two main categories. First, Chapters 1, 2, 3, 4 and 7 deal with matters pertaining to the concentration of power at Westminster, and the operation and activities of the main political parties around this. Second, Chapter 5, 6, 8, 9 and 10 concern themselves essentially with the 'other face' of this, in terms of parties who continually have to come to terms with having limited (if any) access to this concentration of power. Each can be considered in turn, in terms of the likely effect of state aid.

First, in terms of the axis of power at Westminster, we tend to find that this would not be particularly affected by a system of state financing, since the underlying reasons do not hinge on matters pertaining to party funding. For example, Andrew Heywood suggests in Chapter 1 that we do effectively have a dominant-party system, because 'the simple fact is that the Conservative Party has held power alone since 1979 and can . . . expect to remain in government at least until 1996 or 1997'. If Labour did, however, have access to state funds which would put it on a roughly equal footing with the Conservatives in terms of election expenditure, it seems unlikely that this would make any significant difference to its decline. As Heywood suggests, the 'gloom' for Labour lies in the fact that its electoral base of support is being undermined by long-term social and demographic trends.

In Chapter 2, Richard Kelly suggests that the Labour Party has become more centralised, while the Conservative Party has remained highly decentralised – particularly in terms of the organisational autonomy of the constituency associations. Again, however, it seems likely that these post-1979 trends would not have altered substantially if state funding had been in place. The centralist trends within the Labour Party were rooted primarily in the party leadership seeking to 'modernise' the party in the face of continual electoral defeats, and state funding would simply have reinforced this even more. Certainly, a more decentralist trend within the Conservative Party was due to the confidence brought about by the general philosophy of individualism propounded by the centre, and the relative financial autonomy of the constituencies (because of the large membership base of the party – hence allowing it to outstrip the other parties in terms of constituency fund-raising). Thus, state funds paid to Central Office *may* have provided the potential for a centralist counterbalance, although this would not necessarily have led to greater centralisation, since it would have put 'Tory-style' democracy under pressure, because of its traditions of centralism and informal influence from below.

In Chapter 3, Philip Norton suggests that the parties in the House of Commons have become less structured and predictable than before. State funding, however, would also have made little difference to this, since these changes are rooted in factors conducive to back-bencher independence, such as the new departmental select committees and the demands from pressure groups and constituents. Similarly, the party stances and relationships on the 'European' issue, as identified by Alistair Jones in Chapter 4, have little – if anything – to do with the sources of funding. Implicit in Chapter 4 is the suggestion that these stances, and the inter-party 'networking' over the Maastricht legislation, are rooted in complex electoral and ideological factors. Finally, the course of party financing had little influence on the political recruitment trends identified in Chapter 7. As Joni Lovenduski and Pippa Norris suggest, the key factors impacting upon the ability of individuals getting into Parliament is that they must have 'financial security, public networks, social status, policy experience, technical and social skills'.

Second, in terms of the various parties which are to some degree removed from this concentration of power at Westminster, we tend to find a similar situation, in that the post-1979 development for the party system would not seem likely to be affected significantly by a system of state financing. The reason for this, again, is that the motor force for the development of the parties since 1979 has not been the nature of their funding sources. Stephen Ingle suggests in Chapter 5, for example, that for Britain's 'third party' 'ultimately . . . the story is one of failure'. Certainly, it would seem foolish to deny that an injection of state finances into Britain's third party would have no effect – particularly in the light of Johnston's (1986) study of the 1983 general election, in which he found the Liberals to be at a disadvantage because some seats were vulnerable to the amount of money spent. Indeed, parties would not spend the vast sums of money that they do, if it had no effect at all! Nevertheless, it is unlikely that state financing would have a profound effect on the position of the Liberal Democrats, because the two main parties would still have access to funds from their institutional sponsors, and as Ingle suggests, it is essentially the 'first-past-the-post system [which] thwarts the Liberal Democrats today as effectively as it always thwarted the Liberals'.

Similarly, in terms of the fact that the roots of post-1979 party trends lie outside financial matters, the main problem for the SNP and Plaid Cymru, as Roger Levy suggests in Chapter 8, is the 'huge credibility problem' that nationalist parties have in terms of securing a broader appeal. Equally, as Stephen Hunt suggests in Chapter 10, the problem for 'fringe' parties – particularly the Greens – is that they are more like pressure groups, whose ideas have been diffused and partly absorbed by the 'traditional' party system. Certainly, state financing with a 'qualifying threshold' would be likely to bolster the 'larger' nationalist parties and it would confirm the 'fringe' nature of the others (as in Spain), but it would not in itself seem capable of altering the fundamental reasons for their relatively marginal positions. The term marginal can also be used (although not in a pejorative sense) to apply to the party systems in Northern Ireland – as detailed by Arthur Aughey in Chapter 9, and to local government – as discussed by John Gyford in Chapter 6. Again, however, state financing would be unlikely to have any great effect on the post-1979 trends, because *the* issues shaping the development of the parties are (respectively) the struggle between nationalism and unionism over whether Northern Ireland should 'remain a full and integral part of the United Kingdom', and the way that central 'challenges' to the 'traditional workings' of local party politics have resulted in it being more entrenched and creative in its responses.

All of the foregoing seems to suggest, therefore, that a system of state financing would not make a substantial difference to the party system in the post-1979 period in terms of the way that it revolves around matters pertaining to the concentration of power at Westminster. Indeed, in the previous chapters of this book, it is significant that other than Chapters 2, 8 and 10, which refer briefly to the relative financial independence of Conservative constituency units and the financial disadvantage of the 'smaller' parties, the sources of funding for political parties simply do not merit any more than the occasional passing reference. This is not a criticism of these chapters, but rather a recognition that they (rightly) do not see funding as a significant factor in shaping the post-1979 party system.

It would be foolish to assume, however, that sources of party funding are not important. As this present chapter has suggested, the British 'minimalist' system of state funding is essentially 'market-based', and creates underlying problems of (i) distorting representative democracy (allowing at least to some degree for 'wealth to buy power' and helping squeeze out third parties) and (ii) producing a situation where there is the potential for a 'fiscal crisis' of the parties, which are often unable to pay for all the demands made on them. Thus, the issue of *who* finances political parties – the state or voluntary contributions from individual and corporate sponsors – should be seen as a time-bomb ticking away underneath the British party system. Certainly, some sparks have been flying in the summer of 1993, although this is unlikely to result in the introduction of state subsidies because of (i) a £50 billion public sector deficit, (ii) a government committed to the 'voluntary' nature of party funding, and (iii) public opposition to state funding, as indicated by an ICM poll in June 1993 which found 79 per cent against and only 13 per cent in favour (*Guardian*, 9.6.93).

The longer term, however, is less certain. The time-bomb could be sparked off by the need for a second general election in the wake of a hung parliament; a large rise in inflation eroding party incomes; a British-style Watergate scandal (as threatened by Asil Nadir), and other such matters which could expose the underlying vagaries of the system. It would seem wise to remember Heard's (1960: 11) statement, therefore, that 'deeper understanding of political money means deeper understanding of representative government'. If this is the case, then it must be said that representative government in Britain is continually in danger of exposing its own weaknesses. Thus, the question – should parties be funded by the state? – will continue to be a pertinent issue as we move towards the year 2000 and beyond.

## Acknowledgement

The author gratefully acknowledges the research assistance provided by the Faculty of Business at Glasgow Caledonian University.

## Note

1. N.B. A figure of 27 per cent was cited (mistakenly) in this article, but was subsequently corrected in the July (1993) edition of *Business Age*.

## References

Blackwell, R. and Terry, M. (1987), 'Analysing the Political Fund Ballots: A Remarkable Victory or the Triumph of the Status Quo?', *Political Studies*, XXXV: 623–42.

Bogdanor, V. (1982), 'Reflections on British Political Finance', *Parliamentary Affairs*, 35: 367–80.

Butler, D. and Kavanagh, D. (1992), *The British General Election of 1992*, London, Macmillan.

Cahill, K., Kirwan, P., and Siegle, E. (1993), 'Tory Money: The Unexplained Millions That Elected Three Governments', *Business Age*, 32: 40–48.

Cmnd. 6601. (1976), *Report of the Committee on Financial Aid to Political Parties* (Houghton Report), London, HMSO.

Conservative Central Office, *Income and Expenditure Accounts (Years ended 31st March 1989 to 31st March 1992)*, London, Conservative Central Office.

Costello, N., Michie, J. and Milne, S. (1989), *Beyond the Casino Economy*, London, Verso.

Crick, B. (1975), 'Paying for Parties: A Review', *Political Quarterly*, 46: 411–17.

European Parliament. (1991), *The Funding of Political Parties in European Community Member States*, (2nd edn), Luxembourg, Political and Institutional Affairs Division – Directorate for Research.

Ewing, K. (1987), *The Funding of Political Parties in Britain*, Cambridge, Cambridge University Press.

Ewing, K. (1983), *The Conservatives, Trades Unions and Political Funding*, Fabian Tract No. 492, London, Fabian Society.

Hansard Society for Parliamentary Government, (1981), *Paying for Politics: The Report of the Commission Upon the Financing of Political Parties*, London, Hansard Society for Parliamentary Government.

Heard, A. (1960), *The Costs of Democracy*, Chapel Hill, University of North Carolina Press.

Institute for Public Policy Research, untitled submission to the Select Committee on Home Affairs, IPPR, London, May 1993.

Johnston, R.J. (1986), 'A Further Look at British Political Finance', *Political Studies*, XXXIV: 466–73.

Labour Party, *Statement of Accounts (Years 1988–91)*, London, Labour Party.

Leonard, D. (1975), *Paying for Politics: The Case for Public Subsidies*, London, PEP.

Liberal Democrats, *Financial Statements (Years ended 31st December 1988 to 31st December 1991)*, London, Liberal Democrats.

Miliband, R. (1973), *The State in Capitalist Society*, London, Quartet.

Minkin, L. (1992), *The Contentious Alliance: Trade Unions and The Labour Party*, Edinburgh, Edinburgh University Press.

Minkin, L. (1993), Untitled Submission to the Select Committee on Home Affairs, Leeds, Leeds Metropolitan University.

Paltiel, K.V. (1981), 'Campaign Finance: Contrasting Practices and Reforms', in Butler, D., Penniman, H.R. and Ranney, A. (eds), *Democracy at the Polls: A Comparative Study of National Elections*, Washington, American Institute for Public Policy Research.

Pinto-Duschinsky, M. (1988), 'Party Finance: Funding of Political Parties Since 1945', *Contemporary Record*, 2 (4): 20–23.

Pinto-Duschinsky, M. (1981), *British Political Finance 1830–1980*, Washington, American Institute for Public Policy Research.

Pinto-Duschinsky, M. (1989), 'Trends in British Party Funding 1983–87', *Parliamentary Affairs*, 42: 197–212.

Pinto-Duschinsky, M. (1990), 'Funding of Political Parties Since 1945', in Seldon, A. (ed.), *UK Political Parties Since 1945*, London, Philip Allan.

Pinto-Duschinsky, M. (1985), 'Trends in British Political Funding 1979–83', *Parliamentary Affairs*, 38: 328–347.

Richardson, J.J. and Jordan, A.G. (1979), *Governing Under Pressure*, Oxford, Martin Robertson.

Rose, R. and Page, E. (eds), (1982), *Fiscal Stress in Cities*, Cambridge: Cambridge University Press.

Rose, R. (1974), *The Problem of Party Government*, London, Macmillan.

Seidle, F.L. (1980), State Aid for Political Parties', *Parliamentarian*, 61: 79–87.

Taylor, R. (1987), 'Trade Unions and the Labour Party: Time for An Open Marriage', *Political Quarterly*, 58: 424–32.

Ware, A. (1987), *Citizens Parties and the State*, Oxford, Polity Press.

# Index